FORMING THE CRITICAL MIND

Forming the Critical Mind

Dryden to Coleridge

JAMES ENGELL

Harvard University Press
Cambridge, Massachusetts
London, England
1989

Publication of this book has been aided by a grant from the
Hyder Edward Rollins Fund of Harvard University

This book is printed on acid-free paper, and its binding
materials have been chosen for strength and durability.

Library of Congress Cataloging in Publication Data
Engell, James, 1951–
      Forming the critical mind : Dryden to Coleridge /
James Engell.
          p.   cm.
      Includes index.
      ISBN 0-674-30943-X (alk. paper)
      1. Criticism—Great Britain—History—18th
century   2. English literature—18th century—History
and criticism—Theory, etc.   3. Dryden, John. 1631–
1700—Knowledge—Literature   4. Coleridge, Samuel
Taylor. 1772–1834—Knowledge—Literature.   I. Title.
PR73.E54   1989
801'.95'0941—dc19   88-24493
                                                                          CIP

TO GRACE SNYDER

AND

WILLARD SNYDER

PREFACE

Criticism has grown into such a large and yet specialized endeavor that no book can address the subject in its entirety, or even perhaps in its fundamentals. Those intimately knowledgeable about particular approaches and refinements tend to disagree most about what is essential. The subject is like an open city. It does not present just a few gates and entrances with walls that are elsewhere too high to scale. Many roads and thresholds lead in; eventually they all interconnect. Despite the formidable array of terminology and mapmaking that describes the area, no one has jurisdiction over its laws, no traveler needs a special visa; any reader can enter. Yet amid this exhilarating and often confusing welter of critical approaches, certain ideas persist. They change but endure, they never grow obsolete. This book is about some of those ideas and concepts, specifically about their development during the first explosive generations of English critical thought from Dryden through Coleridge.

To look for the absolute origin of any idea may be delusory. During the eighteenth century many seekers after origins and originality—whether concerning language, the social contract, or aesthetic values—encounter the immense frustration attached to that form of intellectual archaeology. But in the process they make important discoveries and create new ideas and methods, many of which we inherit. This book traces a number of important ideas. Their basis might be called theoretical, for criticism in the eighteenth and early nineteenth centuries is frequently and avowedly theoretical in its approach to language, genre, mythology, literary structure, poetic language, universal grammar, effects of composition on readers, the relation between theory and practical criticism, and the function of literature in culture and society, all overarched by a sober consideration of the very limits of critical system and theory.

The tendency of the age, which accompanies these sharpened interests in what were rapidly becoming specialized areas within criticism as a whole, is to make literary criticism accessible to a broad intellectual audience, to exert it as a central form of discourse belonging to a wider critique directed at society, its values and its symbols. (Locke, not Saussure or Peirce, first suggests a full-fledged science of semiotics and introduces the word into modern usage.) Ultimately this critique focuses on nothing less than human nature—individual and social, psychological and spiritual, economic and political. And while critics of the age realize that societies and linguistic structures may to a large degree inevitably dictate (no matter how much one protests) the form, vocabulary, and even values assumed by any writer, those critics never forget that it is still people, not cultural machines, who write. Writing entails individual consciousness and will, individual character and the lonely spaces where hope and fear quest for worthy objects. If there is nothing outside the text, then our lives are texts also, and the individual psyche exists in relation to whatever is inscribed.

I hope in this book to elicit suggestive connections between formative critical concepts developed in the eighteenth century and concepts and theories articulated in the past thirty to forty years. Writers familiar with the two historical bodies of criticism habitually note significant similarities between them. Why is that so? An attempt to answer this question forms one subject of this study.

After the great initial impact of romantic critical theory, criticism in England and the United States went through a century and a half dominated by a series of approaches not especially theoretical. Much eighteenth-century criticism was literally forgotten. In Germany and France, then in the United States and to some degree in England (where the model of the German university was less influential), literary history and historical philology became tremendously important. They served as tools to train the first generations of university scholars and scholar-critics. As social and literary critics, Carlyle, Arnold, and Ruskin turned to individual writers and to the vexing question of culture, European and national. However sophisticated and wide-ranging their positions, they were not oriented toward what today we would call a theory of literature. Nor were they particularly sympathetic to eighteenth-century intellectual life. The theories of Sainte-Beuve and Taine relied so much on history, national culture, biography, or individual character—rather than on language or comparative literary structure—that they now strike most of us, however unjustly, as untheoretical. The hermeneutical inquiries of Schleiermacher, Dilthey, and others failed to alter the mainstream of English criticism. Nineteenth-century aestheticism flagged in its ability to articulate fresh positions in philosophical or psychological terms. Coleridge, Shelley, Kant, the Schlegels, Schiller, Schelling, and Hegel had established intimate bonds between philosophy and criticism. But these loosened in succeeding decades. At one extreme the literary-critical manifestation of aesthetic theory finally emerged as diluted appreciationism. And although modernist critics such as Eliot and Pound articulate views on subjects dealt with by earlier literary theory, their criticism remains largely practical, or is directed at particular authors and broad cultural issues. The few times Eliot mentions Arnold explicitly are inversely proportional to the presence of that ghost and his enduring questions. The History of Ideas movement, all too brief if one regards it as a movement now more neglected than followed, leaned (though not exclusively) on a framework of intellectual history. The New Criticism was largely atheoretical.

In the 1950s, and then increasingly in the 1960s and 1970s, when literary theory steadily gained attention in the Anglo-American world, it was thus not only a birth or an importation but also a phoenixlike rebirth, this time coming after a long quiescence. Naturally the new creature was different, but the ashes remaining, if stirred up, could still give off heat and light. However, since the vast majority of critics and scholars engaged in the new enterprises that followed the New Criticism were themselves primarily trained in romantic and post-romantic literature, criticism earlier than that tended to be represented by a few texts and fewer generalizations.

This book, on the other hand, is about the first century and a half of systematic English critical thought. It is not a narrative history, though a dimension of the past is always present. ("An evolutionary history of criticism," wrote René Wellek, having nearly completed his own monumental *History of Modern Criticism,* "must fail.") The stress is on key ideas and debates, many of which have resurfaced. It is not my contention that these ideas remain the same or always exhibit the same names and vocabulary, but that the underlying issues are similar enough to warrant a closer, more sympathetic examination of eighteenth-century criticism.

In preparing this book, I am indebted to students I have taught in courses on criticism and on eighteenth-century literature at Harvard. I have often become their student. My colleagues W. J. Bate and David Perkins made many helpful suggestions, and I am grateful for their advice. In addition, James Basker, Jerome Buckley, Louis Landa, John Mahoney, Maximillian Novak, Allen Reddick, George Watson, and Howard Weinbrot have generously read or discussed earlier versions of individual chapters, providing aid and insight. My research assistant, Peter Cohen, helped prepare the manuscript with timely skill; Keith Alexander checked references.

A version of Chapter 8 has appeared in *Psychology and Literature in the Eighteenth Century,* edited by Christopher Fox (AMS Press); an earlier version of Chapter 3 and parts of Chapter 4 first appeared in volumes 9 and 12 respectively of Harvard English Studies. Permission to quote the poem "From the Sublime to the Meticulous in Four Stages," *The First Morning* (New York: Scribner, 1950; Westport, Conn.: Greenwood, 1972), is granted by kind permission of the author, Peter Viereck.

CONTENTS

FORMING THE CRITICAL MIND

INTRODUCTION

The Originating Force of Eighteenth-Century Criticism

Literary commentary may cross the line and become as demanding as literature: it is an unpredictable or unstable "genre" that cannot be subordinated, a priori, to its referential or commentating function. . . . A reversal must be possible whereby this "secondary" piece of writing turns out to be "primary."

> GEOFFREY HARTMAN, "CROSSING
> OVER: LITERARY COMMENTARY
> AS LITERATURE" (1976)

The artist and the critic are reciprocally subservient, and the particular province of each is greatly improved by the assistance of the other.

> GEORGE CAMPBELL, *PHILOSOPHY
> OF RHETORIC* (1776)

Our concern is with essentially contested concepts in criticism. These include genre, myth, evaluation, literary history, aesthetics and ethics, the problem of refinement and progress in the arts, the study of rhetoric and the nature of poetic language, the link between literary theory and practice, and even those embarrassingly large questions such as, What is poetry? and What is "literary"?

These subjects are, as Hume describes them, "disputable questions" on which reasonable individuals may—and will—disagree. A significant number of modern critical issues matured during the Enlightenment, and they remain vitally with us.[1]

Critical study implies a present and a future use. Emerson claims that history's true function is to help us see things as they are, so that we may proceed in our actions more justly and with a hope of greater happiness in our own future "histories." Johnson loves biography because it "comes nearest to us" and contains what we can "put to use." If there were no enduring questions and recurring issues in criticism, that would imply an absence of them in literature, art, philosophy, and aesthetics. All literature, really, is literature "of the past," even science fiction and futurist writing. And if literature of the past means something to us, if it is not mere amusement or useless antiquarianism but is at the very least what Eliot calls "superior amusement"—and possibly our vital, best contact with the condition of humanity we have inherited and will, with luck, pass on—then critics who have preceded us and taken that literature for their subject may offer guidance. They may help sustain us in the face of a problematic future. If we disagree with them, they force us to articulate different opinions.

Eighteenth-century writers, mingling pride with anxiety, label their own time a distinctively critical one. It is for them the "age of criticism," as it also becomes for the Romantics. This powerful self-consciousness says something about their enterprise from the start. Johnson calls Dryden "the father of English criticism," and the breathless exclamations, even protests, of the late seventeenth and early eighteenth centuries concerning an unprecedented deluge of criticism are too numerous (and too similar) for all to be cited. It can be argued that criticism, exercised on such a massive scale, ranks with the novel as the most significant "new" mode of writing to enrich English literature between the Restoration of Charles II and the death of George III.

Thomas Shadwell drily prefaces *The Sullen Lovers* with a comment that his is a "very critical age, when every man pretends to be a judge." Or, as Dryden phrased it in 1677, a lament that never seems to go out of date, we live in "an age of illiterate, censorious, and detracting people, who, thus qualified, set up for critics." In a rare instance of expressing the same sentiment as Dryden did, but with more spice and gusto, Thomas Rymer writes: "Till of late years England was as free from critics as it is from *wolves*." For Swift it would be as humdrum "to say this 'critical age' as divines say this 'sinful age.'" Both the Enlightenment spirit of systematic inquiry and the bogus posturing of bad critics attract a steadily and dramatically increasing reading public. People want to read literature, but they also want to read about reading literature. Sometimes the distinction cannot be made. Criticism becomes a major branch of literature and critics produce much of literary merit. And the whole critical spirit of the Enlightenment, which simultaneously affects science, philosophy, government, and the arts, exerts a crucial force in the development of modern, specialized, secular society.[2]

The self-determined intellectual life, the *sapere aude* Kant proclaims, now gains freer rein. Criticism joins those activities of private leisure and social adornment that J. H. Plumb associates with "the pursuit of happiness," a pursuit open in the eighteenth century to a significant part of society for the first time.[3] The critical Pegasus threatens to become a runaway. So many critics argue, explain, and fill sheets that Pope, stung by some of them, wittily suggests their spontaneous generation from mud and dung rather than from the copulation of ideas. He calls these bothersome insects, scholars "For ever reading, never to be read!" When Edward Cave founds *The Gentleman's Magazine* in 1731, London already supports two hundred journals, many with pretense to critical clout. The coffeehouses or "penny universities" serve as critical dens and switchboards. This age witnesses the birth of modern criticism. Most critical approaches developed between 1660 and 1820 are important to us. We still practice them and, although we have enlarged and enriched those inherited approaches, we cannot claim greatly to have expanded their number.

The age of criticism from 1660 to 1820 becomes markedly self-conscious about procedures and goals. Method and principles are frequent topics. How, and by what standards, should a critic judge?

Such concerns haunt the eighteenth century as they haunt us today. Criticism often becomes metacriticism, a critique of criticism, as we see unfold in Hume's deceptively unpolemical landmark essay "Of the Standard of Taste" (1757). And this self-critical habit is adopted by his Scottish and English successors. Of many varieties of criticism, all flourishing by the 1770s, virtually none existed to an extensive degree in what George Saintsbury calls the critical "dead water" of the mid-seventeenth century. Saintsbury's verdict may seem harsh, but his comparative judgment still stands: English criticism before and after the Restoration are different bodies of water, the earlier one a bay leading to a rougher, deep ocean. French and German criticism—and also their critical theory—tend to develop more concurrently with the great swellings of national literature in each of those countries. In France a large body of criticism flourishes contemporaneously with the golden age of neoclassical literature in the seventeenth century. German romantic theory grows inextricably with the "classic" writers of the late eighteenth and early nineteenth centuries.

Far from an enervated or tepid gentility, "polite" literature and learning in the English eighteenth century means what is accomplished, accurate, urbane, correct, methodologically pure, and well-informed. Many scholars continue to pursue these qualities. Most books of criticism now published would be, by those standards, excruciatingly "polite." The term has everything to do with intellectual approach and little to do with etiquette. True, ideas of social class could be invoked—Lord Kames states that those who labor with their hands are incapable of true taste—but the real litmus test is refinement of knowledge. And yet the age questions its own ideals and seeks limits: "Life," says Johnson, "will not bear refinement." There comes a time when the polite specialization of letters may gorge itself like cancer and become one of Bacon's "vanities of learning." Johnson himself, in the *Life of Gray,* freely refers to "the dogmatism of learning."

Umberto Eco suggests that Structuralism originates in the Middle Ages. Stephen Greenblatt has given a new context for artistic creativity and the psychological self-image through studies of literary self-fashioning in the Renaissance. It would oversimplify matters to say that recent critical theories are an efflorescence of concerns that first surfaced in the eighteenth and early nineteenth centuries. But the originating importance of criticism before Coleridge has eluded latter-day Anglo-American theorists even more than it has their continental counterparts. Michel Foucault, Paul Ricoeur, Roland Barthes, Jacques Derrida, Jean Starobinski: much of their grounding locates itself in texts from Racine through Condillac, from Hobbes through Rousseau, Kant, and Hegel. Tzvetan Todorov's *Theories of the Symbol* contends that modern concepts of the symbol and rhetoric develop in the several decades astride 1800. To a mature generation of Anglo-American scholar-critics that includes Northrop Frye, W. J. Bate, M. H. Abrams, E. D. Hirsch, Harold Bloom, W. K. Wimsatt, Paul Fussell, and Hans Aarsleff—and for others "transplanted," such as Isaiah Berlin, Geoffrey Hartman, Paul de Man, and René Wellek—the decades from Pope through Coleridge offered their first and often lasting subjects of inquiry. This period forms the foundation of European critical theory.

The best minds of the age write criticism. In their estimate it is a central enterprise. Edmund Burke, Adam Smith, Thomas Hobbes, Joseph Priestley, Edward Gibbon, David Hume, George Berkeley, Benjamin Franklin, Thomas Jefferson: these individuals are now more associated with politics, science, philosophy, economics, and history, but one of their first—and one of their lasting—interests was the practice and criticism of literature, which for them included the larger relation between language and ideas. They publish extensive literary criticism and become convinced that it is a core intellectual activity, as basic as economics, history, or science in helping us understand ourselves and the world that we perceive and half create.

Strong tendons grow between literary criticism and other genres, between poetics and poetry itself. George Campbell expresses the fact in his *Philosophy of Rhetoric* (1776), the title and overall conception of which I. A. Richards uses for a major work in the 1930s. Campbell says that "the artist and the critic are reciprocally subservient, and the particular province of each is greatly improved by the assistance of the other."[4] The relation between late-seventeenth- and eighteenth-century criticism, critical theory, and the course of poetry during the same period intensifies and grows in value. As Eric Rothstein notes in his history of *Restoration and Eighteenth-Century Poetry,* "Because for the first time in English literature criticism flourished along with poetry, it provides an index of altering taste."[5] This charged interplay of poetry and criticism had not been nearly so active in English literature prior to the Restoration, though it has been vibrant ever since. One means of capturing the symbiosis is through the poet-critic. The English tradition abounds with these, and during its first generations of systematic criticism a constellation appears: Dryden, Addison, Johnson, and Coleridge shine with first magnitude. We could, without violating the poet-critic label, include Pope, Joseph Warton, Fielding, Young, Beattie, Goldsmith, Wordsworth, Shelley, and—if we admit speculative, personal letters into critical discourse—Keats. A large body of lasting criticism in the period comes from good poets. The phenomenon of the poet-critic reminds us that the criticism of the present time that will, in retrospect, be most valued and formative may very well not be academic studies, reviews in learned journals, and rarified theoretical inquiries, but the letters, fugitive essays, prefaces, interviews, and occasional manifestoes of practicing poets, novelists, and other writers—all of which will take a generation or more to sift out.

Furthermore, the critical texts—the touchstones of criticism that constantly provoke and elicit response—are the plays of Shakespeare and the poems of Milton. The effect of this cannot be underestimated. These authors are supplemented, to varying degrees throughout the century, by Chaucer, Spenser, and later Pope. A major impetus for the *Biographia Literaria* is Coleridge's appreciation and judgment of Wordsworth as poet and critic, his "dialogue" with him. In one respect English criticism develops tardily, a century or more after having produced, from Chaucer through Milton, a rich and varied body of literature. When criticism begins to flower in the later seventeenth century, its first instinct (an instinct, for better or worse, characterizing English criticism ever since) is more empirical than theoretical. As Hugh Blair remarks in his *Lectures on Rhetoric and Belles Lettres* (1783), "All science arises from observations on practice. Practice has always gone before method and rule; but method and rule have afterwards improved and perfected practice, in every art."[6] A "high priori road," as Pope derisively calls it in another context in the *Essay on Man,* could not be glorified when such landmarks as *Paradise Lost, Richard III, Hamlet,* and *The Faerie Queene* stood in plain and popular view.

Eighteenth-century critics tend to view evaluation and judgment as paramount. In doing so they subsume generic, structural, and linguistic criteria. Dryden, in his preface to *The State of Innocence,* approvingly notes: "Criticism, as it was first instituted by Aristotle, was meant a standard of judging well." The opening lines of Pope's *Essay on Criticism* (1711) imply the strongly judgmental nature of criticism, as does Johnson's definition of *critic* (a word first used in our modern sense by Shakespeare). Johnson defines "critic" as someone "skilled in the art of judging literature," who is "able to distinguish the faults and beauties of writing." As a measure of how quickly this definition had become established, we can recall that in the first half of the seventeenth century criticism generally did not imply literary criticism; however, by the 1670s and 1680s that usage was universally accepted, and by the beginning of the next century it was settled. When Johnson himself contemplates writing a "History of Criticism . . . from Aristotle to the present age," a remarkable undertaking to be projected at that time, but also a signal that he feels such a history could then, perhaps for the first time in England, be written, he thinks of the undertaking "as it relates to Judging of Authors."[7] Judgment remains the lifeblood of the reviewer, whose existence, seemingly transient, is assured a lasting niche in every literary community. Until that apocalyptic day when a single literary theory becomes universally accepted, criticism will continue to be a diversified affair, and it will include judgments. Its current diversity is a sign of health. We are all pluralists to some degree, at least more than we often care to admit. But we should not lose sight of the eighteenth-century understanding that, in the end, a critic always evaluates, if only by selecting what to discuss, what to make the subject of a book or article, on what to lavish time and energy.

One effect of criticism, or of repeated criticisms, far from fragmenting the experience of literature, can be to organize and unite that experience, at least to make connections, to give us a tradition or traditions. We may form a series of views that, like indices marking angles of refraction, converge until a white light illuminates our experience of the object "as it really is," or at least as it seems to be according to our best efforts at self-education and our refusal to become set in our ways. The echo here is not from Arnold and Pater alone (surprisingly close in their emphasis that criticism should try to see the object as it really is), but also from Wordsworth, Coleridge, and Johnson. *Rambler* 3 personifies Criticism as originally bearing a torch, of which it was "the particular quality immediately to shew every thing in its true form, however it might be disguised to common eyes."

Whether conceived as a single system or as a collective, pluralistic undertaking with varieties and emphases, criticism is analytic and synthetic, practical and theoretical. As a process it resembles what Coleridge says in chapter fourteen of the *Biographia Literaria* about philosophical discourse; it distinguishes in order then to create a schema or sense of coherence:

> The office of philosophical *disquisition* consists in just *distinction*; while it is the priviledge of the philosopher to preserve himself constantly aware, that distinction is not division. In order to obtain adequate notions of any truth we must intellectually separate its distinguishable parts; and this is the technical *process* of philosophy. But having done so, we must then restore them in our conceptions to the unity, in which they actually co-exist; and this is the *result* of philosophy.

For "philosophy" and its cognates substitute "criticism" and its cognates, and for "any truth" substitute "any body of literature." Then this passage describes much of our critical endeavor, the idea Frye has in mind when he says that criticism should stand in the same relation to literature that philosophy does to wisdom.

It has become a maxim that not to have a stated method is to have one anyway—a "hidden agenda." Yet it is also true that the theoretical statement of a method never ensures its practice, and its practice never ensures its intelligent practice. A "wayward" practice may even save us from the rigidities of method and yield insight. These are the very procedural issues that neoclassical theory wrestles with for decades, issues that romantic criticism redefines rather than solves. "It is curious, considering the brilliance of the leading scholars in the field," Northrop Frye told the Modern Language Association in 1984, "how much critical theory today has relapsed into a confused and claustrophobic battle of methodologies, where, as in Fortinbras' campaign in *Hamlet,* the ground fought over is hardly big enough to hold the contending armies."[8] The chapters that follow attempt to enlarge the account of several "essentially contested concepts," and of individual critics who define, recast, and deal with them. With sympathy we can see these critics as individuals caught up in a drama that takes for its subject the expression—in language—of world, culture, and self, of experience, imagination, and action.

Critical studies have as their immediate object other books and publications, many of them written centuries ago, when problems and situations existed for literature and for humanity that do not exist today. In turn, those books, essays, and reviews discuss other poems, books, and essays whose sources may be as varied as "life," "nature," the "fantastic," or yet again other books. An easy way out of this maze would be to argue that all books are ultimately written about other books, that texts are self-enclosed worlds. There is a certain elegance and truth to this proposition. So far as we understand the universe and our own natures, and so far as we both create and understand with words, our understanding and verbal creativity are found in our texts. "Burn but his books," says Caliban of Prospero, and he will become a weak, powerless victim. But Hilaire Belloc, writing in *The Silence of the Sea,* supplies the depressing voice: "Of all fatiguing, futile, empty trades, the worst, I suppose, is writing about writing." The threat of criticism as a "secondary" activity—if we choose to view it as a threat—will not go away by itself. One can use colorful and disturbing adjectives to describe and charge the situation with emotional overtones: for example, criticism is "parasitic" or "marginal." True, criticism must have an object if it is to escape solipsism but, more accurately, criticism—even while "subservient" to the literature or ideas it addresses—is also a vital, concurrent part of literature and ideas. Criticism, according to Eliot, comes to us as naturally as breathing. And while we might observe that anyone continually worried and self-conscious about every breath is already in troubled health, psychically if not bodily, we have little reason to believe our situation different in kind from the one faced by critics and readers preceding us.

Criticism teaches the limits and ephemeral nature of any individual contribution to it. Eventually the critical process unmasks pretense. With precipitate speed, current authorities pass or are completely reinterpreted. In its richness and complexity criticism may promote an insecurity or lack of bearing, which seeks refuge by rushing to establish what is important, new, or exclusive to the "field" and its "cutting edge." But unlike the general procedure of science, where time and repetition bring new, accumulated knowledge, offer hypotheses, or establish theories as natural laws, human experience and its written record come in flux and reflux, constantly renaming and rewriting themselves in texts often read simply because it pleases us to read them, without any discernible sense of ordered progress in the human condition. Into that vortex criticism throws us with all our specialized discourses and recondite distinctions. But it also carries us with a sense of commonness, a community of different voices, of the mysterious power of art so hard to analyze, of our enlargement and connectedness.

In *Rambler* 208 Johnson asserts that "criticism . . . is only to be ranked among the subordinate and instrumental arts." But Campbell sees criticism and the other arts as "reciprocally subservient." Criticism began when a listener said, "That's good" after the singer of tales recited a poem, or when another listener requested "The

Battle" or "The Hunt," or claimed that "Alone at night, my heart holds day-born griefs" was told better than "In fair days, by the fairest of water." As Tzvetan Todorov states in the English edition of his *Introduction to Poetics*, "Discourse about literature is born with literature itself; we find the earliest specimens in certain fragments of the Vedas or in Homer."[9] Criticism begins with natural responses, first with like and dislike—which Henry James says also provide the ultimate test—or, to use Kant's eighteenth-century phrasing, with "pleasure and pain." A dweller of the Dordogne region improved a companion's cave painting, added colors, repeated the scene from another point of view, or interpreted the figures for a child—these are critical acts. Criticism might be considered a twin of art, not identical but fraternal, and it is often hard to tell which of the two is older.

PART ONE

Metamorphoses

CHAPTER 1

Practical Theorist: Dryden's "Variety of Models"

Varietie . . . the rules of it so difficult, that to define or describe it were as to draw one picture which should resemble all the faces in the World, changing it selfe like *Proteus* into all shapes.

HENRY PEACHAM, "OF POETRIE"

Dryden is always *another and the same.*

JOHNSON, LIFE OF DRYDEN

Few critics in any literature have achieved the scope and suppleness, the accessibility and relevance, of Dryden. He synthesizes varied approaches: mimetic, generic, structural, linguistic, and cultural. Yet he combines these without letting any single approach—or its specific vocabulary—get in the way of others. Rarely cluttering or obscuring basic appeals of literature, he embodies a totality of immediate, informed response. His energy turns to technical issues of craft, while also reflecting problematic ideals of a living, not an academic, civilization. In this sense he stands with Dante, Chaucer, and Spenser or, following his own century, with Voltaire, Lessing, and Goethe—in recent generations with James, Eliot, Bakhtin, and Frye.

Of all European critics writing before 1700, Dryden is the most forward-looking and retains power to engage us. In one voice he is Neander—the new man—who refreshes our views more than do Boileau, Casaubon, the Scaligers, Vida, or even Corneille.[1] Compared to contemporaries such as Rymer, who was no poet, Dryden's theoretical statements, like water, seek their own practical level. He combines his undogmatic theory with practice, wringing energy and tension from the two. He will tack and then beat to the wind. Although Dryden's practice as a critic is the subject of this chapter, it is inseparable from his practice as a poet. As Hegel notes in the *Aesthetics,* both a theoretical bent and practical execution "are bound together in the genuine artist."

Some recent studies indicate that Dryden's criticism derives from continental theory, others that his prefaces bolster English or personal traits of composition. This only reveals how dialectical and various his criticism really is.[2] A classicist and a *comparatiste,* instrumental in bringing French criticism to English letters, he encourages selective introduction of continental theory while simultaneously confronting figures who shape English poetry: Chaucer, Shakespeare, Jonson, and Milton. Dryden also knows that much of what is good in English criticism during his own lifetime has come from France, and he acts as the transfer agent.

Yet it is misleading to see Dryden as the champion of an already established national tradition; it is better to say he conceives one—not as a manifesto—but continually over his career. As Eric Rothstein urges, Dryden and his contemporaries are "the inventors of 'English Literature'" and fulfill the desire of the English Renaissance for a vernacular, independent canon backed by literary principles. Envisioning a more capacious and informed tradition, Dryden draws liberally from classical authors, French and Italian critics, and the English past.[3] His achievement is a mosaic fitted together over forty years. If he becomes a coffeehouse arbiter, it is because he spent hours at his desk in the Long Acre house and later, as Pope told Spence, on the ground floor in Gerrard Street. There is hardly one kind of literature he fails to touch and, as Johnson's epitaph says of Goldsmith, does not grace by touching it. And, as Johnson praises

Dryden, "perhaps no nation ever produced a writer that enriched his language with such variety of models"—drama and dramatic criticism, translation, lyric, narrative, and meditative verse, comments on genre, and several types of discursive prose. "Variety of models" describes his critical stance, too.

Wearing Virgil's armor more comfortably than Swift pictures him in *The Battle of the Books,* Dryden expresses his love of classical literature through useful reference and translations.[4] His awareness of the past never drags him into stale nostalgia; he remains open to the educative and formative functions of criticism, realizing that readers and writers are not like the younger Pitt, on whom Macaulay, echoing Coleridge, passed the admiring but ultimately negative verdict that Pitt did not grow but was "cast." Literature, asserts Taine, lives only through the individuals it animates and changes. Similarly, Erich Auerbach contends that "what we understand and love in a work is a human existence, a possibility of 'modifications' within ourselves." And although it may be impossible to define such changes or modifications, they are not random. Dryden never loses sight of Aristotle's first observation in the *Poetics:* humans are animals who imitate. Life and art are linked—both ways, as Wilde pointed out two centuries later—by our drive to imitate and, in the process, to fashion ourselves. Dryden speaks of a "just and lively image of human nature" and prefers to see living "character" and "life-touches" in a work. One danger now is that Dryden will be seen with a literal mind: distant in time, a figure in "the history of criticism" providing raw ideas that others refine. That view has fractional truth, but his ability to hold many approaches in solution makes him particularly appealing. He speaks of "character" in a work, and his own shines through his criticism.[5] Johnson notes how in Dryden's prose we sense inevitable ease and timelessness. Congreve says his friend's writing seemed, like gold, incorruptible, an image Eliot echoes when he speaks of Dryden's "uncorruptible sincerity of word."

Taken singly, Dryden's observations prove insufficient for understanding his critical response. If he is inconsistent and contradicts himself, the same applies to Hazlitt or even Johnson, who changed his mind as the decades passed. Systematic consistency seems no more valid a criterion of criticism than of art. Dryden proceeds by accretion, assimilation, comparison, and re-comparison, by a friendly tug-of-war between practice and theory. He has the method of an artisan. Working with refractory materials, he realizes that "method," once mastered, must often be modified or abandoned. For him the critical precepts of the ancients were drawn first from practice. In the preface to *Aeneis* (1697), he refers to "those many rules of imitating nature which Aristotle drew from Homer's *Iliads* and *Odysseys,* and which he fitted to the drama."

My concern is with the relevant strategies Dryden uses to maneuver between theory and practice, critical and creative acts: how he retains integrity without losing pluralism.[6] Part of his attraction is that he brings criticism out of the scholar's closet. Although Pope and others note that Dryden in person was not "conversible," and that his acquaintance and conversation were limited mostly to literary topics and figures, he lived in the world of affairs and fits his criticism for a generally educated—not a specialized—audience. He does this without sacrificing either depth of thought or delight of expression. Auden says poets wish to be read by the rich, the beautiful, and the powerful, when in fact they are more generally read by the pimply boy sitting alone in a corner of the school cafeteria. Dryden succeeds in winning an audience of wide cultural influence. His criticism still seems to talk to us, participating in a world where we do not need an expert's passport to travel.

In large part Dryden pilots English criticism out from its "dead water" to "a vast ocean." Near the end of his career, he describes the disorientation he felt at the beginning: "As I may say, before the use of the loadstone, or knowledge of the compass, I was sailing in a vast ocean, without other help, than the polestar of the Ancients, and the rules of the French stage amongst the Moderns, which are extremely different from ours, by reason of their opposite taste." Faced with a mixed, comparatively thin heritage of English

criticism, little of it systematic, yet with strong English poets rang-
ing back more than 250 years, Dryden and his contemporaries could
simultaneously feel attracted to, but distanced from, the organized
criticism practiced on the Continent. Ironically, the Interregnum
eventually increased the impact of French thought on English culture. If Charles returned directly from Netherlands soil, his court
brought French ideas. True, "the rules of the French" were "extremely different from ours," but the appeal was that such rules
could exist—and could improve poetry (as they did Dryden's poems
of the 1680s). English literature could then find its own principles,
something, at any rate, to calm and order the growing chaos Pope
would envision as a force that "buries all." The Restoration seemed
an ideal time to shape a strengthened poetic practice according to
systematic criteria drawn from the classics and the learned spirit of
French intellectual criticism—and thus for the first time publicly
to yoke critical theory with poetic (and critical) practice. Dryden
remarks in his dedication of the *Aeneis* that, "Impartially speaking,
the French are as much better critics than the English as they are
worse poets."[7] Could one not legitimately strive for the best of both
worlds?

Criticism Methodized: An Adaptable Discourse

Dryden's "method" of discourse, the way he combines theoretical
ideas and a practical eye, is a gift we are in danger of losing from
lack of practice. It is tempting, though not quite accurate, to apply
to him a phrase that Burke, in the *Speech on American Taxation,* uses
in a different context: "consistent in theory and valuable in practice." Yet in Dryden's case it would likewise be false to say "*in*consistent in theory" and let the matter drop. The truth lies in a degree
of play present between the compass of theory and the rudder of
practice. Perhaps it is not far-fetched here to see Descartes as a
presence. The *Discourse on Method,* and rationalist philosophy in general, helped to pressure literary criticism into a posture where it felt
more eager than ever to generate and defend "method." Hence Rap-

in's famous reply, echoed by Pope, that critical rules "Are Nature still, but Nature methodiz'd." The perpetual drift of some critics toward a "scientific" approach reenacts this tendency. Dryden genuinely appreciates the new science, but realizes it can form no template for criticism. He quips that Hobbes's version of Homer was "bald" (it is), and said in the "Preface to Fables" that Hobbes studied "poetry as he did mathematics, when it was too late." But Dryden read Hobbes and Descartes carefully.[8] Like those English critics more exposed to science than their peers—Johnson, Coleridge, Shelley, Emerson, Richards—Dryden knew science could not provide a strict pattern for literature. He sensed the temptation of it, and the irony as well. For literature and criticism do need to borrow materials and intellectual perspective from technical fields; letters must take cognizance of science. Yet too often it is a high-school understanding of science that leads to an "imitation" of it in criticism. Those who have done scientific research see up close that "method" is a fluid, exasperating, often plural set of procedures and assumptions difficult to define even for a restricted subarea. Those who read in the history and philosophy of science are unenthusiastic about something as large and diverse as "scientific method" becoming a model for criticism.

Most of Dryden's critical efforts are prefatory. They explain, defend, or comment on his poetry or translations. He writes in an easy tone of semiformal but personal address, or in the series of familiar addresses, which form the *Essay on Dramatic Poesy*. "It is all," Bonamy Dobrée notes, "beautifully conversational . . . he is talking to, not at, the addressee of the essay."[9] We might quibble over an exact characterization of such prose, but it is universally admired, as Mark Van Doren long ago pointed out. In addition, this use of the preface was, Johnson notes, "a kind of learning then almost new in the English language."[10] Dryden is a critic who shares. He shares as he moves from one point to another, providing a reader the courtesy of making his points as clear as one would do for the sake of a friend. And in sharing he hovers between talking as a reader and responding as a writer—and so do we. In Dryden's prefaces the audience and artist, reader and critic, critic and scholar, are dissolved in dia-

logue. This is disciplined conversation; and in that sense it is dialogic criticism.[11]

Reflecting on Dryden's "negligent" method of preface and personal address (to patron, friend, or fellow artist), we can see how
vitally it unites theory and practice. Other examples are well
known: Horace's *Ars Poetica* to Piso, Longinus' *On the Sublime,* which
is addressed to a friend or group of artists, Corneille's three *Discours,*
Davenant's Preface along with Hobbes's reply, and naturally the
1800 Preface to the *Lyrical Ballads.* Constantly using the modern
shorter title of Johnson's *Lives,* we tend to forget they were originally *Prefaces, Biographical and Critical, to the Works of the English
Poets,* first printed as introductions to separate volumes of each poet's
work.

The prefatory method, often similar to the verse epistle, remains
a dominant mode of critical discourse from *Joseph Andrews* and Johnson's edition of Shakespeare through Arnold's 1853 Preface, the exquisite pieces of Henry James and Conrad, and Wilde's underrated
preface to *Dorian Gray.* That flawed masterpiece the *Biographia Literaria* began specifically as a preface to *Sibylline Leaves,* and Coleridge
intended to defend and to correct Wordsworth's Preface to the
Lyrical Ballads. (Coleridge even insisted that a type face identical to
Wordsworth's Preface be used). Then, as Coleridge enlarged his
"preface," he planned it as a companion volume to the poems; it
grew into a separate work. Letters form a rich body of criticism:
Voltaire, Rilke, Keats, Byron, Wilson—these are often personal,
individual, one reader to another, and hence speak universally.
Goethe's *Conversations with Eckermann* presents another case of
method that follows the discourse found at the heart of a literate,
civilized community: speaking to one another about what we read.

Discussing catachresis, but in a remark taking on greater scope,
Dryden has Eugenius say, "that wit is best conveyed to us in the
most easy language; and is most to be admired when a great
thought comes dressed in words so commonly received that it is
understood by the meanest apprehensions, as the best meat is easily
digested." This is the precept under which Dryden conducts criticism, and a lesson we often miss. What he says of Cleveland, in

line with his bias in favor of a more natural, passionate language, could be applied to many academic styles: "we cannot read . . . without making a face at it, as if every word were a pill to swallow." We are fed "many times a hard nut to break our teeth, without a kernel for our pains."[12] Anticipating Johnson's aversion to mere bookishness, Dryden touches on the masquerade of academic discourse when he describes Ben Jonson's Truewit as "a scholar-like kind of man, a gentleman with an allay of pedantry, a man who seems mortified to the world by too much reading. The best of his discourse is drawn not from the knowledge of the town, but books. And, in short, he would be a fine gentleman in an university." We would be less than honest if we failed to admit that Dryden voices this implicit rebuke.[13] Of course the style of criticism is immeasurably important. Goldsmith notes in *The Bee* that Dryden's pen "formed the Congreves, the Priors, and the Addisons . . . and had it not been for Dryden, we never should have known a Pope." He goes on to add that "Dryden's excellencies, as a writer, were not confined to poetry alone. There is in his prose writings an ease and elegance that have never yet been so well united in works of taste or criticism."[14]

Dryden's critical achievement includes the prologues and epilogues to his plays. They run in verse "a course parallel to the essays in many ways."[15] In these short poems we hear direct address to the audience, an utterance acutely aware of—and attempting to influence or to humor—reader response. There could be no more compact resolution of theory and practice in verse criticism. Dryden also exposes the sinews and ligaments that connect social behavior with the stage, and cultural values with literature and language at large. With the frank and open address, the lack of affectation and literary posing (things he elsewhere indulges in), the rapid jabs at—and alternate complicities with—the reader, then the scolding of crude "popular" tastes, these poems and their varied tones might remind us of *Don Juan,* as Byron was reminded by them. Taken as a separable body of work, the prologues and epilogues form one of the finest examples in English of the conscious, articulated relation of a poet to all levels of his audience. They reveal how much Dryden felt he had to please the most uninformed taste, and how much he calculated to elevate and refine it.

Terms of Lasting Questions

A rough measure of the shift in Anglo-American criticism is that, in the 1930s, T.S. Eliot could speak explicitly of Dryden as a theorist and of his propensity "to theorise," while thirty-five years later, in his introduction for the Regents Critical Series, Arthur Kirsch stresses the pragmatic side of Dryden's prefaces and essays. In light of an increased theoretical orientation of English criticism, beginning with Wellek and Warren's *Theory of Literature* in 1949, Dryden now appears less theoretical than he once did. Unless we seek attention through discourse and opinions that are determinedly outlandish, or unless, like the Wizard of Oz, we mystify our audience more than our subject requires, no controversial reassessment of Dryden's criticism seems likely. Though many of its judgments have been questioned or rejected, the last complete revaluation of him is in Saintsbury's *English Men of Letters* volume more than a century ago (1881). Interesting views and fresh connections have been uncovered, but no revolution is likely to shake our attitude toward Dryden as a critic.

However, Dryden holds principles and interests that qualify him as a broker of theory. We may speak about his idea of the delight or pleasure of the text, of his dialogic foreshadowing of Bakhtin, especially on the subject of Menippean satire, of his interest in the nature of literary genre and structural principles. Theoretical concerns arise when we observe that Dryden is among the first English writers to understand, at least implicitly, the conditions imposed on a literature that is primarily printed and read—that is, written as well as heard—where books and writing are the main instruments of transmission. In the preface to *Annus Mirabilis* he reverts to a "School distinction" (in the way Kant would use terms coined by the schoolmen). Dryden revives the distinction between "wit written" and "wit writing." Yet his application has, I believe, connections with what is now referred to as "arche-writing." In addition, Dryden pays attention to at least two other issues of language and structure that have haunted English criticism since the Renaissance: poetic diction (the language of poetry seen in contrast to the language of prose), and especially the desire for a more "natural" language.

Dialogue, Variety, and the Everyday

Of all Dryden's works in verse or prose, the most familiar are *Absalom and Achitophel* and *Mac Flecknoe,* which are anthologized with greatest frequency. As soon as historical pointers are given and a few words glossed, the poems become accessible even to a reader only vaguely aware of political and literary intrigues in Restoration England. Now it is just these two poems of his own that Dryden classifies as Varronian or Menippean satire, placing them in that genre along with Apuleius' *Golden Ass,* Erasmus' *Praise of Folly,* and Spenser's *Mother Hubbard's Tale.* In his exploration of literary "kinds," perhaps his comments on this genre or mode—the satiric, the style of which, as he is quick to point out, is multileveled and various—retain most relevance. We should include Dryden's prologues and epilogues here, for they are best seen as satiric in nature, much in the sense Dryden calls Chaucer of *The Canterbury Tales* a satirist. Dryden's own account of Menippean or varied satire bears striking resemblances to twentieth-century commentary, especially to that of Mikhail Bakhtin in *The Dialogic Imagination.*

Although Dryden contends that "an Heroic Poem is certainly the greatest work of human nature," and then compares the heroic to the epic and tragic, concluding that the heroic exceeds them because it "forms a hero,"[16] his longest essay on any genre is the *Discourse concerning the Original and Progress of Satire.* This preface, admittedly with its share of padding and flattery to the Earl of Dorset, runs about one hundred pages, longer than the famous *Essay on Dramatic Poesy* published twenty-five years earlier in 1668. It is here, in the *Discourse concerning Satire,* that Dryden explores Menippean or Varronian satire. Before examining the implications of his position in this essay, let us consider parallels with Bakhtin who, though employing a somewhat different vocabulary, covers the same territory in his essay "Epic and Novel."

In looking at the roots of the novel, Bakhtin takes up the whole nature of seriocomic writing, or what the ancients called *spoudoge-loion*. Here, he says, "belong Roman satire (Lucilius, Horace, Persius, Juvenal) . . . and finally Menippean satire (as a genre) and dialogues of the Lucianic type." These are precisely the subjects and writers whom Dryden treats in his essay. The idea of the Menippean satire, according to Bakhtin, is "to put to the test and to expose ideas and ideologues," which is what occurs in a poem such as *Absalom and Achitophel*. For him, this genre grasps "the 'todayness' of the day" and emphasizes it "in all its randomness." For Dryden, in a similar vein, this genre arises from "chance and jollity," and includes characters about whom "stories . . . were told . . . in bakehouses and barbers' shops." Dryden calls it "a sort of *ex tempore* poetry" or "their clownish extemporary way of jeering" and connects it with the speaking, raillery, and verbal sparring of individuals caught up in celebrations and feasts, especially the saturnalia. For him the origin is carnivalesque. So, too, for Bakhtin, a direct connection exists with the saturnalia, and the "central hero of the genre," typified first by Socrates, is "a speaking and conversing man." Thus, both critics link the genre with the historical and social setting of the carnivalesque, and Dryden, by way of translating a paragraph from Dacier, also links Socrates with the central figure or archetype of this kind of satire.[17]

Perhaps the closest parallel comes in an insistence that this kind of literature, which Bakhtin explicity identifies as the forerunner of the modern novel, contains a variety of styles, a series of voices, a "dialogized story" that is "full of parodies and travesties, multistyled." For Dryden, too, such variety is the key element. As Bakhtin sees "heteroglossia" as characteristic of these texts, Dryden points to the "mixture" of verses encountered in such satire: "And if variety be of absolute necessity . . . yet it may arise naturally . . . in the several subordinate branches of it [satire], all relating to the chief. It may be illustrated according with variety of examples in the subdivisions of it, and with as many precepts as there are members of it; which, altogether, may complete that *olla,* or hotchpotch, which is properly a satire."

We should not push the parallels between Dryden and Bakhtin so far that we forget, first of all, that it would be quite natural for them to come to similar conclusions when looking at the same satiric dialogues by the same writers. Second, Dryden was leaning on those Renaissance scholars who had preceded him, just as Bakhtin was immersed in literary history. And third, Dryden does not speculate about the novel or novelistic form. In many places we could find appropriate parallels to the idea of dialogue in poetry and in criticism. Plato and, more recently, Martin Buber come to mind. A suggestive statement by Feuerbach connects the larger philosophical process of dialectic with that of dialogue: "The true dialectic is not a monologue of the solitary thinker with himself, it is a dialogue between I and Thou."[18]

Still, though Dryden does not have the terms "dialogic" and "heteroglossia" (instead, "dialogue," "mixture," and "variety" were at hand), several ideas of the two critics move together in emphasis and outlook. Even while arguing for the final, fluid irreducibility of Bakhtin's terms and concepts, two of his best English-speaking commentators connect "heteroglossia" and "polyphony" with "his several attempts to find a single name for *variety,*" sheer variety in literary voice, language, and perspective.[19] The spirit of mixture, of what Bakhtin calls "novelness," emerges in the *Discourse concerning Satire.* At one point Dryden is commenting on Boileau's *Lutrin.* It combines, he says, "the majesty of the heroic, finely *mixed* with the venom of *the other.*" Dryden applies the highest aesthetic and moral terms to this form of writing which is, after all, not tragic nor heroic nor epic: "This, I think, my Lord, to be the most beautiful, and most noble kind of satire." Here we might recall how Dryden, though giving the two etymologies for "satire" and Isaac Casaubon's arguments for distinguishing them, sees some value in the one from "satura," a Roman dish filled with a variety of fruit. It could be argued that in Dryden's time "variety" meant not primarily the quality of variousness but more a change or succession. However, the definition Johnson gives includes "intermixture," and I believe it is this intermixing quality that Dryden and others, especially novelists who constantly use the term "variety" to defend the genre in their prefaces, have in mind.[20]

It is tempting to think of Dryden, writing in the last decade of his life, as turning more to the idea of dialogue, mixture, and variety typified by his theoretical view of Menippean satire and also by his own poetry. His later, more adroit and varied prologues and epilogues indicate this shift. So does *Absalom and Achitophel*, a poem affecting the last twenty years of his poetic practice and one in which Mark Van Doren says Dryden "realized at once that he had woven patches of verse which would wear like iron, and proceeded to acquaint himself with all the varieties of texture which the new weave would admit."[21] Like Pope, he never writes the epic poem he hoped to achieve. And although he translates the *Aeneid*, his later critical work and "translations" also turn toward Chaucer and ancient fables. In this, Dryden responds to a sense that poetry and criticism are shifting to fresh scenes and an accompanying fresh investigation of the past. He may also be following his impulse for a narrative art that shows, in dramatic form, a full range of passion and the "life-touches" of action and emotion imitated with immediate directness. At any rate, Dryden orients his critical bearings more in this new direction during his last twenty years.[22]

Bakhtin says "contemporary reality," with its direct gazes at "everyday life" and with the "living people" in their "diversity of speech and voice" before us in "a zone of crude contact, where we can grab at everything with our own hands," serves as the basis for the novelistic. We might equally turn with Dryden, in his "Preface to Fables," to his encounter with Chaucer's creations: "I see . . . all the Pilgrims in the *Canterbury Tales,* their humours, their features, and the very dress, as distinctly as if I had supped with them at the *Tabard* in Southwark." Dryden identifies Chaucer as "a satirical poet," though, more important, "he must have been a man of a most wonderful comprehensive nature" (as Shakespeare had a "comprehensive soul"). Dryden is recognizing in Chaucer these same qualities highlighted by Bakhtin's observations. The passage concerning the pilgrims is almost too famous to continue quoting—how Dryden praises "the matter and manner of their tales," how they "are so suited to their different educations, humours, and callings, that each of them would be improper in any other mouth." This is "heteroglossia" by an older name, but smells as sweet. "'Tis sufficient to say, according to the proverb," adds Dryden, with the right spirit for his subject, "that *here is God's plenty*."[23] The same impulse to admire the range of passion and voice in everyday life is behind Dryden's opinion of Shakespeare—as it is behind Johnson's of Shakespeare and Hazlitt's of Shakespeare and Chaucer.

Dryden obviously held "variety" as a conscious value throughout most of his career. Neander prefers English to French drama for several reasons; specifically, English plots "are fuller of variety." And it is no coincidence that Dryden stands near the chronological verge of the English novel. One of his young readers, who spent much time writing satires and dialogues for one party or another but in later years wrote his famous novels (or proto-novels), is Daniel Defoe. Significantly, two of the more eloquent, earlier defenses of the novel in English—the preface to *Joseph Andrews* and the apologia in *Northanger Abbey*—stress the novel's characteristic stamp of variety. Fielding's definition rests on this quality and, however familiar, is worth noting again: "Now, a comic romance is a comic epic-poem in prose; differing from comedy, as the serious epic from tragedy: its action being more extended and comprehensive; *containing a much larger circle of incidents, and introducing a greater variety of characters*." Austen reemphasizes this hallmark in an aside that closes chapter five. Novels are works "in which the most thorough knowledge of human nature, the happiest delineation *of its varieties* . . . are conveyed to the world." From the start, the novel is associated with this quality. In his prefatory remarks Defoe assures readers of *Robinson Crusoe* that they will encounter "Wonders" of great "Variety."[24]

Although T. S. Eliot's affinities with Dryden will be discussed later, let me interject here that *The Waste Land* may be read as the great modern Menippean satire, a poem of varied levels, of "fragments . . . shored," which Eliot originally entitled (even there borrowing from Dickens' *Our Mutual Friend*), "He do the police in different voices." The variety of styles and levels in much modernist writing casts that whole movement in a Menippean mode, for, unless we insist on a straitjacket definition, works such as *Ulysses, The Sound and the Fury,* Pound's *Cantos,* and novels such as Vonnegut's *Slaughterhouse Five* all rely on the technique of varied voices caught in juxtaposed immediacy. Faulkner originally wanted to use a variety of type faces and ink colors to capture the different voices in his novel. Petronius, with whom Eliot finally, after Pound's editing, begins *The Waste Land,* represents an archetypal Menippean mode. And Dryden, with what Johnson calls his "variety of models," acts as a powerful center of gravity for Eliot throughout the 1920s.

In Dryden we have a critic who engages himself in dialogue with what he reads, whether Virgil, Bouhours, Chaucer, Shakespeare, or Oldham. He expresses interest in what is characteristic of an author, the "character" of a work and what he repeatedly calls an author's "turns" of thought—what makes a writer's voice distinct. The *Preface to Ovid's Epistles* outlines this attitude: "Nor must we understand the language only of the poet [to be translated], but his particular turn of thoughts and of expression, which are the characters that distinguish and, as it were, individuate him from all other writers."[25] He sounds as if he were distinguishing characters in the dialogue of a play. This emphatically does not mean reducing a writer to anecdotes or biographical squibs, the kind of "character" Graham Greene justly deplores in the press's treatment of Evelyn Waugh. Dryden's term "character" is not what makes a celebrity, but rather features of style and thought that, taken in aggregate, uniquely establish the quality of an author's writing.

It is no accident that the scene of *Mac Flecknoe* is a stage, and that *Absalom and Achitophel* includes pronounced theatrical elements in speeches and characters. Though rarely noted, Dryden's major critical principles (imitation, pleasure, characteristic yet varied voices) are those we would expect of a practicing dramatist. His experience in the theater, his sense of audience, the critical comments in his prologues and epilogues, the fact that his first piece of criticism is in effect a small play about dramatic poetry—all these contribute to the dialogue and friendly confrontation encountered in his criticism. We find a connection with the novel here, too, for dialogue taken from the theater later sharpens the fiction of Fielding, and even Richardson explains to readers approaching *Clarissa* that his epistolary novel is actually "written in the Dialogue or Dramatic Way."[26]

More than other English critics of his stature, early in his career Dryden is closely familiar with the theater. Eliot strives for it with success, but nearer the end of his last productive phase; Wilde earnestly achieves it in several instances, including the tone and method of *The Decay of Lying* (itself a dialogue play) and parts of *Dorian Gray*. Hazlitt loved verse tragedy above other genres and founded many of his critical bywords on it—imitation, passion, and nature. Fielding and Goldsmith exhibit the dramatic and speaking sense of criticism in brief, brilliant flashes. The criticism of these writers—Dryden first among them—reflects, in varying degrees, their sensibility and apprenticeship to the theater. They are critics in dialogue, or often capable of it, a manner essentially foreign to Johnson, Arnold, Pound, and even Coleridge. For instance, of all romantic critics who admire Edmund Burke, Hazlitt is particularly sensitive in commenting on the dramatic nature and structure of Burke's speeches and presence in the House of Commons.

The Pleasure of Texts *as* Structure

It has become a commonplace—a correct one—to observe how Dryden remains flexible within his standards and rules, how he rejects flat formulae (what Johnson in his *Life of Dryden* calls "theorems"), yet how he embraces principles by which to judge literature. One reason for this flexibility within classical bounds is his belief that poetry must be passionate, that truth to feeling—not a copy of action—but truth in the "*life-touches*" of art is not only important but fundamental, and must come first. This is what Dryden chooses to paraphrase from Davenant on the subject of heroic poetry: "*That it ought to be dressed in a more familiar and easy shape; more fitted to the common actions and passions of human life . . . and figuring a more practicable virtue to us than was done by the Ancients or Moderns.*"[27]

Auden observes that Dryden avoids violent personal emotion except in some passages throughout the plays. The pervasive thrust, similar to Eliot's, aims at formal values and objectivity (the external, not necessarily the eternally true), a use and recasting of the past, plus a molding or shaping of emotional response into more intense and universalized expression. This has little to do with self-expression in the romantic sense, yet Dryden puts great weight on the value of feeling and emotion. This is not contrary to, but a part of his "formalism." Part of the structure—the most *necessary* part of it, in fact—is based on feeling. It is emotive.

At the end of *Heads of an Answer to Rymer,* Dryden notes that Rapin (in his *Réflexions sur la poétique d'Aristote,* 1674) "attributes more to the *dictio*, that is, to the words and discourses of a tragedy, than Aristotle had done." And Dryden closes the *Heads*, if we follow most editors' arrangement of its paragraphs, by quoting Rapin's "remarkable" words: "'Tis not the admirable intrigue, the surprising events, the extraordinary incidents that make the beauty of a tragedy; 'tis the discourses when they are natural and passionate." But then, actually, there follows a short, final paragraph of three words referring to "natural and passionate" discourses in the tragedies of one poet: "So are Shakespeare's."[28] In the *Heads* we hear this explicit theme many times. It is "new passions" and "all the passions in their turns" that create the excellence and individual stamp of modern, particularly English, tragedy. Dryden does not publish these observations, but they indicate, as they indicated to Johnson, who admired them, a premium on the direct and essential in feeling as a quality in poetic speech. The prime example held up is Shakespeare, who influenced English criticism more than any critic. Not plot nor "the justness of the occasion" give him his force, but "the raising of . . . passions . . . from the excellency of the words and thoughts."[29] The extensive, published defence of passion, of a psychological depth of "anger, hatred, love, ambition, jealousy, revenge" that distinguishes characters themselves, comes in "The Grounds of Criticism in Tragedy." And, though Dryden begins his discussion with plot and manners, he concludes it with feeling— with Shakespeare again, if only because the essay is prefaced to an adapted *Troilus and Cressida* (1679).

Little more than sixty years after Shakespeare's death, Dryden takes a critical line that continues through the eighteenth century, strengthens in the Romantic period, and remains emphatic: the power of expression and feeling in individual phrasing and parts of discourse. This becomes so embedded in English criticism that Arnold eventually warns against undue emphasis on it. Yet despite this warning, even Arnold's touchstones provide an emotional register of high seriousness. (It often goes unnoticed, even in sympathetic accounts, that his touchstones reverberate with sharply pitched *emotion* over life and death more than they do with any grandiose or "high"—in the sense of superior—code of ethics, philosophy, or morality.)

To some extent the New Criticism, and also Russian Formalism, the Prague Circle, French Structuralism, and deconstruction do not speak about human feelings with the direct intensity Dryden does. Modern formalism and textualism seem to harbor a certain timidity—or lack of felt acquaintance—in the face of what the eighteenth century calls the passions. At its basic level Dryden's sense of genre is the contrast between tragedy and comedy, which is in turn based on feelings of pleasure and pain—the states of consciousness—produced or elicited by actual reading. His formalism is oriented to the disciplining, sharpening, and intensifying of passion. (Is it too much to speculate that this is one origin of Eliot's stress on passion rather than on subjective, personal feeling?) But much modern formalism seems to have wrung emotion out or left it on the sidelines, a criticism sometimes more passionless than dispassionate. If a theory of literature becomes, in essence, schematic or classificatory, without regard to human feelings and values, then feeling and value, suffering and pleasure, will receive less attention in literature.

For Dryden a play is a *"just and lively image of human nature, representing its passions and humours, and the changes of fortune to which it is subject."* The emphasis falls first on passion, action second. He lauds Seneca for "the scene in the *Troades* where Ulysses is seeking Astyanax to kill him." It "bears the nearest resemblance of any thing" in Roman tragedy "to the excellent scenes of passion in Shakespeare." And in imitating the images of nature, it is not that Shakespeare makes us see them; "bare imitation" is not enough.

When "he describes any thing, you *more* than see it, you feel it too."[30] This sounds like Hazlitt on gusto: Chaucer makes us feel, not see, the atmosphere surrounding his pilgrims.

Dryden particularly emphasizes, as Johnson also will, the feeling of pleasure and delight poetry can bring. Frost, echoing Horace in his own rural voice, says a poem should begin in delight and end in wisdom. This is as good a short version of Dryden's blend of delight and didacticism as we are likely to get. Arthur Kirsch shrewdly points out that of all critics whom we might call neoclassical, it is first Dryden, then Johnson, who understand that pleasure and delight, the desire to read and to continue reading, must come before any ethical or intellectual point is driven home. "The notion that classical rules and precedents ultimately derive their authority from an ability to please centuries of readers is the root assumption of all neoclassical criticism, from Sir Philip Sidney to Samuel Johnson. But with the exception of Johnson, only in Dryden does that assumption really operate; in the others it is often solely an uncompromising appeal to authority."[31] Rymer's determined method of formalizing English dramatic literature could not work because, as Dryden points out, it is contradicted by the experience and the response of audiences.

Dryden's high valuation of pleasure in literature can be seen as early as the *Essay on Dramatic Poesy*. As often with the expression of his principles, it becomes more open, more direct as he grows older. Without forgetting literary form, he supplements concern for it with increased emphasis on the characteristic powers and voices of individual poets. This soon governs his ideas of form.[32] "The Grounds of Criticism in Tragedy" and the *Heads* come at the crucial turning point of the late 1670s. Later, in the *Discourse* on satire (1693), Dryden uses the issue of translation to reflect on what exactly in a text is the pleasurable part—what is essential to its enjoyment (which a translator may overlook or mangle): "A noble author would not be pursued too close by a translator," he says. What exactly it is cannot be pinned down like a specimen. In this escape of Dryden's lies an affinity with Barthes' *jouissance:* like sexual pleasure it consists in a certain free play, personally felt, and would not be pursued or interpreted either microscopically or literally. We go back to variety, for at the "moment he takes his pleasure," Barthes' reader "mixes every language."[33]

After discussing translations of Juvenal by Holyday and Stapylton, Dryden pauses to make a general reflection: "They who will not grant me, that pleasure is one of the ends of poetry, but that it is only a means of compassing the only end, which is instruction, must yet allow, that, without the means of pleasure, the instruction is but a bare and dry philosophy: a crude preparation of morals, which we may have from Aristotle and Epictetus, with more profit than from any poet." Dryden's argument in favor of tragicomedy, a century before Johnson's, leans heavily on basic psychological inclinations and on the emotional (and therefore concomitant structural) impact that tragicomedy has on the audience. So we get imitation, pleasure, structure, and "reader-response" all sheaved together. "Our variety," says Neander (again that term *variety*), "if well ordered, will afford a greater pleasure to the audience." There is more play. To express a simple passion without its natural interminglings will not appeal to "the concernment of an audience." A "bare imitation" cannot "excite the passions."[34]

An emphasis on pleasure and suggestive, natural language at the level of phrasing cannot be overestimated. Dryden protests against words and clauses "placed unnaturally, that is, contrary to the common way of speaking," especially "without the excuse of a rhyme to cause it." He makes the same point about similar attempts to "poeticize" the obvious. Given the line *"Sir, I ask your pardon,"* some, he says, "would think it sounded more heroically to write, *Sir, I your pardon ask."* He quickly follows this with the charge of "unnatural," even in cases where the word order must be altered to rhyme. Later, Dryden admitted that some of his own plays fell short of this developed standard. The remarks anticipate Johnson's laughter at Thomas Warton's use of Miltonic inversions: *"Gray evening* is common enough; but *evening gray* he'd think fine." In blank verse Dryden advises that "Variety of cadences is the best rule" because it helps actors and refreshes listeners. If we put aside his sometime preference for rhyme (especially in tragedy), we see that he gravitates to the advantages of English blank verse or, as he calls it by the French and Latin names, *prose mesurée* and *sermo pedestris*.[35]

Wit Writing, Wit Written / "Colours of Speech" and People Reading

Dryden apparently had difficulty reciting his own lines in company. He seemed shy. But in an age when poetry was so often read aloud, he seems to have been one of the first English poets to realize that poetry was being read as much as heard, and that every hearing of it also constituted a new reading. Dryden knows he is writing for readers as much or more as for listeners. He underscores this awareness not only through his prefaces but by specific asides. For instance, in Chaucer's "Wife of Bath," we find this apology:

> Now wolden some men seye, paraventure,
> That for my necligence I do no cure
> To tellen yow the joye and al th'array
> That at the feeste was that ilke day.

Dryden renders it directly: "Perhaps the reader thinks I do him wrong / To pass the Marriage-Feast and Nuptial Song," which implies a written, not a spoken narrative.[36]

In addition, the older Dryden takes increasing pains with his prologues and epilogues: he insists that folio copies of them be circulated among the audience before the play starts and before any recitation begins—so that even these poems are read before heard. The practice, though not uncommon, Dryden pursues with vigor.[37] He intentionally turns the poems into texts for response and examination, to reinforce the effect that the prologues and epilogues have on the way the play was received, criticized, and remembered.

Religio Laici is usually considered as a statement by Dryden about his religious belief. But it also represents some of his thoughts on the interpretation of written texts. Though this is not the place for a full-scale examination of the poem, which deals with biblical hermeneutics, we see in it Dryden's recognition of interpretive communities of readers (religious sects), and of the power of writing over speech:

> *Tradition written* therefore more commends
> *Authority,* than what from *Voice* descends.

He concludes that in issues "needful" for faith the Bible is clear, but that in many other instances it is impossible to interpret with precision: not *"every where* / Free from Corruption, or intire, or clear." He thus sees the difficulty and even impossibility of univocal interpretation, or of discerning all the authors' intentions. It is enough for him that there is sufficient agreement "In *all* things which our needfull *Faith* require." He painfully admits the influence of speculation or prejudice on interpretation, and of the importance and difficulties raised by canons and authority.

We should not place too much emphasis on this, but there are indications that Dryden thought consciously and systematically about the special circumstances of inscribing and interpreting texts. The test is the effect on reader or audience.[38] A passage in his letter to Sir Robert Howard prefacing *Annus Mirabilis* points up the issue:

> The composition of all poems is, or ought to be, of wit, and wit in the poet, or wit writing (if you will give me leave to use a school-distinction) is no other than the faculty of imagination in the writer which, like a nimble spaniel, beats over and ranges through the field of memory, till it springs the quarry hunted after; or, without metaphor, which searches over all the memory for the species or ideas of those things which it designs to represent. Wit written is that which is well defined, the happy result of thought, or product of imagination.

The end, however, is not a particular kind of text, but a particular kind of effect on the reader:

> But to proceed from wit, in the general notion of it, to the proper wit of an heroic or historical poem, I judge it chiefly to consist in the delightful imaging of persons, actions, passions, or things. 'Tis not the jerk or sting of an epigram, nor

the seeming contradiction of a poor antithesis (the delight of an ill-judging audience in a play of rhyme), nor the jingle of a more poor paronomasis; neither is it so much the morality of a grave sentence affected by Lucan, but more sparingly used by Virgil; but it is some lively and apt description, dressed in such colours of speech that it sets before your eyes the absent object as perfectly and more delightfully than nature.

Here wit means capacity of mind generally (OE *witan*). The "wit in the poet, or wit writing" is a prewriting or mental process that involves memory, conception, and invention—with the final aim being the act of inscribing itself, of "wit written," the specific inscribed words of the text, words which are a "well defined" product and belong properly to a particular species of composition, to a particular kind of text (such as heroic stanzas or the dialogue in drama). But furthermore—and here Dryden's intelligence goes beyond an otherwise common set of observations—the written words, the figures and tropes, the "elocution" must be "sounding and significant." (He repeats this phrase five years later in the *Defence of the Epilogue* as "more sounding, and more significant," and yet again almost thirty years later in his preface to *Aeneis*). What is written must be varied and apt, with the stipulation that no matter what kind of text is composed, the written words are "dressed in such colours of speech" that they set before the reader's "eyes" the absent object. In other words, the wheel comes full circle: readers find their own minds and senses returned, through a "lively" hint of the act of speech, to the immediacy of "nature," now presented even more delightfully, because accompanied with the greater "accuracy" only "wit written" can provide. The reader's imagination has been directed and sharpened. But in this sharpening process any "remoteness" or impression of "labor" should be avoided—the qualities that texts might exhibit if left in the realm of what is only inscribed in texts and, as a result, ignored the need to draw upon and inscribe the liveliness of speech. We are left with the pleasure of the text, with what Barthes finally calls *Writing aloud,* the "sounding" part of composition that throws "the anonymous body of the actor into my ear."[39]

Confronting Past Poets: "that affable familiar ghost"

Dryden became a great English critic, but not because he was the first. Sidney, Jonson, Henry Reynolds, and numerous others precede him. Yet Dryden is undoubtedly a seminal figure. Johnson, aware of the English lineage—and of earlier Continental critics including the younger Scaliger, Vida, and Castelvetro—pointedly calls Dryden "the father of our criticism." Eliot echoes this assessment in the 1930s: "Dryden was positively the first master of English criticism" and wrote "the first serious literary criticism in English by an English poet." And Auden, asked by Eliot's firm Faber and Faber to select and introduce a volume of Dryden's verse, avers that his critical prose retains "the highest historical and aesthetic importance."

The connection with Eliot's publishing house is more than coincidental. Dryden's considerable influence on twentieth-century poetry comes primarily through Eliot. The full influence of Dryden on Eliot, for whom in some respects he acts as a model, has yet to be recognized.[40] Finishing the decade of his poetic transformation, Eliot begins three essays on "John Dryden: the Poet, the Dramatist, the Critic" (1932, originally five talks for the BBC in 1930) with the self-conscious proposition that Dryden might best be approached in the context of English letters precisely by tracing "his *influence*."

Eliot then makes a personal anticipation of W. J. Bate's *The Burden of the Past and the English Poet* (1970) and Harold Bloom's *The Anxiety of Influence* (1973). He states: "For 'influence,' as Dryden had influence, a poet must not be so great as to overshadow all followers. . . . It should seem then no paradox to say that Dryden was the great influence upon English verse that he was, because he was *not* too great to have any influence at all. He was neither the consummate poet of earlier times, nor the eccentric poet of later. He was happy both in his predecessors [precursors] and in his successors." Francis Jeffrey put the situation succinctly more than a century earlier. Speaking of the hopeful poet, he said: "He is perpetually haunted and depressed by the ideal presence of those great masters, and their exacting critics. . . . Thus, the merit of his great predecessors chills, instead of encouraging his ardour."[41] Many of Eliot's aims are conscious foster children of Dryden's. ("Conscious" is a key word in Eliot's description of Dryden himself, as Pechter says Dryden was "conscious" in styling himself a modernist.) The one who went before is great enough to guide, but not so great that he smothers or stunts the imaginative space of those who follow. Goethe said he would not like to be an Englishman, because the example of Shakespeare would prove too overwhelming.

One week after Eliot died, the *Times Literary Supplement* pointed out affinities between the great Modern and a long-deceased other Modern: "Mr. Eliot resembled Dryden in the apparently casual and informal movement of his thought rather than Dr. Johnson in his orderly argumentation and combative briskness. He perhaps also resembled Dryden more as a person." The parallel is extended into areas of religion, cultural concern, technical craftsmanship and interest in poetic drama. During much of his career Eliot consciously paid homage to Dryden through the sincerest form of flattery. By a considerable margin he wrote more on Dryden than on any other author. In addition to the three essays on "John Dryden: the Poet, the Dramatist, the Critic," there is also "John Dryden" (1922), "Homage to John Dryden" (1927), first published by Virginia and Leonard Woolf's Hogarth Press (and dedicated to George Saintsbury), and the curious "Dialogue on Dramatic Poetry" (1928). The title for "Homage" likely came from the *Life of Pope,* where Johnson relates how Pope, as a young poet, paid "homage" to Dryden by visiting him. Eliot loosely models his "Dialogue" on Dryden's own *Essay on Dramatic Poesy.* Throwing in a dash of Oscar Wilde's "The Decay of Lying" along the way, Eliot ends his "Dialogue" with a toast: "And meanwhile let us drink another glass of port to the memory of John Dryden." Then there are the 1931 pieces in *The Listener* (V: 118–120), going over similar ground but showing Eliot's continued interest and admiration. Dryden becomes Eliot's "complete man." The hundred-plus pages of criticism he devotes to him thus form the single largest cohesive body of criticism written about any single author by a major poet of the Modern movement.

When Eliot concludes that "Dryden gives what is the soundest and most commonsense view possible for his time and place," we are in part reading Eliot's program for himself. The image of Dryden as a poet and man of letters shares in Eliot's familiar, compound ghost.

Eliot admits that his own opinion is no discovery. But while he does not "pretend that Dryden as a critic is often profound . . . the more I consider contemporary reflexion upon poetry, the more thankful I am for what we may call Dryden's critical orthodoxy," an orthodoxy which has now become an anomaly. Dryden's brand of criticism, unextravagant yet wonderfully varied, lucid, and informed by the same pen with which he wrote poetry—some of it mediocre but much of it excellent and some of it timeless—this kind of criticism is unorthodox and rare today. Perhaps because it appears deceptively easy, like a perfect pas de deux we imagine doing if only someone would "show us the steps." Eliot praises Dryden for setting a "good example for critics by practising what he preached." In imitating him, Eliot is consciously leveraging the burden of the past and the anxiety of influence to advantage. Viewed in one light, the basic concept of "Tradition and the Individual Talent" is nothing less than a strategem to handle anxiety, a way to defuse and deflect, then to redirect and deal successfully with the burden of the past and one's predecessors.

It is interesting to see how Eliot turns the situation to advantage by taking not an overpowering nor a supremely great predecessor or precursor, but one whom he can intentionally imitate and admire without being faced, in his own words, by one "too great to have any influence at all," a poet on whom he had modeled at least one critical essay as early as 1922—not coincidentally, I think, the year of *The Waste Land*. This is part of Eliot's strategem of defense, his way of wrestling with and finally turning the psychological heritage of greatness to advantage by the use of conscious leverage. The strategem seems to have worked well enough for Eliot to continue using it across the arc of his career.

Dryden is the first English poet consciously to confront, in an extended fashion, the ghosts of his English literary past, to wrestle with them first as a critic and then to bring them into service, particularly Shakespeare and Chaucer, though also Jonson and Milton, with whom Dryden establishes his personal, critical relations. He is the first English poet to handle the anxiety of influence and the burden of the past in a self-conscious way. Eliot recognizes this.

Saintsbury notes that in the *Defence of an Essay of Dramatic Poesy* Dryden disparages the older dramatists. His tone is unusually flip and dismissive; he is prosperous and on familiar terms at court. He had even lent King Charles £500. "It was at this time, and at this time only," Saintsbury says, "that he spoke disrespectfully of his great predecessors."[42] This assertion oversimplifies Dryden's changing attitudes, and some of his later favorable remarks about Shakespeare harbored political motives. Yet if we put aside that *Defence* and perhaps, too, the *Defence of the Epilogue,* it is clear that Dryden becomes engaged not only in a give-and-take struggle of emulation with Shakespeare, Jonson, and Fletcher but also with a wider admiration of Milton and Chaucer. In effect, he selects strong poets before him, then highlights one or two things that attenuate their pressure: Chaucer is obscure and needs translating; his meter is rough (then still misunderstood); Shakespeare has faults and lacks certain refinements of judgment and language; Milton is unlike Dryden in temperament and conviction. Thus, no poet poses a crushing threat to Dryden's own sense of what he wishes to be. There is a difference to be achieved. Furthermore, there are several models (including Virgil, the Latin satirists, and French dramatists) to draw upon. So the past is not summed up in one specific poet who becomes a single idol and therefore a more inhibiting presence, as Shakespeare seems to have acted upon Coleridge.

"Those milder studies of humanity"

Dryden is generally not classified as a humanist in the way More and Erasmus are. The archaeology of humanism has as many levels as the city of Troy. Dryden is not remarkably erudite, and his view of civilization does not engage philosophical questions in a sustained fashion. He is not a seminal thinker, but he is an intellectual, a master of language and the purposes of poetry. The claims of his criticism appear modest, even nonchalant. But the geniality of manner should not obscure a fundamental quality: he examines the value of language and literary structure in the context of human feeling and ethical value. "Qui dit langage," says Lévi-Strauss, "dit société." In Dryden's case this maxim is particularly apt. His criticism searches out the self-image that a culture and a civilization create through literature. In him there is always—as in Virgil, whom he loves so deeply—a wider reference. Criticism is a humane social enterprise before; after, it is a professional one.

Dryden believes "moral truth is the mistress of the poet as much as of the philosopher." This does not mean inculcating a code; nor is it a moralistic pose. All it assumes is that the poet should consider the end and effect of writing to be important along with the means and forms by which it is carried out. Making a distinction as valuable as it subtle, Dryden says that "poesy must resemble natural truth, but it must *be* ethical."[43] That is, poesy or art cannot copy or give us exact reference to life, to our ideas, to things or to experience. It simply *re-sembles* these to our minds and feelings. But in its essence it therefore presents us with a pattern analogous to experience. Furthermore, the poet must choose what to represent and how to do it. That is unavoidable unless the poet becomes a purely mechanic instrumentality. And Dryden would contend that this process could be "free" from ethics only if the imitation in no way resembled "natural truth" or experience.

Time and again Dryden successfully uses criteria of human interest, experience, motivation, and, above all, delight and amusement. The Interregnum is summed up once this way: "we have been so long together bad Englishmen, that we had not leisure to be good poets." The hopeful, equitable insertion here of the word "together" puts much in perspective. It is to "those milder studies of humanity" and "life-touches" of art that Dryden wishes to turn.[44] Whom we admire at once reflects and shapes our being. Of all authors in English— questions of versification and polish aside— Dryden loves two, Chaucer and Shakespeare, and admires Milton.[45] In his criticism and translations he always seeks the particular stamp, the "character" of an author with the particular "turns" of thought and expression that combine to make an individual voice, the individually creating soul.

Dryden's achievement poses, at least implicitly, a disturbing question. Are his range, scope, ease of reference, and knowledgeable participation possible only in the relative infancy of a body of national criticism, or in a culture that, compared with ours, is small? Must specialization and refinement, the compartmentalization of university departments and the looser-knit, more pluralistic structures of politics, theater, scholarship, and "culture" (whatever we now understand by that word), necessarily drive the individual critic to attain an ever smaller stature?

Whenever we read an eighteenth-century critic, we are reading Dryden as well. His views on refinement of language, and yet his intensely ambivalent attitude toward refinement when offered the alternative of rough greatness and sublimity; his consideration of poetic diction and "natural" language, of Shakespeare and Chaucer, of a capacious sense of imitation and the end of pleasure; his thoughts on tragicomedy and the progress of arts and literature in the stream of time, on the nature of readers' psychological "assent," and the importance of passion in poetic language: all these preoccupations of 1700 through 1820, and later, Dryden first encounters and gives a varied, often modern voice. Here is a critic with whom we can still enter into dialogue, a writer whose every concern and judgment we may not wish to repeat or scrutinize, but whose method and attitude extend to us opportunities we are in danger of losing. His criticism is not a product but a process, and his readers are made to feel indispensable partners in that process. He wishes to make a tacit compact, with latitude for disagreement. In taking up any subject he is in dialogue with his several readers, with other critics and authors, and ultimately with the larger human community that our acts of reading imply.

CHAPTER 2

The Paradox of Refinement: Progress and Decline in Literature

As with the greater Dead he dares not strive,
He wou'd not match his Verse with those who live:
Let him retire, betwixt two Ages cast,
The first of this, and hindmost of the last.

DRYDEN, PROLOGUE TO
AURENG-ZEBE (1676)

For nearly two centuries one manifold idea haunted criticism, and it will inevitably do so again. This idea or issue proves so elusive and complex that it can never be expressed in a single, simple formula, but only by a matrix of related concerns. During the late seventeenth and eighteenth centuries these concerns underpin nearly all intelligent discussion of literature and European culture. They surface repeatedly in literary criticism: Are the arts progressive? Do they improve in overall quality, and, if so, what conditions encourage fresh achievements of individual genius? Or does refinement, at first a blessing, inextricably grow excessive? Does continual refinement stifle creative power under a veneer of perfected technique until the arts, potentially synthetic and humane, grow "decadent" in their narrow specialization, limited audiences, and increasingly self-referential, even self-mocking, pursuits?

Poets and thinkers of major stature are preoccupied with these unresolved, perhaps unresolvable, queries.[1] Such questions guarantee no new insights and lend themselves to simplistic answers, but are not concocted by failed versifiers turned guardians of taste. Any culture old enough to remember segments of its own past as distant, and mature enough to realize that some of its splendid achievements occurred under bygone circumstances—or any culture turning back to Greece and Rome—would ask self-conscious questions and make comparisons. Ben Jonson proclaims Bacon as one "who hath fill'd up all numbers, and perform'd that in our tongue which may be compar'd or preferr'd either to insolent *Greece* or haughty *Rome*."[2] Two decades later young Dryden brings his panegyric on Lord Hastings to a fever pitch (Hastings died of smallpox) by asserting

> . . . had he liv'd his life out, his great Fame
> Had swoln 'bove any *Greek* or *Romane* Name.

And in his lovely later poem to John Oldham, Dryden invokes the ghost of this "young Marcellus of our tongue" through Virgilian echo. Association with ancient authority becomes an imprimatur. Today at Stowe, where eighteenth-century busts of British Worthies adorn a garden monument, visitors see the head of Pope, but with an effort: his likeness is placed out of view, around a corner, because he was considered too modern for such an honor. Nevertheless, the inscription reassures us with its final verdict: "equal to the Originals, the best Poets of Antiquity." Pope himself would play on the comparison with classical poets in complex fashion. In the *Epistle to Augustus* he parodies the sentiment of refined superiority in five proud lines, then whips them all into irony with a sixth about the popularity of pantomime:

> Tho' justly Greece her eldest sons admires,
> Why should not we be wiser than our Sires?
> In ev'ry publick Virtue we excell,
> We build, we paint, we sing, we dance as well,
> And learned Athens to our Art must stoop,
> Could she behold us tumbling thro' a hoop.

For Enlightenment Europe the issue of new achievement or inevitable decline becomes vital and baffling. "To feel oneself born in 'an age too late' was the great emotional aftermath of the Renaissance."[3] Post-Renaissance Europe had, in addition to the ancients, its own immediate and detailed past to look back on and ponder. Time had loaded a double-barreled gun. T. S. Eliot, confronted with the statement that we now know much more than previous writers did, replied: yes, and they are what we know. As early as 1672 Dryden voices this awareness, that "one age learning from another, the last (if we can suppose an equality of wit in the writers) has the advantage of knowing more and better than the former. And this, I think, is the state of the question in dispute."[4] But, as Dryden himself is aware, no stable answer to the question of progress in the arts leaps out. Yet the question cannot be dismissed or ignored. The issue grows too prevalent for denials.

The eighteenth century turns questions of progress and decline in literature into an obsession. Why this preoccupation diminishes in the mid nineteenth century is puzzling. The rapid triumph of technology, urbanization, and the sense of progress as material accumulation and social amelioration are factors. So is the unprecedented establishment of the bourgeosie as Europe's dominant cultural force. Molière's *Le Bourgeois gentilhomme* long ago exposed a class more concerned with "getting" culture than with asking in what state or condition it exists. Colonialism and imperialism provided increasing and detailed contacts with cultures outside Europe. These partly replaced comparison with one's own past. Unfortunately, comparisons with Asia and Africa—and with America—reinforced a sense of European superiority. Then, as we move into the twentieth century, the Greco-Roman heritage that deeply characterizes the neoclassic period seems less telling and important. In our cosmopolitanism, we may have found ourselves in the position of Pope's young man on the grand tour, "All classic learning lost on classic ground."

Critics in the period from 1650 through 1825 possess, as part of habitual consciousness and response, an acute sensitivity to cultural direction and quality. In literature *The Dunciad* strikes the apotheosis of this concern. Racine, Dryden, Cowley, Addison, Voltaire, Diderot, Johnson, Goethe, Rousseau, Hume, Hazlitt, Schiller, Shelley: each enters the debate over decline and progress. Many figures write long essays on the subject. *Spectator* 160 explores the difference between natural and refined genius. Addison's essay influenced Schiller's *Über naive und sentimentalische Dichtung* (1795). Rymer's *Tragedies of the Last Age* (1677, 1678 on title page) and Dennis' *Advancement and Reformation of Modern Poetry* (1701) contrast previous achievement with present possibility. Dryden writes *Heads of an Answer to Rymer* in his own copy of Rymer's book, but apparent timidity prevents him from publishing them. As Johnson and others recognize, though, the *Heads* rank among Dryden's most perceptive statements. Dryden does publish an "Essay on the Dramatic Poetry of the Last Age," which compares his day to an earlier, golden period of the British stage. And Goldsmith accomplishes the same thing in another key with "On Laughing and Sentimental Comedy." He specifically discusses the decline of the arts in his *Enquiry into the Present State of Polite Learning in Europe* (1759). Hume's essays "Of the Rise and Progress of the Arts and Sciences" and "Of Simplicity and Refinement" are aimed at the question of cultural health, and at the paradox of elevating both "refinement" and "originality" as desirable ends. Hazlitt's trenchant essay "Why the Arts Are Not Progressive" misleads some readers to regard him as a snob; but one of his thrusts is simply that a mass-market appeal of art does nothing to ensure quality: "The diffusion of taste is not the same thing as the improvement of taste; but it is only the former . . . that is promoted by public institutions and other artificial means." Among these means of mere diffusion Hazlitt characterizes "the study of the antique, the formation of academies, and the distribution of prizes," which covers a swath of current higher education. Peacock, of course, prompts Shelley's *Defence* by claiming in *The Four Ages of Poetry* (1820) that for any society the literary age of gold comes early, with the paradox that any later refinement produces metals less precious.

Rousseau's genius capitalizes extravagantly on ramifications of cultural progress and decline, on tensions between a hypothetical or ideal state and an advanced, often luxurious and corrupt, society. He draws comparisons in government, education, philosophy, and human behavior. The *Discours sur les arts et sciences* (1749), which first brought him so much fame and attention, answers the prize question set by the Dijon academy: what is the effect of the progress of civilization on morals? Perhaps Diderot originated the negative response, but Rousseau's discourse could not have succeeded so well had it not crystallized and articulated prevalent feelings.

The controversy surrounding ideas of progress and decline in English literary culture fascinates the strongest minds, however hesitant they are to pronounce on the fate of that massive, shifting series of concepts we call "the arts" or "civilization." Already Davenant in his Preface to *Gondibert* (1650) is worried: "Whilst we imitate others, we can no more excel them than he that sails by others' maps can make a new discovery." Dryden echoes the thought— and copies the cartographer's image—in "Of Heroic Plays" (1672). In the eighteenth century no solid consensus on the nature of cultural and literary progress emerges. Crosscurrents of theory and speculation fail to generate one tide of opinion. But to enter the debate is to get at the heart of literary values at that time. Some individuals, such as Dryden and Johnson, are large-minded enough to be of two minds. Eager to indicate advantages of the present, they also lament inevitable losses and weakening.[5] The question remains among those intractable and "disputable" ones Hume envisions existing at the center—the elusive, unlocatable *presence*—of the critical process itself.

At least two methods or levels of thought were combining. One was a newly sharpened critical awareness starting, in England, with the Restoration, though earlier in France and Italy. The second was the birth and rise of literary history. The establishment of a newly expanded criticism we now take for granted. As long as we remind ourselves that English criticism existed before 1660, we can see that the Restoration introduced an exponential growth—an explosion, really—of critical interests and critics. The second way of thinking, the sense of literary history and cultural consciousness that developed in the late seventeenth century, sought to place—and to judge—literature in the context of cultural values as they evolve over time. Working in prose free from technical terms and open to a generally educated reader, critics register changes in literary form and language as indicators of changing social and humane values. The pervasive, judgmental tendency of a young criticism—displaying "beauties" and finding "faults"—combines with a historical awareness of literature as a barometer of the polished—or barbarous—condition of the age that "produced" it. Dryden could claim "the wit of this age is much more courtly" than that "written in the last." He undertook to turn "some of the *Canterbury Tales* into our language, *as it is now refined.*"[6]

In judging the contemporaneous, one is driven to judge the past and to make comparisons, either impressionistic or at times self-serving. Systematic English criticism and a historical consciousness of cultural productivity went hand in hand. Perhaps they always do. Earlier proto-critics such as Jonson, Puttenham, Wilson, Daniel, and Sidney had distinguished themselves by a degree of historical awareness and learning not only through the classics but also in their concern to foster modern vernacular literature. As a further complication and enrichment for the English situation, Shakespeare stood out as critically untutored. He rose supreme by nature, not artifice, a trait emphasized by a string of writers including Addison, Warton, Goethe, and Arnold. In contrast, other European poets who articulated the soul of a culture—Dante, Voltaire, Racine, Goethe himself—seemingly wrote from larger critical knowledge and literary self-consciousness. From the beginning English criticism faced a unique situation: the poet most loved in the language stood "above" the headaches of criticism and advantages of refinement. No one needed to postulate or to forge what the greatest natural poetry in English would be like. It already existed.

With Shakespeare and his age fixed in the literary psyche as golden, cries of protest arose when critics looked at Restoration writers with their (often unwanted) critical tools imported from Paris. How old this attitude is! In *Critical Observations on Shakespeare* (1746), John Upton complains, "'Twere to be wished, that with our restored king, some of that tast of literature had been restored, which we enjoyed in the days of Queen Elizabeth. But when we brought home our frenchified king, we did then, and have even to this day continued to bring from France our models."[7] The sense of a golden Elizabethan age is commonplace. "On the Golden Age of Queen Elizabeth" (1759), where Arbuthnot is Richard Hurd's persona, epitomizes the conviction that England's true self-expression began long before the eighteenth century and its systematic criticism.

No single perspective on the huge subject at hand will satisfy a desire for precision, but let me delineate four attitudes: progress, decline, cycles, and, for lack of a better term, indeterminism. As we have seen with Dryden, few thinkers subscribe wholeheartedly to one exclusive judgment. But even fewer, if any, dismiss the issue and its varied turns. The different ways to consider a historical evolution and morphology of the arts are in constant interplay.

"A still superior culture" or "A wintry world of letters"?

Those convinced that the arts were, at least in some ways, improving, used words such as "refinement" and "correctness," "fixing" or "establishing," "polished" and "elegant." Earlier ages were labeled "barbarous." Dryden's poem "To my Dear Friend Mr. Congreve" affirms a genuine advance in art over "the giant race, before the flood." Put simply, "The present Age of Wit obscures the past." Congreve manages to combine the excellencies of several playwrights, among them Jonson, Fletcher, Shakespeare, Etherege, Southerne, and Wycherley. Dryden, though certainly indulgent to his friend, is not flattering him in the way he flatters his own patrons. He is not just making the best of a diminished thing but advancing a genuine critical claim, one largely based on a sense of craft and perfected effort.[8] Not long after, William Walsh extends that notion of craft as "correctness." He advises Pope "that there was one way left of excelling . . . we never had any one great poet that was *correct;* and he desired me," Pope later told Joseph Spence, "to make that my study and aim." When T. S. Eliot included seventy lines of rhymed couplets in *The Waste Land,* Pound slashed the passage, writing "Too loose" in the margin. But the verses were good, and later Pound told Eliot the real reason why the section should be deleted: "Pope has done this so well that you cannot do it better; if you mean this as a burlesque, you had better suppress it, for you cannot parody Pope unless you can write better verse than Pope—and you can't."[9]

Some critics sympathetically condescend to the influence crude manners once exerted on literature. This self-puffing, where a writer claims for merit what time has distributed by accident, continues for decades. "As Chaucer became dissatisfied with Gower," Sharon Turner asserts in her *History of England* (1814–1815), "we have long since become dissatisfied with Chaucer . . . Hence, rich and varied as our Parnassus has become, and beautiful and sublime as are many of its productions, they are but the pledges of a still nobler vegetation, of a still superior culture."[10] But as Turner blew the trumpet of culture, Mr. Escot in Thomas Love Peacock's *Headlong Hall* (1815), like his counterpart Mr. Forester in *Melincourt* (1817), announced an "absolute, universal, irremediable deterioration" in everything—not surprising from the author of *The Four Ages of Poetry.*

Yet from the mid-eighteenth century forward, popular "general" histories proclaim a positive "march of mind." The phrases in Keats's famous letter to J. H. Reynolds, "general and gregarious advance of intellect . . . really a grand march of intellect," probably crept in from such books or the talk they generated.[11] The theme is common enough; histories written from the 1760s through the 1790s exude this confidence. Their authors are influential: Adam Ferguson, Lord Kames, James Dunbar, John Logan, and George Thomson. The titles, too, are predictable: *Essay on the History of Civil Society* (1768), *Sketches of the History of Man* (1774), *Essays on the History of Mankind* (1780), *Elements of the Philosophy of History* (1781), and *The Spirit of General History* (1791).

The pith of this confident attitude is apparent in Francis Jeffrey's 1802 review of Madame de Staël's *De la Littérature considerée dans ses rapports avec les institutions sociales* (1800): "*there is a progress . . .* letters and intelligence are in a state of constant, universal and irresistible advancement." Jeffrey repeats the idea in several guises, stating that "writers who adorned the beginning of the last century have been eclipsed by those of our own time," and that "the general taste of every successive generation is better than that of its predecessors."[12] Such confidence, though unattractive today, occupied a large place in the critical landscape, so large that Tolstoy attacks it in his epilogue to *War and Peace*. Tolstoy's remarks reveal how pervasive the faith in universal literary and cultural progress remains throughout the nineteenth century. He contemptuously refers to "a certain kind of European enlightenment called 'progress'" and berates "so-called historians of *culture*" who follow "the writers of universal history." He sees what we often call "spiritual activity, enlightenment, civilization, culture . . . are all vague, indefinite conceptions under whose banner" such historians "conveniently employ words having a still less definite meaning and which can therefore be readily adapted to any theory."[13] Tolstoy punctures the bubble of "universal historians and historians of culture who fail to answer the essential questions of humanity." They "only serve as currency for sundry purposes of their own—in the universities and among the legions who go in for 'serious' reading, as they are pleased to call it." The idea of unmitigated progress, though prevalent and popular, never succeeded in winning profound hearts and minds. Before Tolstoy lashed out, Hume, Johnson, Hazlitt and others had kept their distance from cultural perfectibility and easy generalization.

But some notions of progress did make sense: attaining "smooth" versification, avoiding crude jokes or tired clichés, the new flexibility of prose under the influence of Dryden, Clarendon, Halifax, and Addison. These achievements could be consolidated and continued. Speaking with anyone from Jena or Weimar in 1825, it would have been insulting not to praise, let alone concede, the progress and achievement in German literature and culture during the previous century. English critics could hope to produce a literary culture rivaling the ancients and outshining Europe. From the perspective of the mid-eighteenth century this goal seems plausible. Significant names come to mind: Chaucer, Milton, Shakespeare, Jonson, Bacon, Dryden, and Swift. It depends on perspective. As Johnson notes in *Idler* 91, "We consider the whole succession from Spenser to Pope, as superiour to any names which the continent can boast." Several critics, including Addison in his *Account of the Greatest English Poets* (1694), think poetry would only improve, or at least respond to the defeat of superstition and ignorance; that what pleased a "barb'rous age" would "charm an understanding age no more." Samuel Cobb's "Of Poetry: Its Progress" (1700) and Judith Madan's "The Progress of Poetry" (1721) indicate the drift. In 1737 Elizabeth Cooper's preface to the *Muses Library* claims English literature is now at "the highest perfection it has hitherto attained." *The Critical Review* later runs pieces similar in theme. Gray explores the possibility of a new British poetry in his twin odes "The Progress of Poesy" and "The Bard."[14] Even Johnson, who looks back to the Elizabethan age as the wellspring of "English undefiled," sees an advance in the social reception of literature: "The English nation, in the time of Shakespeare, was yet struggling to emerge from barbarity . . . literature was yet confined to professed scholars, or to men and women of high rank. The publick was gross and dark."[15]

And if the ancients "excell'd the Moderns in the greatness of Poetry," Dennis submits, it was only because they grounded tragedy and the loftier ode in subjects no longer available, not because they enjoyed "any External or Internal advantage."[16] Hurd claims "that the fancies of our modern bards are not only more gallant, but, on a change of the scene, more sublime, more terrible, more alarming, than those of the classic fablers."[17] The avowed purpose of the *Spectator* was to bring taste and cultivation into common drawing rooms, in short, to civilize. And it is, coincidentally, Addison's "fairy way of writing" that prompts Hurd's apostrophe to gothic taste. The notion of poetry retaining its greatness, of progressing and refining, could seem not only plausible, but inevitable—given a receptive frame of mind.

The idea of decline, like its progressive cousin, did not encourage single-minded formulation. Nor did it hinge on the one obvious comparison (surfacing often enough) that Shakespeare and Milton are dead, and what now equals them? Naturally, as the decades, then centuries, passed, that question exerts more leverage. But a sense of decline already had a long pedigree, even in England. Ben Jonson complains in *Timber* that after the death of Bacon, "Now things daily fall; wits grow downe-ward and *Eloquence* growes back-ward."[18] As the idea becomes obsessive, it stirs more than glances at two or three immortal authors with a plaintive *ubi sunt* added on.

Some eighteenth-century writers, such as Joseph Smedley in his "Complaint," simply feel inadequate in face of a distant past.

> When Graecians lived, auspicious Times!
> Glory inspired the sacred rage:
> How faint the Muse in Albion's clime
> Now glitters in th' enervate page.

But a deeper, more intelligent unease takes shape. James Thomson sees that refinement produces progress but also notes the "forced and unaffecting fancies, little glittering prettinesses, mixed turns of wit and expression, which are as widely different from native poetry as buffoonery is from the perfection of human thinking." He forecasts an unseasonably "wintry world of letters."[19]

The spectre of decline visits Goldsmith, who claims in exasperation that "the race of [English] poets is extinct," that Pegasus "has slipped the bridle from his mouth, and our modern bards attempt to direct his flight by catching him by the tail." Actually, although Goldsmith observes, "it has been so long the practice to represent literature as declining, that every renewal of this complaint comes with diminish'd influence," he devotes energy to reiterating this very point in his *Enquiry into the Present State of Polite Learning in Europe.*[20] Boswell told Johnson that Goldsmith complained, "he had come too late into the world, for that Pope and other poets had taken up the place in the Temple of Fame; so that, as but a few at any period can possess poetical reputation, a man of genius can now hardly acquire it." Johnson, contrary to his habit of debate, replies: "That is one of the most sensible things I have ever heard of Goldsmith."[21] In effect, we have what Murray Krieger calls "the propagation of two myths, the myth of origins, which leads to the idolatry of the ancients by attributing 'original genius' uniquely to them . . . and the myth of the 'advancement of learning,' which was to account for the superiority of the moderns in those areas in which . . . learning would have to be enough."[22] In his *History of the Idea of Progress* Robert Nisbet observes that the quarrel between Ancients and Moderns remains essential for our understanding of the Enlightenment foundation of modern concepts of progress.[23]

The Paradox of Refinement

The topic of progress and decline naturally occupies Johnson. But for him, as for Dryden and Hume, the question never degenerates into a simple choice. A greater principle of dialectic and apparent opposition is operating. As part of his "Dissertation" on poetry and poets, Imlac admits to Rasselas:

> it yet fills me with wonder, that, in almost all countries, the most ancient poets are considered as the best: whether it be that every other kind of knowledge is an acquisition gradually attained, and poetry is a gift conferred at once; or that the first poetry of every nation surprised them as a novelty, and retained credit by consent which it received by accident at first: or whether, as the province of poetry is to describe Nature and Passion, which are always the same, the first writers took possession of the most striking objects for description, and the most probable occurrences for fiction, and left nothing to those that followed them, but transcription of the same events, and new combinations of the same images. Whatever be the reason, it is commonly observed that the early writers are in possession of nature, and their followers of art: that the first excel

in strength and invention, and the latter in elegance and refinement.

Here is the double edge of elegance and refinement. Always cutting both ways, it is, to use Patrick Brantlinger's phrase in *Bread
and Circuses,* "the paradox of progress as decadence." Johnson does
not venture exact reasons for this undoubted paradox, but he for-
mulates it clearly: the kind of progress known as elegance or refinement automatically registers a decline or reduction in scope. Taste
cannot but reflect this "contradiction" or "contrary." In the 1755
Dictionary he defines "elegant" as "Pleasing with minuter beauties."
To illustrate this he quotes Pope and his own *London.* The second
definition specifies manners: "Nice; not coarse; not gross" (significantly, Pope is again quoted). Definitions of related words show
that for Johnson the nature of elegance is "to please without elevation," to be "soothing rather than striking," to be "without grandeur." We get a sense, to borrow the French proverb, that advanced
civilization "has the defects of its qualities." The more refined and
elegant it becomes, the more it prizes those "advances," the more
it may lose strength, power, and scope. With his usual irony, Swift
selects his favorite adjective in *A Tale of a Tub:* it is "refined." A
concordance reveals that virtually all his uses of it are negative or
ironic in signification.[24]

In condensed form, without Swift's bitterness but yet with "wonder," Johnson expresses the paradox that refinement must involve
progress and decline simultaneously. We advance to diminished
things. When he writes about Addison and Steele, he uses "refined"
to carry the double meaning of polished and weakened. To illustrate
"elegancy," the *Dictionary* quotes *Spectator* 477: "My compositions
in gardening are altogether Pindarick, and run into the beautiful
wildness of nature, without the nicer *elegancies* of art." Johnson's
several definitions for "refine," "refinement," and "refiner" all betray
a split between purification and affectation, between "improvement" and "superfluous subtilties."[25] The two-edged sword of refinement could be seen as a chiasmatic opposition between taste and
poetic power. Thomas Barnes, in his essay "On the Nature and

Essential Character of Poetry as Distinguished from Prose," concludes "that the *strong poetic character* may be expected to decline, as TASTE improves." While we may "excel in . . . refinement," this precludes "bursts of honest nature" and the imagery, the enthusiasm, which exalt works "to the *first order* of poetic excellence."[26]

In Imlac's dissertation, Johnson also draws a telling comparison between poetry—a general, synthetic, and intuitive form of knowledge—and other forms of learning, such as science, which are more specific, analytic, and empirical. Wordsworth will do the same in his 1800 Preface. The point is that even if refinement and "advancement" could be kept up in poetry, they would be kept up with diminishing returns while science and factual knowledge would rush ahead exponentially as the years passed. The pace of any improvement in poetry, first granted it is an improvement (itself a huge concession), will be outstripped by accelerating progress in other areas of human endeavor.

Dryden, whom Johnson praised as having "refined the language," was the first to face the paradox of refinement with awareness throughout his career. In the epilogue to the second part of *The Conquest of Granada* he writes:

> If Love and Honour now are higher rais'd,
> 'Tis not the Poet, but the Age is prais'd.
> Wit's now arriv'd to a more high degree;
> Our native Language more refin'd and free.
> Our Ladies and our men now speak more wit
> In conversation, than those Poets writ.
> Then, one of these is, consequently, true;
> That what this Poet writes comes short of you,
> And imitates you ill, (which most he fears)
> Or else his writing is not worse than theirs.
> Yet, though you judge, (as sure the Critiques will)
> That some before him writ with greater skill,
> In this one praise he has their fame surpast,
> To please an Age more Gallant than the last.

This epilogue, an admixture of flattery, self-conscious calculation, and problematic self-awareness, is one indication of Dryden's dilemma. He ominously remarks in the "Preface to Fables," that it is more in "the genius of our countrymen . . . to improve an invention than to invent themselves."[27] Here, in an epilogue addressed to those who felt he undervalued Jonson and Shakespeare, he makes himself a prisoner of his age, though it is not clear that he thinks the age truly superior in anything but a certain kind of wit. (Recall what he says in "Anne Killigrew" about his "lubrique" age and its degraded theater.) We infer that the "height" of the previous age, though unsustained, was high indeed. The advent of scrutinizing critics seems both a plus and a minus. They are part of the refinement that has occurred, yet some of these critics may judge that earlier poets wrote (having no critics to "assist" them) with "greater skill," a phrase Pope will vary to open his *Essay on Criticism* as "greater want of skill."

Finally, the would-be syllogism near the end of Dryden's epilogue implies what he could hardly believe without uneasiness: either he is not mirroring the newly refined wit and superior language of his age, or else he is "not worse" than poets before him. The contrapositive will hold, and the paradox becomes, naturally, that as society "improved," poetry declined—or so Dryden represents himself in the eyes of critics. He makes this paradox inescapable: it is not possible both that he be a better poet than previous ones *and* that he also please readers; nor is it possible both that he fail to please and be worse! A troubled undercurrent of irony flows; perhaps the age is not better in qualities that foster powerful art. If Dryden most fears not imitating the present age of gallantry, then what he fears least is being judged "not worse" than his predecessors. He adeptly uses the audience as a fulcrum to extract himself from an uncomfortable position. We infer that his taste differs from his audience's—ever so "refined" as that has come to be.

By the mid-eighteenth century Hume warns in "Of Simplicity and Refinement" that "the *excess* of refinement is now more to be guarded against than ever."[28] The more a civilization advances, the further it removes itself from what Johnson calls "Nature and Passion." Then, paradoxically, it is redrawn to "nature" as an idealized quality it no longer possesses, or else must redefine in order to recapture. For example, in *Sketches of a History of Literature* (1794), Robert Alves claims that, since Shakespeare and Milton, "the study of good criticism . . . and a sound knowledge of the rules of good writing" have improved but, despite this advance, Shakespeare and Milton remain incomparable. Moreover, earlier human nature, though less learned in criticism and hence "unpolished," was—for that very reason—admirably "simple" and "undebased."[29] This thirst for the primitive in an ever sophisticated and sophisticating culture led Leslie Stephen to comment on such a "futile attempt to revive old modes of thought and feeling amidst an environment fatal to their real vitality."[30]

Significantly, in the Enlightenment we find almost exclusively a cult of primitive poetry and literature, but not primitive music, painting, or dance. Literature seems to have become older, more refined, sooner. Of all the media in the arts, words became least susceptible to technological innovation. Fingal, darling of Europe and supposed bard of James Macpherson's wildly popular *Ossian,* and poets such as Stephen Duck the Thresher, Mary Collier the "Poetical Washerwoman," or Henry Jones the "Poetical Bricklayer," were perceived to be uncontaminated by enigmatic cultural questions that plagued critics and poets possessing higher levels of sophistication. The human thirst for the authentic produces for us, as it did for eighteenth-century poetry, a cult of folk art liberated de facto from institutional memory and the influence of other art. Even cosmetic companies, which today Ben Jonson might attack as the epitome of civilized pampering and refinement, find an upscale market for "primitive colors" with "desert" or "jungle" hues.

As a poet whose identity is rooted in a "primitive" or unpolished past, Chatterton presents the strangest, saddest example. Unlike Collier or Duck, he makes headway by forging an excellent naïveté. Yet, as a child, his genuine refuge and recreation was the old parish church St. Mary Redcliffe in Bristol, where his ancestors acted as sextons for nearly two centuries. There among the tombs, parchment manuscripts, monuments, inscriptions, and black-letter Bibles, he shaped his first inventions and self-consciously entered their world. Keats understood how unjust it was to view him simply as a calculating forger or fake. And so Chatterton becomes caught in a vise of conflicting literary values, a victim of the paradox of refinement. On the one side his work attracted those who desired something authentic, heartfelt, and near the wellsprings of spontaneous emotion and "poetical" action. Sidney long ago had commended the ballad of Percy and Douglas, *Chevy Chase,* and Addison wrote two *Spectator* papers explaining the merits and force of that native poem. Such poetry would unquestionably seem "original" to an audience jaded by a deluge of bad imitations and modish, delicate magazine verse. Yet on the other side, the age ended by judging too nicely. When Chatterton was "discovered," meaning when he was finally "found out," the rising premium on novelty and originality became his enemy, though not one word of his verse had changed. Instead of a bracing alternative to overly refined verse, he was now seen as one who had cheated the expectations of a knowledgeable, polite audience whose very "sophistication" resulted from their less engaged, more superficial hunger for the past. "No man," Johnson warned in *Rambler* 154, knowing it useless to weigh the justice of the fact, "yet became great by imitation." The idea of *aemulatio,* however, was another case, as Dryden recognized when he spoke of emulating, not imitating, Shakespeare. An inventive emulation, which bypassed the sense of formal and generic recapitulation suggested by *imitatio,* became one way to combat the increasingly narrow focus of repeated refinements. Hence throughout the eighteenth century, while imitation of particular works of previous authors becomes less prized, Longinian emulation of their spirit grows.[31]

Burns, knowing better than young Chatterton how to exploit the desires of a civilized mob of readers, imitates neither Virgil nor Theocritus. Instead, he shrewdly introduces the 1786 Kilmarnock edition of his poems in humble tones:

> The following trifles are not the production of the poet who,
> with all the advantages of learned art, and perhaps amid the

elegancies and idlenesses of upper life, looks down for a rural theme, with an eye to Theocritus and Virgil. . . . Unacquainted with the necessary requisites for commencing poetry by rule, he sings the sentiments and manners he felt and saw in himself and his rustic compeers around him in his and their native language.

For another purpose, but with a remarkably similar vocabulary and message ("rustic," and "a selection of the language really used by men"), Wordsworth would defend the *Lyrical Ballads* fourteen years later. As late as 1820, John Clare's publisher, John Taylor, assures readers that "The following poems will probably attract some notice by their intrinsic merit; but they are also entitled to attention from the circumstances under which they were written. They are the genuine productions of a young Peasant, a day-labourer in husbandry, who has had no advantages of education beyond those of his class."

The situations are different—Clare, Wordsworth, Burns, Chatterton—yet all expose the tension between literature recognized as derivative (that is, imitated), polished, codified, and refined, and writing that is fresh, direct, and untrammeled by false models or "superfluous subtilties." Could a culture prize refinement and originality at the same time? Comparing Shakespeare to "other poets," John Newbery, in *The Art of Poetry on a New Plan,* claims that those others "had ancient authors too much in view, and, by frequent imitation, lost the spirit of originality."[32] Could critics and the public demand of writers a power mysteriously reserved for "primitive" and relatively untutored bards—such as Beattie's minstrel and the old woman poet who teaches him to sing—while simultaneously preening themselves in the advancement of collective knowledge and the honing of critical power?[33]

Primitivism aside, whether genuine or affected, we can see the Horatian ideal, the eighteenth-century version of the Sabine farm, the flight from what Cowley calls "that monster London," and what Coleridge promises his child in "Frost at Midnight" he will never have to endure: growing up in a grimy city—we can see all these as reactions against urban values that are literally overcivilized.

Pomfret's *Choice, The Task,* Gray's *Elegy, The Seasons,* Cowley's essay "Of Obscurity," Johnson's *London,* and Pope's Man of Ross: none can be called a plea of behalf of primitivism. Instead, all rely to some extent on a classical ideal of self-sufficient retreat and natural, even agrarian virtue. They may also be seen as part of an immediate protest against social refinement that brings with it competition, bureaucracy, and scrambles for fame and "reputation." This protest is not the covenient imitation of classical *topoi,* but a sincere outcry. Echoing Gray's *Elegy,* Johnson in his late poem "On the Death of Dr. Robert Levet" (1782), elevates the values Levet followed. He was "innocent, sincere . . . coarsely kind." As distinguished from "letter'd arrogance," this humble physician of the London poor possessed "merit unrefin'd."

Yet, later writers, as contrasted with those Johnson called "the first," could entertain the notion that the possibilities most open were ones that tended to eloign them farther from nature and what Tolstoy calls "essential questions of humanity." Addison, in discussing epic poetry, refers to "the *false* Refinements of later Ages."[34] And Johnson, concentrating on literary form as a reflection of this paradox, invokes in his *Drury Lane Prologue* a vigorous Elizabethan stage, now "crush'd by rules, and weaken'd as refin'd." To refine upon Pope's versification, he said elsewhere, would be "dangerous." One could also argue that Pope's idiom and techniques, perfected and compressed further, would collapse, become opaque, and lose more than gain, including a loss of readers. We find this sentiment repeatedly: refinement of poetic form eventually becomes unsatisfactory: Gilchrist's *Beauties of English Poetry* (1786) warns that "in labouring to polish the verse, the strength and vigour of the thought is lost, and the boldness and animation of genius is overlooked in the fondness for meretricious ornaments."[35]

In 1790 Henry James Pye became poet laureate. Two years earlier he had produced *The Progress of Refinement: a Poem in three parts.* A better member of Parliament than poet, "Poetical Pye" nevertheless expresses the widespread sense of hope balanced with unease. This ardent believer in progress harbors misgivings about the luxurious refinements accompanying the progress he holds dear:

If life's severer evils they subdue,
And smooth the rugged mind, they
    weaken too,
If savage hate they quell, and wild desire,
They damp the Poet's and the Patriot's fire.
               (Part III, ll. 293–296)

Refinement and elegance, what is "polite" and "polished," appear as remaining avenues for achievement, but can the stick be whittled forever? The effect is to subdue and to limit, and then to turn to sheer novelty or shock as a way out. Johnson thought one remark of Joseph Warton deserved particular attention: "In no polished nation, after criticism has been much studied, and the rules of writing established, has any very extraordinary book ever appeared."[36] How long can one go on refining? Perhaps Pope was not a good model, and this may be one reason why he later is attacked as being no poet at all. In his article on Pope for the *Encyclopaedia Britannica,* De Quincey contends that, after the Elizabethan age, "passion begins to wheel in lower flights . . . observing, refining, reflecting," three things in which Enlightenment culture vested so much critical effort. Archibald Alison, Condillac in his *Traité de l'art d'écrire,* and John Moir in his *Gleanings,* are just a few who feel criticism is actually becoming pernicious to art. In 1826 Goethe tells Eckermann that no Shakespeare could arise in England now, "in these wretched days of criticizing and fragmentizing journals"—a virtual paraphrase of Dryden's epilogue to the second part of *Granada.*

"Refinement" and "elegance" could—and often did—mean two related things at once: refinement in artistic technique and also in social manners. The two values are linked. This is one of the fascinating socio-literary phenomena of the modern world. Johnson captures the negative possibilities in his phrase "elegance refined into impatience," perfectionism and subtlety carried to a point where attention no longer feels any exertion worth the reward and the whole project becomes literally insufferable (in + *patiens*). Whoever has seen the film of *Pride and Prejudice* relishes the moment when

Greer Garson (Elizabeth) eyes Laurence Olivier (Darcy) and counters one of his remarks about the unrefined nature of the middle classes at play: "Oh yes," she says, "to be *really* refined you have to be dead!" Aldous Huxley's screenplay brings to mind Austen's favorite author, Johnson. Boswell reports that Johnson advised him "not to *refine* in the education of my children. 'Life (said he) will not bear refinement: you must do as other people do.'" The essence of refinement is that it is repeated, it goes on, hardly knowing where to stop, a self-serving value, a universal prey that mistakes a particular, minor end for all ends. So Elizabeth's sister Mary we find "as usual," Austen writes, "deep in the study of thorough bass and human nature." In art or education, specialization and narrowed perspective can drastically reduce the receptive audience. Yet to some degree such refinement is necessary; the point is to know when it applies. Highlighting the inherently contrary and paradoxical nature of the whole issue, Boswell—years after Johnson's comment to him about doing as other people do—argued categorically "that a refinement of taste was a disadvantage, as they who have attained to it must be seldomer pleased than those who have no nice discrimination, and are therefore satisfied with every thing that comes in their way." But Johnson now champions personal effort and replies, "Nay, Sir; that is a paltry notion. Endeavour to be as perfect as you can in every respect."[37]

In the arts, refinement and elegance arrive in the form of more exquisite technique, vocabulary, versification, structure, self-conscious experiment, and in perfecting what Henry James sums up as "devices"—in short, the care with which a writer invents, selects, organizes, revises, and chisels.[38] This attitude produces superb effects. It also promotes the situation Peter Viereck catches in his poem "From the Sublime to the Meticulous in Four Stages":

> Dante: We were God's poets.
> Burns: We were the people's poets.
> Mallarmé: We were poets' poets.
> Today (preening himself): Ah, but we are critics' poets.

Damning with faint praise, Johnson says "*Addison* speaks the language of poets, and *Shakespeare,* of men." Archibald Alison crisply offers this situation in his *Principles of Taste* (1790): the writer will be tempted "gradually to forget the end of his art, in his attempt to display his superiority in the art itself." The audience will experience a "gradual desertion of the *end* of the art for the *display* of the art itself."[39] The artist Frank Stella has commented that at a certain time in Renaissance art the subject of imitation gradually ceded prime importance to the technique of imitation, and then began mannerism and a major trend in modern art. Modern sociologists such as Pierre Bourdieu repeat the conclusion with reference to audience: "Formal refinement—which, in literature or the theatre, leads to obscurity—is, in the eyes of the working-class public, one sign of what is sometimes felt to be a desire to keep the uninitiated at arm's length."[40]

Thomas Blackwell, in his *Enquiry into the Life and Writings of Homer* (1735), suggests that "a People's Felicity clips the Wings of their Verse"; in other words, great poetic actions are refined out of a settled, caring society.[41] The explanation becomes a sour favorite with Hazlitt. "It cannot be concealed," he says in one of his 1818 *Lectures on the English Poets,* "that the progress of knowledge and refinement has a tendency to circumscribe the limits of imagination, and to clip the wings of poetry." Keats attended that lecture. We hear an echo in *Lamia* (written the next year) about systematic knowledge eroding poetic spirit: "Philosophy will clip an Angel's wings." The potentially contracted range of poetry later occupies Arnold in his 1853 Preface. It troubles Nietzsche in another way: in the *Birth of Tragedy* he sees that the death of mythology means all will be converted into "history" or "criticism."

When Hazlitt asks "Why is Shakespeare popular?" his answer immediately redounds: "Not from his refinement . . . so much as from his power." Perhaps the secretly feared result of refinement was—and remains—the reduced popularity and diminished emotional power of poetry, a loss felt sharply by those who love it and believe it retains genuine promise for the human condition. Francis Jeffrey, reviewing Scott's *Lady of the Lake* in 1810, saw consequences of a long trend:

we think that modern poetry has both been enriched with more exquisite pictures, and deeper and more sustained strains of pathetic, than were known to the less elaborate artists of antiquity; at the same time that it has been defaced with more affectation, and loaded with far more intricacy. . . . Modern poetry, in this respect, may be compared . . . to modern sculpture. It is greatly inferior to the ancient in freedom, grace, and simplicity; but, in return, it frequently possesses a more decided expression, and more fine finishing of less suitable embellishments.

Whatever may be gained or lost, however, by this change of manner, it is obvious, that poetry must become less popular by means of it.[42]

The first history of English poetry, Thomas Warton's, put the situation baldly: "Ignorance and superstition, so opposite to the real interests of human society, are the parents of imagination."[43] William Collins in the "Epistle addressed to Sir Thomas Hamner" (1747), Edward Jerningham in "Rise and Progress of Scandinavian Poetry" (1784), and George Richards in "Songs of the Aboriginal Bards of Britain" (1792) all celebrate how important and highly regarded poetry once was, but no longer.

William Duff and John "Estimate" Brown (the nickname derives from his *Estimate of the Manners and Principles of the Times,* which went through seven editions within a year of its 1757 publication) postulate a cultural decline that sets in like arteriosclerosis. The English, Brown says, have become "vain," "luxurious," and "selfish." A "general decay of taste and learning" infects the land. "Progress" he regards as mixed, even bad or tyrannical. Thomson catches the paradox of human beings going from prey to predator, leaving behind their primitive vulnerability but substituting for it "the savage arts of life, / Death, rapine, carnage, surfeit, and disease." Blake comes to mind, with progress depicted in Night the Seventh [B] of *The Four Zoas:*

    . . . intricate wheels invented Wheel without wheel
To perplex youth in their outgoings & to bind labours

Of day & night the myriads of Eternity. that they might file
And polish brass & iron hour after hour laborious
   workmanship
Kept ignorant of the use that they might spend the days of
   wisdom
In sorrowful drudgery to obtain a scanty pittance of bread[44]

And Wordsworth attacks the sensationalism and degraded artistic taste of his own day even as he tries to rest poetry on "the language really used by men."

Furthermore, as another indication of trouble and decline, or at least of obstacles, the pressure for originality, growing as the hegemony of classicism waned, drives poets as dissimilar as Cowley and Coleridge to lament that the modern poet works under extraordinary strains.[45] "It is almost impossible," wrote Cowley, "to serve up any new Dish" from the "boasted Feasts of Love and Fables," as moderns attempt: all are "but the Cold-meats of the Antients, new-heated, and new set forth." Addison, in *Spectator* 253 (December 28, 1711), takes the same line: "It is impossible for us," he says "who live in the latter ages of the world" (adapting Boileau's similar statements) "to make observations . . . which have not been touched on by others. We have little else left us but to represent the common sense of mankind in more strong, more beautiful, more uncommon lights." And in *Guardian* 12, Steele joins the chorus with a third "it is impossible": "Now nature being still the same," he asserts, "it is impossible for any modern Writer to paint otherwise than the Ancients have done." Richard Hurd, later discussing *Gondibert,* could speak of the "affectation of originality in lettered and polite poets," as if it necessarily produced a contradiction in terms.[46]

Coleridge thinks poetic style has become ingrown. "So countless have been the poetic metamorphoses of almost all possible thoughts and connections of thought," he confided, that poetry became all too easy, and therefore "so very difficult . . . in the present day. I myself have for many years past given it up in despair."[47] Johnson, in *Rambler* 36, contends that nature offers but a finite number of images to ear and eye. To be freshly imitated by a modern poet, nature must be considered "philosophically." In this context, we might think of Coleridge's repeated praise of Wordsworth not as the poet of visible nature, but as the poet capable of writing "the first genuine philosophic poem." It was not only plausible, it was imperative for critics to worry how poets could avoid giving up under the dual pressure of knowing so much and trying to be so original.

The value of refinement, so highly prized by the Restoration and earlier eighteenth century, submits to increasing pressure until it finally becomes questioned, dissected, and diminished. Unlike originality, which could seem open-ended in time, never wearing itself out, refinement, by definition, looks backward and becomes increasingly fragile. The rise of primitivism and a more "natural" poetic diction are directly connected with the self-strangulation of refinement as a premium value for style and subject matter. In fact, those values of the primitive, the natural, and the original, became logical replacements for a concept that ran the course of its natural —one could say, doomed—life. It is during the relatively barren period in poetry, from the 1760s to the 1790s, that refinement reaches its burnt-out end. The most interesting poets—whether those rediscovered in Percy's *Reliques,* "Fingal," Goldsmith, Robert Fergusson, Chatterton, Burns, Blake, Cowper, or Crabbe—seem in various ways to minimize or reject refinement.

Cycles and Genres

The idea of a cycle or determined series of events is as old as the observation of seasons and the yearly dance of stars. Successive "ages" of civilization and poetry are familiar: iron, gold, silver, and brass. Some schemes place silver before gold, or replace brass with bronze. Thomas Hakewell proposed a cyclic theory of nature, and writers such as Dryden seem aware of it, or of similar schemes, in viewing the arts. The cyclic theory, an analogy to vegetable or natural growth, applied not only to art but to language itself. Seventeenth-century writers such as Edward Phillips could envision a seemingly endless maturation. In his preface to *Theatrum Poetarum* (1675), Phillips relishes "the smooth style of our present Language, taken to be of late so much refined," and projects "two or three Ages hence, when the Language comes to be double refin'd." Yet Phillips warns, too, that refinement of language may undercut strength of verse. "If no Poetry should Pleas but what is calculated to every refinement of a Language," then works will soon become "obsolete and thrown aside."[48] By the later eighteenth century the warning pause becomes, as we have seen, a worried one. Easy confidence in refined language vanishes. Instead, we find frequent assertions that earlier, more primitive languages are actually more poetical because less refined—hence relying more on metaphor and images. Or, to use Jakobson's definition, there will be more of a projection of the axis of selection onto the axis of combination as a result of the simple fact that there is less to select from in the first place, and therefore combinations of poetic language must occur more frequently. Leonard Welsted claims in "A Dissertation concerning the Perfection of the English Language and the State of Poetry" (1724) that "it is with languages, as it is with animals, vegetables, and all other things; they have their rise, their progress, their maturity, and their decay." Welsted concludes that English "is not capable of a much greater perfection that it has already attained." What would come next appeared problematic, unless one returned to the less refined, the more natural.[49]

A specific consensus concerning the time of an English golden age in literature never develops. Apparently contravening his professed confidence in the progress of authors and taste that we noted earlier, Jeffrey identifies "the brightest in the history of English literature" as "the sixty or seventy years that elapsed from the middle of Elizabeth's reign to the period of the Restoration." Goldsmith considers the zenith in "the reign of Queen Anne, or some years before."[50] (It was this period, or not long before, that Ben Jonson had, in his later years, judged to be "downe-ward.") But even if no specific decades receive most votes for this unofficial award, the remembered golden age falls between 1550 and 1700.

In his criticism Dryden quotes the Roman thinker Velleius Paterculus, as Hume later would. (Johnson also recommends reading him.) Velleius envisioned cycles of human achievement reaching their peaks when individuals emulate one another in a contagion of work and excellence—in short, when conscious comparison, evaluative judgment, and personal striving converge. Adam Smith thought a "high" cycle blessed Scotland in his day, and he was right. That nation quite suddenly emerges in belles lettres, philosophy, and economics. Its relative barrenness for several previous centuries may be one reason. Scotland was not concerned with the enervating effects of refinement on its own immediate past. This helps to explain why Johnson enjoyed traveling there, while he declined to attend cultural festivities such as Garrick's Shakespeare jubilee at Stratford in 1764, which he considered, in a real sense, decadent.

The cyclic theory of poetry was well-worn but influential. Unlike Stephen Gosson's *School of Abuse,* which helped prompt Sidney's *Defense,* Peacock's *Four Ages of Poetry* did not attack poetry per se. Yet it could seem more devastating because it implied that the enemy was within: poetry inevitably follows a course of events, a cycle of rise and decline in which the poet is a passenger. The question amounted to one's judgment of the contemporary scene. Where did the present fit in? Was poetry—were the arts in general—enjoying an upswing or a downturn, and how long would it last? The Renaissance recaptured and used the spirit and learning of the ancients. But could writers continue to turn to an earlier period and receive encouragement without falling into the slavish imitation Horace mocks in *Ars Poetica:* the crazy or poor poet hoping to achieve grandeur by mere variation, *delphinium sylvis appingit,* painting a dolphin in the forests? How could one use Milton and Shakespeare as models? Blake and Keats showed that the attempt could liberate more than constrict.

At one time or another many critics take a position of practical indeterminism, increasingly common as the prizing of refinement subsides. They refuse to dismiss the possibilities of decline, progress, or cycles, but neither do they make poetry behavioristically or culturally determined. And who can say, after all, which grand judgments about art and culture are accurate? Isn't the important thing to try to encourage poetry and to ask how that might be done?

"I am always angry," Johnson protests, "when I hear ancient times praised at the expense of modern times."[51] As late as 1818 William Roscoe produces a level-headed analysis *On the Origins and Vicissitudes of Literature, Science, and Art, and Their Influence on the Present State of Society,* in which he sees no "inherent tendency towards either improvement or deterioration." Like Hume, he cites factors that engage the polity and economic well-being of societies; thus, Roscoe avoids concentrating on a narrow history of literature.[52] All sorts of qualifications spring up. If poetry were suffering decline, then what about music? And if poetry is progressing in new forms such as the shorter lyric, what about visual art? The "fine" or "sister arts" might be related, but do they all rise and fall on one curve? Aren't the propositions too snarled to draw axioms—so many cultures, countries, arts, and so many genres or kinds within arts? In this complex situation a critic might hold four concepts—decline, progress, cycles, and a hands-up-in-the-air indeterminism—all at once, applying each as it seems appropriate to the situation at hand. Dryden does so, emphasizing one or another as it suits his purpose. The ideas work simultaneously, as the paradox of refinement reveals they often must.

Ideas of rise and decline lead to ideas of generic transformation. Each genre within one branch of the arts could be considered in this light. If lyric poetry revives in the later eighteenth century, could that also be said of tragedy or the epic or, after Sheridan, of comedy? Surely the novel gains popularity if not stature. John Brown's *Dissertation on the Rise, Union and Power, the Progressions, Separations and Corruptions of Poetry and Music* (1763) examines how—through time—the arts become more specialized and self-enclosed. The result is a study in genre development, the historical morphology of literature as one line that traces cultural values and how that culture renders its self-image. Ideas of rise and decline, of refinement and sublimity, intimately affect genre criticism. And the place of social manners becomes important here as well; Johnson recoiled from the pastoral because it ceased to reflect "real life" and therefore, for him, became a degenerate form. A new, more realistic pastoral—such as *Michael* was for Wordsworth—would need to restore the genre to social realities; *Michael* itself is dramatically keyed to the destructive refinement of urban life contrasted with less refined rural purity. Goldsmith, later echoed by Hazlitt, predicts the decline of English dramatic comedy after Sheridan. In 1773 he warns "by our being too fastidious"—too refined in social manner—"we have banished humour from the stage." In thinking about the question of advance and decline and genre, Joseph Warton spies a silver lining: "If the Moderns have excelled the Antients in any species of writing, it seems to be in satire."[53] If we hold to Northrop Frye's idea that satire comes last in the mimetic modes, this observation fits with a sense of chronological sweep. In the eighteenth century, the last age in which classical mimesis dominates English literature, it could be argued that its greatest perfection in a single mode of literature is satire.

Myths That Shape the Present / Promethean Science

Evaluations of the arts become most revelatory when critics apply them to their own age, not to the past. For instance, it is one thing to call a style or an age "decadent" when it is past history, but another, more formative act to consider—as the fin-de-siècle movement did—that the present time is decadent. Such evaluations gain power as myths of self-fashioning, not only for an individual but for culture at large. In this sense critics become mythmakers. Thus, in his novel of a culture experienced during his own time, George Santayana ends *The Last Puritan* not with a pronouncement of objective values, but with a statement about cultural meaning and individual worth that not only resides in but is created by the narrative forms through which we tell our story: "After life is over and the world has gone up in smoke, what realities might the spirit in us call its own without illusion save the form of those very illusions which have made up our story?"

A number of ancillary topics cluster around the fundamental one we are discussing. These include imitation and translation, the consolidating spirit of a national literary tradition that will outstrip its classical ancestry, the polarization of "natural" and "artificial" values, and the issue of primitivism. Literary motifs and social realities of high and low life, or city and country, can fruitfully be seen in light of progress and decline, refinement and elegance. We are not going far afield if we ask why Hume divided even virtues into "natural" and "artificial."

William Duff, among others, fears that refinement in colloquial language might signal the end of an evocative, metaphoric power essential to strong poetry. Burke sums up this concern in his *Enquiry* (part IV, section 7, "How Words Influence the Passions"): "It may be observed," he says—and it was being observed, uneasily, countless times during his lifetime—"that very polished languages, and such as are praised for their superior clearness and perspicuity, are generally deficient in strength." Typically, Dryden grasps the problem near its inception when he speaks of language now "more refined and free," which, however, produces poets less sturdy than those nurtured in the rough-hewn Elizabethan tongue. In short, judgment on the general health of the arts begins to create a nexus of concerns: poetic diction and linguistics, urbanization, classical scholarship, genre, and many more.

More factors come into play, one in particular that humanists rarely forget but seldom mention. During the decades after 1660, science steadily piles one achievement on another. In the late seventeenth century many intellectuals, such as William Wotton in *Reflections upon Ancient and Modern Learning* (1694), assume that natural philosophy, science, and mathematics will grow without bound. To some it seems obvious that science is progressing, quite simply, while the arts and morals appear in flux. For these reasons La Bruyère thinks a new, vital literature will be difficult to achieve, but new science is visible on the horizon. Swift unwittingly makes fun of Kepler's laws of planetary motion in *Gulliver's Travels*; Thomson incorporates science in his verse. The arts now find themselves in a novel situation relative to another massive area of human endeavor. Science could accumulate; technology could wield matter with power. Natural philosophy could prove its progressive nature (perhaps it was identical with progress), but art could never attain such confidence or such exponential expansion. Goldsmith summarizes the situation in his *Enquiry into the Present State of Polite Learning*. At one time, he says, the "arts and sciences grew up together, and mutually illustrated each other. But when once Pedants became lawgivers, the sciences began to want grace, and the polite arts solidity; these grew crabbed and sowre, those meretricious and gawdy; the philosopher became disgustingly precise, and the poet, ever straining after grace, caught only finery."[54]

Goldsmith is too severe. Science and scientific method are mazes in themselves, subject to historical and even biographical qualifications. Also many Enlightenment figures could justifiably be considered both scientists and critics: Priestley, Benjamin Thompson (Count Rumford), Franklin, Adam Smith, Jefferson, and Gray, whom Johnson called "one of the most learned men in Europe." Yet the stunning fact remains: Prometheus is now more scientist than poet, as prose romances would soon discover.

Hazlitt in particular urges restraint in mixing science and art. Science depends for its lifeblood on refinement, the essence of which is repeated effort building on earlier ones. Art depends on fresh approaches to nature, human conduct, and the medium of the art itself. "It is often made a subject of complaint and surprise," remarks Hazlitt, "that the arts . . . in modern times, have not kept pace with the general progress of society and civilization . . . First, the complaint itself . . . proceeds on a false notion, for the analogy . . . totally fails; it applies to science, not to art." Any critical expectation of progress in the arts will therefore become wrongheaded and subversive. We must keep in mind "the peculiar distinction and privilege of each, of science and of art; of the one, never to attain its utmost summit of perfection, and of the other, to arrive at it almost at once." As if acknowledging the endless refinement that advances scientific fact, and the excessive refinement that threatens the pleasure of literary pursuit, Johnson suggested, "if you are to have but one book with you upon a journey, let it be a book of science. When you have read through a book of entertainment, you know it, and it can do no more for you; but a book of science is inexhaustible."[55]

Questions of progress or decline in the arts and society are neither ushered in nor sustained by a conservative cabal wishing to retain older, classical values in literature or class structure. These questions preoccupy spirits zealously liberal and reform-minded: Hazlitt, young Coleridge, Priestley, Blake, Shelley. Poet-critics bring home the questions in popular publications. Warton's *History of English Poetry* opens with a generality that reveals how the role of poetry (and other pursuits) has been elevated to a major issue in a society that considers itself sophisticated: "In an age advanced to the highest degree of refinement, that species of curiosity commences, which is busied in contemplating the progress of social life, in displaying the gradations, and in tracing the transitions from barbarism to civility. That these speculations should become the favorite pursuit, and the fashionable topics at such a period is extremely natural."

Discussions and comments on the state of the arts secure for themselves a place in widely circulated periodicals and books. We may feel that the progress and decline of art is too metaphysical and ungrounded in fact, too biased by individual taste to permit solid determination, and awkwardly out of place in a pluralistic, diverse culture. The question may be viewed as untextual criticism, hollow theorizing, intellectual posture. But this issue and its related debates improve eighteenth-century criticism, make it more suspicious of itself. And whenever criticism dismisses the question of progress and decline, or whenever it grows unaware of the paradox of refinement, it blocks with one stroke an informed evaluation of historical process and of its own historical consciousness.

CHAPTER 3

"So Far Retir'd from Happy Pieties": The Rise of Modern Myth

Wer sichert den Olymp? vereinet Götter?
Des Menschen Kraft im Dichter offenbart.

Who makes Olympus sure, and gives the gods one life?
The power of humankind, as in the bard revealed.

FAUST I 156–157

The eighteenth century sets the patterns of thought for romantic and modern concepts of myth. Its writers are the first to claim that classical mythology, passively received and used largely for stock ornament and allusion is, in Coleridge's phrase, "exploded mythology." The new critical maturity is summed up in Johnson's disdain for Granville's poetry: "He is for ever amusing himself with the puerilities of ancient mythology."[1] The Renaissance, which revived, explored, and embellished classical myths, and romanticism, which, as Emery Neff says, created the "classics of the modern world," flank the comparatively thin bar of the eighteenth century like two massive weights. But picking up this bar we extend the Renaissance traditions and also grasp the rise of modern approaches to mythology with all their creative and cultural potential.[2] And the century connecting the two great mythopoeic periods is thin only if we are looking at poetry alone,[3] for in sharp contrast to the conventional view of it as a valley between two Olympuslike summits, the eighteenth century rethinks literary and critical assumptions of mythology and transforms them into modern views.

The eighteenth century neither blindly worshiped nor utterly rejected the gods. As Frank Manuel says, it confronted them.[4] Its many intellectual premises concerning mythology were exactly those from which romantic poets gained direction and confidence. Historical research, comparative mythology, the sociology and anthropology of myth, its linguistic and psychological origins, and the poet as mythmaker engaged critics and poets. Such a thorough and multiple investigation was intensified by a dilemma faced for the first time in the eighteenth century, a dilemma we have not escaped. What can we do as we find it increasingly difficult to create original myths of the kind we admire in earlier, popular writers, when, at the same time, we find it just as hard to retell those older myths because, for the purpose of the poet writing at the present time, they are "exploded" and unoriginal?[5] Does a premium on literary originality spell doom for an enduring modern mythology?

However we classify the various eighteenth-century treatments of mythology, we discover, as writers then discovered, that each approach is a matter of emphasis, not exclusivity. Bishop Warburton could not demonstrate the divine legation of Moses, a religious and even dogmatic conclusion, without considering historical evidence. When Lowth discussed the "sublime" quality of the Hebrews' "mystical allegory," he engaged an aesthetic sense of style applicable to contemporaneous poetry. Newton constructed his chronology with curiosity about belief in the literalness of ancient religious myths. The relation of critics and poets to mythology became like Keats's apostrophe to the urn: it is a "sylvan historian" recording the past, but around its shape haunts a "leaf-fring'd legend" engaging the beholder's imagination to create more than the eye can see. Hume might have been on the skeptical side of mythology whether Greco-Roman, Christian, Hebrew, or Chinese, but he analyzed beliefs in order to understand myths.

Some, like Blackwell and later Hazlitt, held that myths originally were not necessarily stories of the gods that were meant either to entice or to oppress the unlettered majority into religion. Myths could be seen as the original poetic vehicle of philosophic speculation, of all ideal discourse concerning human nature and its first cause. Psyche, a myth about the nature of the human mind and inner spirit, was, after all, introduced by Apuleius' *Golden Ass* in the second century A.D. as—self-consciously—the last goddess. Classical mythology had at last symbolized its own introspection. Bacon indicated that philosophic wisdom, not religion, was the key; for him, as Blackwell noted in *Letters Concerning Mythology* (1748), mythologies were the "Wisdom of the Ancients" and "a constant Source of Pleasure to a speculative Man, as they represent some of the grandest Ideas in Nature and Art."[6] Mythology, said Blackwell himself in the *Proofs* (1748) following his earlier *Enquiry into the Life and Writings of Homer* (1735), is actually the grand and universal allegory of nature, the imaginative narrative of the cosmos, the world's creation in narrative form. It became the "majestick Method" of the poet's creative power.[7] The same definition is re-echoed today by Carlos Fuentes in his assessment of two modern novelists: "As for his master William Faulkner, for Garcia Marquez a novel is the fundamental act we call a myth, the re-presentation of the founding act." In *One Hundred Years of Solitude,* the history represented is "all the things that men and women have dreamt, imagined and desired and named."[8]

End of an Epoch

Paradoxically, increased literacy in the eighteenth century diluted rather than strengthened the presence of classical mythology. The reading public is more modern (*modo,* just now): knowledge of the original tongues of mythology often meant school grammar and a smattering of easier texts. Young Wordsworth and others still immerse themselves in Ovid's *Metamorphoses* (for whom Wordsworth maintained a lifelong preference to Virgil), and Keats translates part of the *Aeneid* as a schoolboy.[9] (All the major romantic poets studied classical mythology in the original, at least in Latin.) But in his note on the *Ode to Lycoris* (1817) Wordsworth admits that in the seventeenth century "an importance and a sanctity were at that period attached to classical literature . . . that can never be revived. No doubt the hacknied and lifeless use into which mythology fell towards the close of the seventeenth century, and which continued through the eighteenth, disgusted the general reader with all allusion to it in modern verse."

Yet what Wordsworth says had been noted often—and more acutely—by critics and poets frustrated with classical mythology in contemporary writing. With Akenside, as with most (and later with Wordsworth himself), this disgust mixes with nostalgic admiration. But the essence of nostalgia is irretrievability. Poets and readers familiar with previous borrowings know that to borrow again would be pointless, and that to change a borrowing slightly would not offer novelty but only offend expectation and violate custom. Johnson hammers this home repeatedly. Waller, he says,

> borrows too many of his sentiments and illustrations from the old mythology, for which it is vain to plead the example of ancient poets: the deities which they introduced so frequently were considered as realities, so far as to be received by the imagination, whatever sober reason might even then determine. But of these images time has tarnished the splendor. A fiction, not only detected but despised, can never afford a solid basis to any position, though sometimes it may furnish a transient allusion, or slight illustration. No modern monarch can be much exalted by hearing that, as Hercules had had his *club,* he has his *navy.*

Even "of the ancient poets," Johnson contends, "every reader feels the mythology tedious and oppresive." It is, he quips, a "school boy's" subject (though Keats would make great imaginative use of his relatively simple handbook learning). Alternately bored and offended, we recoil at "the inefficacy and incredibility of a mythological tale."[10]

Johnson is writing this at the time when Wordsworth attends

Hawkshead Grammar School and Coleridge was soon to enter
Christ's Hospital. Even earlier, in 1746, Akenside admits in his
note MM to *Hymn to the Naiads* that "the mere genealogy, or the
personal adventures of heathen gods" has no place in new poetry
and is "but little interesting to a modern reader." As Johnson puts
it, not even sharing Akenside's wistful attempt to give naiads British citizenship as protectresses of the Thames, the renovation of
classical and even gothic deities and fairies smacked of an enervated
culture and literary heritage unable to face "real life." This was not
a poetry of experience. In T. S. Eliot's transposed key, "The nymphs
are departed." Even in Gray's Welsh *Bard,* which makes a case for
genius and power in the individual poet, Johnson denigrates "the
puerilities of obsolete mythology."[11]

In the critique of Wordsworth and poetic diction in the *Biographia,* Coleridge states that Gray's "Sonnet on the Death of Mr. Richard West" should not be censured for outmoded diction—as Wordsworth had done in the Preface to *Lyrical Ballads*—but for the use
of "an exploded mythology."[12] The line in question is Gray's "And
reddening Phoebus lifts his golden fire." Yet Coleridge is again echoing Johnson's phrase that Thomas Tickell's *Kensington Garden* is
populated by "Grecian deities and Gothick Fairies" in which "neither species of those exploded beings could have done much."[13]
Coleridge himself is castigated by his schoolmaster James Boyer
(who also taught Charles Lamb) for mythological allusions in his
juvenile poetry: "*Harp? Harp? Lyre? Pen and ink, boy, you mean!
Muse, boy, Muse? your Nurse's daughter, you mean! Pierian spring? Oh
'aye! the cloisterpump, I suppose!*"[14] Mythological allusion is usually
associated with an archaically trite diction. James Beattie, in *Essays
on Poetry and Music* (1778), scoffs that with certain authors "a country maid becomes . . . a *nymph of the groves*; if flattery sing at all, it
must be a *syren song;* the sheperd's flute dwindles into a *oaten reed,*
and his crook is exalted into a *scepter.*"[15] In his 1800 Preface, Wordsworth reverses the procedure of Beattie (whom he read) and italicizes
the diction of Gray that does *not* offend. Classical mythology becomes a dead weight encumbering not only narrative but a natural
language of passion and experience.

Throughout the eighteenth century the most successful use of classical mythology is in comedy, surfacing especially in mock-heroic work. *The Rape of the Lock*; *The Dunciad*; *Joseph Andrews,* that "comic epic in prose" where Fielding spoofs the idolatry of Homer; and *Tom Jones,* where comically inflated chapter openings parody not books of the *Iliad* but Homer's later mechanical imitators—all this is fun and it works. Eliot achieved a similar effect in *The Waste Land* simply by changing diction. Lines from the *Parliament of Bees* by John Day (1574–c. 1640),

> A noise of horns and hunting, which shall bring
> Actaeon to Diana in the spring,

become

> The sound of horns and motors, which shall bring
> Sweeney to Mrs. Porter in the spring.

In the eighteenth century serious allusion to mythology begins to fail regularly. Dryden's *Astraea Redux,* echoing Virgil's fourth *Eclogue,* pleased in 1660, but, as Wordsworth notes, the next century grows increasingly impatient with contrivance and parallelisms. Granville's *Heroic Love,* Spence's *Polymetis,* and Prior's *Solomon* are received as tepidly as Rowe's *Ulysses,* Gay's *The Fan,* and Thomson's *Agamemnon.* This last trio Johnson dismisses with similar condemnations: to show heroes such as Ulysses, "as they have already been shown is to disgust by repetition; to give them new qualities . . . is to offend by violating received notions." *The Fan* "is one of those mythological fictions . . . of little value. The attention naturally retires from a new tale of Venus, Diana, and Minerva." *Agamemnon* "had the fate which most commonly attends mythological stories, and was only endured, but not favoured."[16] The repellent nature of common mythology in modern poetry became a constant theme of Johnson's *Lives.* Some new relevance to modern life is needed, as Tennyson later attempts, or some complete overhaul into a totally new telling, as Joyce reworks *Ulysses,* or as Mann revitalizes the old legend of *Doktor Faustus.*

In the 1700s the success of "mythological works" with a serious tone nearly vanishes. In the preface to *A Tale of a Tub,* Swift pokes fun at those who in a "grand Committee" had "mythologized" the meaning of his tub and explains it as a diversion thrown to Hobbes's *Leviathan*! Only the mock-heroic and satiric inversion, or, as Johnson admitted, the frolicking inventions of Pope's *Rape,* support the machinery of supernatural beings.[17] Abstract personifications (Fame, Avarice, Hope, and so forth) often replace the gods. And ironically, what Peter Gay calls the "pagan" enlightenment is modern enough to reject pagan deities, yet religious enough to feel uneasy about Christian mythological fiction that strays beyond and hence potentially violates the Bible. We shall return to the crucial question of faith, for the flight of the "damned crew" of deities from the divine-human Jesus in Milton's *Hymn* signals what Johnson sees as the end of "mythological allusions . . . with sentiments which neither passion nor reason could have dictated, since the change which [monotheistic] religion has made in the system of the world."[18] This change, combined with new literacy and new premiums on originality and the representation of "real life," create the end of an epoch. The importance of this cannot be overstressed. The literary world is thrown into a kind of long trauma, and poets and critics struggle to regain their coordination.

As the century progressed, an escape route develops. It is not, after all, the stock diction, the frozen or hackneyed images, or even the worn narrative line, the "fable" of classical mythology that captures admiration. More important is the individual poet's ability, the spirit or the genius that invents a work of power. In Yeats's metaphor, it is not the "circus animals" that count, but the "foul rag-and-bone shop of the heart." The poet's ability to make myth out of experience and materials at hand—that was what surpasses the names, however wonderful and resonant, of old gods. The poet's power to create new myths is highlighted in a series of articles in the *British Magazine* (1762), credited to both Goldsmith and Smollett.[19] Instead of a cultural heritage of common values and images, "mythology" begins to be seen as a call to natural individualism. Ezra Pound would proclaim this cosmopolitan and modern sense in Canto 81, "What thou lovest well is thy true heritage / What thou

lov'st well shall not be reft from thee." At times this natural individuality rebels against society and culture by ironically taking
refuge in the older and admittedly inert myths, as in Wordsworth's
cry, "I'd rather be a pagan suckled on a creed outworn."

Historicism and the Hellenic Revival

To recapture the ideal of the mythmaking poet who followed natural
rather than artificial impulses, the yoke of Rome had to be cast off.
Roman models could not revive the mythmaking power in modern
form, yet the tenor of early eighteenth-century literature is, on balance, more Roman than Greek. Dryden tries Virgil's helmet,
Twickenham becomes a rough equivalent to the Sabine Farm, and
Johnson turns to Juvenal for the pattern of his two longer poems.
The Roman world had passed on all ancient mythologies: Agrippa's
Pantheon remains the most perfectly preserved of major public
buildings of the Empire. No other exterior better exemplifies the
adage that Augustus found the city brick and left it marble.[20] But
the gods inside were Greek in origin and Aeneas was Priam's son.
As far as original, *inventive* strength was concerned, the Roman legacy—for the eighteenth century—moved into satire and contem-
plative verse. When the high satiric mode waned in the 1740s,
poet-critics turned to Greece. After *The Vanity of Human Wishes*
(1749) no major English poem of the century overtly derives from
a Roman model.

Longinus and Pindar attracted critical attention from the late
seventeenth century on. Fénelon's *Avantures de Télémaque* proved
popular[21] and, in addition to influencing Andrew Ramsay's *Travels
of Cyrus,* it prompted Thomas Russell's excellent sonnet on Philoc-
tetes, *Suppos'd to be Written at Lemnos.*[22] Ramsay (also known as the
Chevalier de Ramsai and not to be confused with his compatriot
Allan Ramsay) communicated with Nicolas Fréret, the famed
French mythographer, knew Fénelon personally, and, in his *Conversations with Fénelon,* claimed a conversion experience. His new religious sensibility shines through the *Travels of Cyrus* and informs two
important essays Ramsay affixed to the *Travels:* "Of the Mythology

of the Antients" (1728) and "A Discourse upon the Theology and Mythology of the Pagans" (1730). Under the Grecian influence William Whitehead, following Akenside's *Hymn to the Naiads* (1746), wrote *Hymn to the Nymph of Bristol Spring*. Blackwell's *Memoirs of the Court of Augustus* proved far less successful in sales than his studies of Homer. Addison's *Cato* gave way to Thomson's *Agamemnon,* and Aeschylus became something of a rage, his most colorful admirer being Parson Adams. Swift's retelling of Greek myths counterpoint his Horatian satires. Psyche becomes the subject of Gloster Ridley's poem *Psyche* (1747), as well as of the notable mythological chapter "The Vision" in Abraham Tucker's *Light of Nature Pursued* (1768–1777). Collins tries to mythologize the passions collectively and separately in his odes and asks British poets to look to Greece and "confirm the tales her sons relate!"[23] The progress poems of Gray and others begin with Greece and end with Britain (Philip Freneau's ends appropriately with California.) John "Estimate" Brown, who takes Greece as his model for the rise of poetry in primitive societies, abhors the standard of Augustan Rome.[24] Add to this Hellenic revival the rising interest in Hebrew poetry and myth reflected as early as Milton and carried through Ramsay's *Travels,* Warburton's *Divine Legation of Moses Demonstrated* (1737–1742), and Lowth's *Lectures on the Sacred Poetry of the Hebrews* (1753), and we can see that Hebraism and Hellenism are crowding out Augustanism. This helps greatly to generate a new view of mythology.

But the Hellenic revival, at its best, declines any *close* imitation of Greek, or other ancient, mythology. As Edward Young states in his famous dictum, quoted as often in his own day as in scholarship now, "To imitate the *Iliad* is not to imitate Homer." In 1735 Blackwell himself pointed this out in his *Life and Writings of Homer,* where he criticizes Trissino's blank verse *L'Italia liberata* (1524) as a noble failure precisely because it imitated the *Iliad* and not Homer's genius.[25] The aim of imitation should be more ideal than formal. The power of invention, not gods or heroes, was what was wanted. Horace's advice in the *Ars Poetica* that "it is better to dramatize the *Iliad* into acts than to offer a subject unknown and unsung" no longer sat well. The Greek cast of mind and its mythopoeic force, not the myths themselves, became the higher object of emulation. Although Young's *Conjectures* (1759) alludes repeatedly to classical mythology, his real point is that, despite Pope, nature and Homer are *not* the same. Look to nature, Young says, for "the true Helicon" is not earlier literature but "the breast of Nature." The goal is not another *Iliad* but "a capacity of accomplishing a work so great." Granted, direct imitations of Greek fable endured, but, as Johnson noted, they were more endured than favored.

The turn to Greece results in increased historical consciousness of mythology. The rise of modern mythology and the rise of systematic literary history go hand in hand. Moreover, the fables not only were *older* by the Ilissus than by the Tiber, they seemed more genuine and less borrowed, however much of Greek mythology was derived from cultures that thrived centuries earlier. Pushed further, even Greece could be seen as young. "To allegorize," Blackwell says, "is an Egyptian invention."[26] All one had to do was open the *Timaeus* and read Solon's conversation with the Egyptian priest (or Hesiod's *Theogony*). By old Nile the myths seemed oldest of all. A kind of historical oneupmanship now operates. Blackwell expresses it in *Letters Concerning Mythology:* "The Greeks and Romans had their Religion at second hand from powerful and knowing Nations, but who had departed from their first Establishment, before their Intercourse with European People. It is not therefore to be expected, that *these* should be wiser than their Masters, and exercise a Purity they had never received."[27]

It was comforting to view Greece as a latecomer by hundreds, even thousands, of years in the realm of mythology. It offered hope that to be first is more accident than distinction. (Johnson says *Paradise Lost* "is not the greatest of heroic poems, only because it is not the first.") Ramsay and Warburton try to explain the still undeciphered Egyptian hieroglyphs in terms of symbol and myth. In 1730 Ramsay mentions the scholar Thomas Hyde (1636–1704), who helped bring to light Persian mythology. Ramsay also extends himself to a discussion of the Vedas, the Yking (*I Ching*), and North American myths. Bernard Fontenelle already had studied Peruvian myths. The historical approach leads to comparative mythology. Antoine Banier (1675–1741) claims that all myth, unlike allegory, has a historical basis.[28] Ramsay's historical curiosity, in his *Discourse upon the Theology and Mythology of the Pagans*, reveals a more syncretist approach: "We see then that the doctrines of the primitive perfection of nature, its fall and restoration by a divine Hero, are equally manifest in the Mythologies of the Greeks, Egyptians, Persians, Indians and Chinese."[29] Later Johnson himself projects a *History of the Heathen Mythology, with an explication of the fables, both allegorical and historical, with references to the poets.* He admitted "good reasons" for reading mythological romances, primarily the poet's "fertility of invention" and "beauty and style of expression."[30]

The very idea of "pastness," if not essential to myths, seemed to enhance them. Clio is the muse of history and epic poetry. The temporal enemies of the mythmaking imagination are a historical sense based purely on fact and, at the other extreme, an antihistorical stance proclaiming the relevance of the modern only. So Blackwell regretted the "meer *Historical* Use (setting aside higher Considerations)" of comparative mythology. A speculative admixture open to literary style, philosophy, and religion was needed. Spenser— and Chatterton—knew the value of a generalized sense of the past and its archaic poetic language. Sidney admitted in his *Apology* that he loved to hear some old crowder singing the "Ballad of Percy and Douglas," and that while in Hungary (much like twentieth-century scholars of the oral tradition who went there), he admired oral poets reciting stories generations old. In both Marlowe's and Goethe's *Faust* the hero immerses himself in dusty tomes and searches for secret knowledge locked in the past. Thomas Mann's Adrian Leverkühn resorts to medieval magic number squares and an arcane, private alchemy of symbols and mathematical relations. Somewhere between factual knowledge of history and disregard of it lay the suggestive and partial awareness conducive to myth. Alfred North Whitehead remarks that the Renaissance knew about classical mythology just as much as was good for it. The eighteenth century knew more, but it concentrates on the poet's ability to create myth in the first place.

Primitivism

The Hellenic revival and much of the historical approach to mythology were symptomatic of something larger and harder to define: primitivism. Blackwell prefaces his *Letters Concerning Mythology* with an engraving of the bust of Homer and contends that all great poets have had "a *simple country* Look," like the *"plain rustick* Look" of this bust. (Much to Coleridge's dismay, *rustic* was the word Wordsworth later stressed in his 1800 Preface; and *plain* became a positive description of poetic diction for Coleridge himself.) Blackwell even praised the Appalachian Indians for their primitive mythology: "Their daily Worship is simple and pure."[31] Had complexities of civilization choked mythology? Were not Blake's "dark satanic mills" negative images of "the green and pleasant" pastoral world often associated with myths? When the curtain goes up on Goethe's *Faust,* the great man turns from his books and wishes himself far from esoteric learning. He wants to escape into a clear, direct, and inviting pastoral world.[32] In Keats's 1817 volume of poems his dedicatory sonnet to Leigh Hunt (who made careful notes in Blackwell's *Life and Writings of Homer*) expresses the link between a primitivistic pastoral setting and the power to make myths. Although "Glory and loveliness have passed away" from a world where there is "no crowd of nymphs" and where "Pan is no longer sought," Keats hopes, as the remaining poems in the volume testify, to revive the magic of nature interpreted through myth. Hazlitt also hypothesized that the pastoral world originated mythology, but lamented, "We have few good pastoral poems in the language."[33]

Underneath all of this lay a grand paradox: primitivism reflected, as Arthur Lovejoy has noted, "the discontent of the civilized with civilization." Yet no self-respecting poet, as Keats and others before recognized, wanted to revive mummies of parched fable. One could try to negate the course of history that was debilitating classical mythology by reviving the myth of a *timeless* golden age, one so old as to be perennial. But by the eighteenth century this myth was itself becoming trite. An alternative became the glorification of the child, the only "civilized" being not spoiled by civilization. Wordsworth addresses the child as "thou best philosopher," and Novalis proclaims, "Wo Kinder sind da ist ein Goldnes Zeitalter," where there are children, there is a Golden Age. Later, in Dickens, Melville, and Twain, settings devoid of (or opposed to) the pressures of commercialized society and a focus on childhood (frequently an orphan—even Ishmael becomes one) add to the archetypal and mythic dimension of their work. Coleridge could, with some nostalgia, invoke the "fair humanities of old religion" and long for their return, despite his later criticism of an "exploded mythology." Wordsworth's sonnet "The world is too much with us" is, Douglas Bush states, "the keynote of a mass of mythological poetry of the nineteenth and twentieth centuries; the old antagonism between Pan and Christ has become a contrast between the ugly materialism of our . . . industrial civilization and the natural religion, the ideal beauty and harmony, of Hellenic life."[34] As early as Akenside's *Hymn to the Naiads* (which Bush calls "the most remarkable mythological poem of the century"), the poet hoped to escape the "unhallow'd rout" and "profaner audience" of modern civilization. But this occurs before the cult of primitivism reaches epidemic proportion; Akenside's nymphs encourage British commerce, its getting and spending, and provide for "the maritime part of military power." Gray, Goldsmith, Cowper, and Blake become less sanguine about the bonds linking myth, money, and power.

For all its vaunted virtue of simplicity, much primitivism arrived on the back of arduous historical scholarship. The prizing of the *Volk* could be an easy sentiment, but the work of Gray and Percy came painstakingly. (It was to be one of Wordsworth's great strengths as a poet that he was surrounded by the rustic; he did not learn it from books.) Academic and antiquarian research created a thirst for a new mythology based on earlier, "purer" times. In a sonnet written in a copy of Dugdale's *Monasticon,* Thomas Warton styles himself "of painful Pedantry the poring child," but envisions the pedant melting into the pensive bard; true, much antiquarian research, such as William Stukeley's, achieves more invention than accuracy. Like Gray and Collins (see *Ode on the Popular Superstitions of the Highlands*), Warton turns not only to Greece but to Britain for new mythology. The conclusion of Warton's *Pleasures of Melancholy* rejects the Greeks and praises the Druids. His sonnets "Written at Stonehenge" and "On King Arthur's Round Table at Winchester" reveal a primitivistic, mythic urge. Warton read Stukeley's *Stonehenge, a Temple Restor'd to the British Druids* (1740), and the Druidic line continues through Blake. Although "early English poetry was still too near to fall completely under the category 'primitive,'"[35] a poem such as Collins' *Ode on the Death of Mr. Thomson* suggests this ancient British mythology. The last stanza combines nostalgia, a pastoral world long lost, and a mythmaking poet (Thomson himself) as the object of yearning for British mythology:

> Long, long, thy stone and pointed clay
> Shall melt the musing Briton's eyes;
> "O! vales and wild woods," shall he say,
> "In yonder grave your Druid lies!"

Yes, the British past could seem mythic. As Richard Hurd relates in *Letters on Chivalry and Romance* (1762), Milton wrote *Paradise Lost* only after abandoning "his long-projected design of Prince Arthur" (Letter 12).

Rational Inquiry

A contemporaneous and not always sympathetic analysis probes the validity of primitivism. As early as 1690 Sir William Temple's *Of Poetry* and *Essay upon the Ancient and Modern Learning* use the age-old theory of cyclical cultural change to explain current literary development.[36] Cultures reaching a sophisticated plateau look back to giants in the earth. The irony is that the ancient periods longed for by modern primitivism glanced backward themselves. Much "ancient" mythology, in fact, concerns earlier fables and heroes. Even the gods experienced cultural revolution: the Olympians supplanted the Titans. Temple asks, will poor humankind never learn: must imagination streamline history to conform it to patterns of strong, archetypal emotions? Even cultured people, he concludes, must, like aging children, be amused by simple stories.

In the *Life and Writings of Homer* Blackwell divides mythology into "natural" and "artificial," the latter the result "of great Search and Science." But "natural" mythology "is the Faculty that . . . invents and creates it." Blackwell considers his own century largely "artificial," with polished manners and apparently degenerated literary power. In his dedication he remarks that heroic poetry belongs to a rougher age; he is persuaded that in all likelihood "*we may never be a proper Subject of an Heroic Poem.*"[37] Blackwell, whose *Enquiry* Gibbon called "an effort of genius," becomes influential in Germany through Herder.

In 1763, the year James Macpherson purveys *Temora,* his second "translation" of Ossian (*Fingal* appeared in 1761), John Brown's *Dissertation on the Rise, Union and Power, the Progressions, Separations and Corruptions of Poetry and Music* reinforces cyclical theory. Brown derives his argument from Greece and the prototype of Hesiod's *Theogony,* which Blackwell himself discussed.[38] *Ossian* vindicated such theories. It was, in Brown's words, a "noble confirmation" of an earlier, mythologically superior age. But opponents snickered; aside from not having seen original manuscripts, Johnson was probably suspicious because he knew Percy's genuine research. The myth of the noble savage rankled Johnson as well. He scoffed at Rousseau (who actually never uses the term), and took the view that this was old stuff indeed—culture hoodwinking itself, developing a New Style calendar with one hand and turning back a pseudo clock with the other. Rousseau's view, popularly understood, was not new. Dryden's lines from the *Conquest of Granada,* nearly ninety years before, reveal a vision already in circulation:

> I am as free as Nature first made man,
> Ere the base laws of servitute began,
> When wild in woods the noble savage ran.

William Duff explicitly makes the connection with mythology that lurks behind the debate over primitivism. The last section of his *Essay on Original Genius* (1767) defends its long title: *That original Poetic Genius will in general be displayed in its utmost vigour in the early and uncultivated periods of Society, which are peculiarly favorable to*

it; and that it will seldom appear in a very high degree in cultivated life.
Early societies, Duff argues, had an advantage in composing mythologies and inventing symbols. Life was simpler, emotions more
forcefully expressed. Smaller vocabularies made figurative speech
common and natural. Greek mythology, "a system of ingenious fiction," and the "remarkable boldness of sentiment and expression
. . . the most poetical figures of speech" in Eastern and Egyptian
mythologies were attributable to their "primitive" state.[39]

Hume, agreeing with Blackwell that mythology was originally
used to exploit the fear of the common people and to control them
(anticipating Marx's "opiate of the masses"), resurrects arguments of
the first-century rhetorician Velleius Paterculus.[40] Cultures follow
cycles, he says, in his *Essay on the Rise and Progress of the Arts and
Sciences.* Perfection in the arts will "necessarily decline." The fact
that Hume could revive a seventeen-hundred-year-old argument favored that very argument's premise. The question remained whether
a new mythology could be created in the face of predetermined
cycles that controlled literature and society.

Rational inquiry into primitivism and mythology thus cut two
ways. It could deflate or buoy up. Kames, for instance, in *Sketches
of the History of Man,* attacks Paterculus. The Highland Society of
Scotland, perturbed and embarrassed by the *Ossian* controversy, established a commission to judge the work—and not to render the
Scottish verdict "not proven." In 1805 the commission's report,
compiled by Henry Mackenzie, was generally favorable. But that
same year Malcolm Laing, who five years earlier had attacked Macpherson, produced a heavily annotated *Ossian* that revealed clear
echoes not only of Homer and Virgil, but of Waller, Prior, and
Pope.

Perhaps an inevitable cycle did produce an age of myth and was
now grinding or "polishing" down a veneer. At any rate, a "revolution" had occurred. The century finds itself entering a new cycle.
Thomas Warton, in *Observations on the Fairy Queen* (1754) calls Spenser "a romantic poet," the last champion of allegory. Then, after
Milton's sublimity, "imagination gave way to correctness" (sec. 10,
"Of Spenser's Allegorical Character"). In 1762 Hurd repeats the

lament: "What we have gotten by this revolution, you will say, is a great deal of good sense. What we have lost is a world of fine fabling, the illusion of which is so grateful to the *charmed spirit* that, in spite of philosophy and fashion, *Faery* Spenser still ranks highest among the poets." Hurd feels that cultural determinists ignore the human factor. The *"charmed spirit"* means more than good sense. One might express it in Thoreau's later words: "This lament for a golden age is but a lament for golden men." The problem is to stir the poet to heroic effort, not to fiddle with theories that minimize psychological freedom.

Crucial Terms for Culture

When Hurd says that the "revolution" in poetry leaves "fine fabling" by the wayside, he means mythmaking. The eighteenth century and the romantics never speak of *myth* or *myths;* the closest usage is *fable.* Not until the 1820s and 1830s did *myth* and *mythic* enter the language.[41] For the eighteenth century *mythology* carries assumptions that are often overlooked. It implies a body of interconnected creations and, according to Johnson's *Dictionary,* their "explication," or unfolding. The connected creations give each other resonance and meaning (Duff's *"system* of ingenious fiction"). We are really verging on a structuralist view of mythology. Although myths isolated from other myths did not yet exist for the eighteenth century as they do for us, the new historical and comparative awareness erodes the more complex, structural awareness of different versions of the same fable taken together. Modern pluralism of culture is beginning to destroy the sense of a mythology and to foster separate myths. A "myth" is more easily understood. It is one story—or even one ideology. So Theseus, that quite modern ruler and man of reason, says: "I never may believe / These antique fables, nor these fairy toys." But "mythology" is, properly speaking, what it is for the romantics and the eighteenth century: a whole narrative body or series of stories so layered that their connection becomes something of *universal* import. Hippolyta gently corrects her consort:

> But all the story of the night told over,
> And all their minds transfigur'd so together,
> More witnesseth than fancy's images,
> And grows to something of great constancy,
> But, howsoever, strange and admirable.[42]

Like many Shakespearean insights, this one is repeated by contemporary intellectuals, in this case by Claude Lévi-Strauss, who affirms that "The 'meaning' of mythology cannot reside in the isolated elements which constitute the myth, but must inhere in the way in which those elements are combined, and must take account of the potential for transformation that such a combination involves." For Lévi-Strauss as for Northrop Frye, the combination creating Hippolyta's "something of great constancy" ("certainty" in Elizabethan usage) is nothing less than a narrative of human culture itself. Or, more than that, it is the merging of the cultural and the natural into narratives that are not only created by society and its individuals, but in turn become formative of society, and are its deepest educational resource. As Frye remarks in *The Secular Scripture,* "Myths stick together to form a mythology, a large interconnected body of narrative that covers all religion and historical revelation that its society is concerned with. . . . Myths take root in a specific culture, and it is one of their functions to tell that culture what it is and how it came to be, in their own mythological terms."[43]

Although *myth* was not yet a word in the eighteenth-century, writers employ many other terms and debate their slippery meanings. The value of such discussions seems less in forming clear definitions than in providing critical tools and interpretations. No norm or standard is reached, but the nature of mythology acquires a contour and surface relief from the pressure of these increasingly learned debates. Ephraim Chambers' *Cyclopedia* (which Rousseau notes is the original for Diderot's and d'Alembert's *Dictionnaire encyclopédique,* "at first to be only a sort of translation of Chambers"),[44] contains in its 1728 and later editions a structural definition of *fable* as plot or narrative, the essence of which "is to be a symbol" itself, "to signify somewhat more than is expressed by the letter," a metaphoric plot. Influenced by Banier, Chambers subdivides fables into rational, moral, and mixed types.

A dozen years later, Warburton conceives of mythology as a vast system of allegories, each of which uses various "symbols," themselves nothing more than "improved hieroglyphics." In turn, hieroglyphics are either "tropical" or "proper," the latter the simplest kind of literal pictures. The teaching of the ancients often involved feigning "a *divine original* for hieroglyphic characters." This meant backtracking to develop larger allegories to explain each single symbol or character rather than seeing all symbols emerge from one original allegory. This strategy of interpretation suggests a method of composition (not necessarily written) in which the poet invents an allegory or narrative to explicate or to place in context an already received, though obscure, symbol. Such a narrative becomes an exegesis or explication (as Johnson notes) in fictive form.[45] This is what Roland Barthes means, I think, when he says "myth is a peculiar system, in that it is constructed from a semiological chain which existed before it: it *is a second-order semiological system.*" Myth is a metalanguage constructed from language.[46] A myth becomes a supersign, containing within itself a system of language with its own signs. In myth, language thus assumes a deeper or second-order resonance. The plots as well as the language of mythology are also analogic or even anagogic in their structure and interpretation. Lévi-Strauss notes that the "savage" mythmaking mind "builds mental structures which facilitate an understanding of the world in as much as they resemble it. In this sense savage thought can be defined as analogical thought."[47] In a similar vein, Andrew Ramsay, while agreeing with Banier that allegory and mythology are different, questions Banier's conviction that mythology must have a historical basis. Could it not be part of a larger interpretive effort not necessarily rooted in actual events? In his *Discourse* prefixed to Fénelon's *Avantures de Télémaque,* Ramsay decries that symbol, allegory, and hieroglyph are all degenerating and, by a process of critical secularization, losing religious import.[48] Already the battle lines of later debates—such as Creuzer's religio-allegorical school versus Lobeck's historical interpretations—are being drawn.

Coleridge's Symbol is Lowth's Mystical Allegory

Robert Lowth's 1753 definition of "mystical allegory" is virtually identical with Coleridge's famous definition of symbol in *The States-man's Manual* almost sixty-five years later. Both discussions, embedded in the context of sacred history, rely on examples from the Old Testament prophetic books. In the mystical allegory, Lowth says, "The exterior or ostensible image is not a shadowy colouring of the interior sense, but is in itself a reality; and although it sustain another character, it does not wholly lay aside its own." Each view, the literal presence of the thing or image and its figurative signification, "whether conjunctly or apart, will be found equally agreeable to truth." For Coleridge, "a system of symbols" are "harmonious in themselves" but are also "consubstantial with the truths, of which they are the *conductors*." The symbol, unlike the allegory, is thus "tautegorical": it is its literal self but also has "a two-fold significance . . . It always partakes of the Reality which it renders intelligible." For Coleridge, this twofold nature separates symbol from allegory, as for Lowth this same twofold significance separates "mystical allegory" from lower forms of allegory. Paul de Man, urging a Hegelian distinction between symbol and allegory (which basically reverses Coleridge's terms and reverts to Lowth's usage), contends that Coleridge overlooks the temporality of the symbol. Yet the context of Lowth's and Coleridge's respective definitions of mystical allegory and symbol makes it clear that for both men these figures of speech partake of the history they are empowered to reveal. They permit the intersection of the eternal with the temporal. Lowth's "mystical allegory" and Coleridge's "symbol," central to prophetic texts, urge, as Blake will urge, a larger and more complicated grasp of temporality within eternity.[49]

Schelling, who made a distinction similar to Coleridge's (and later praised Coleridge's for its deeper insight), left suggestive remarks still unfamiliar to most English readers.[50] They reveal a close theoretical attention behind the romantic achievements. Schelling defines *schema* (a Kantian term) as the presentation of a class of individual particulars by a generalized one; conversely, *allegory* presents a general idea, value, or concept by an individualized character or image; and a *symbol* mediates perfectly between these two. A symbol holds the equilibrium between an intellectual world of eternal, universal ideas and a material world of transient, particular individuation. Mythology is the totality of nature living in the human mind, the existence of nature expressed as the mind's independent poetic or imaginative experience. "Mythology" is a *state of mind*—which then generates literary works as products. Mythology as an outlook of the psyche is "the first condition and necessary material of all art."[51]

The eighteenth-century and romantic debates and definitions create an atmosphere in which these concepts are crucial and relevant to literature, an atmosphere in which the poet desires to forge a new mythology and new symbols, not only on paper but in a mental vision of the world. Yet in doing this the poet inevitably needs to handle the questions of religion and modern philosophy. Milton felt an uneasy truce between Pan and Christ, and afterward, as we have seen, classical mythology began to break down. The "damned crew" of old gods fled, but "time," as Milton hoped, did not "run back, and fetch the age of gold." In the greatest of English epics Milton expressed the essential Christian myth, but later poets (with the exception of Blake) fail to regenerate its power at length. Deists and pantheists produce a spate of epics, odes, and effusions in the eighteenth century. They are too abstract and full of moralizing.[52] *The Seasons,* one of the excellent long poems in the language, is not "myth" as usually understood. In philosophic poetry the tendencies of natural religion secularize and intellectualize the mythological elements. *Ossian* would puzzle admirers and detractors alike by what Thomas Warton calls a "perplexing and extraordinary circumstance": the northern bard has no religion at all![53]

Johnson asserts that no writer could break the taboo of mixing profound religious truths with literary fiction. In a sense the Christian religion killed off the religious content of myth. One could try to smile with the ancient authors (let alone Renaissance poets) who smiled indulgently at the suggestion that they literally believed their stories. But, among other considerations, they had no Bible always putting literary treatments to the litmus test of a single holy text. Or one could argue about the religious origins of ancient myths, but what did that offer to the struggling poet writing at the present time? In Johnson's words, "The change which [the Christian] religion has made in the whole system of the world" altered forever our view of mythology. Schelling and other Germans agree, and accordingly construct new interpretations of historical and cultural evolution.

Yet, although someone devout or simply familiar with the Bible might be offended or bored by inventive fables of Jesus, Moses, or St. John (by and large Blake avoids biblical figures in his myth-making), one "Christian" character could always be treated mythologically—the devil. This fact is behind Blake's remark that Milton was of the devil's party, for the devil leaves room for the imagination. Richard Steele's *Christian Hero* (1701) is reprinted many times, but as an ensign in the Cold-Stream Guards he had asked, "Why is it that the Heathen struts, and the Christian sneaks in our Imagination?" Wordsworth in his 1815 Preface to *Lyrical Ballads* and Coleridge in his Shakespeare Lectures, to exemplify how the imagination works in poetic description, select passages from *Paradise Lost* that portray the devil and death. Burke did the same in his *Enquiry.*

Myths not believed or half believed enjoyed a pleasing quality, a distance, a "pastness," or, to use Burke's term, an "obscurity." Myths held devoutly to be true eventually suffered by comparison because they did not elicit that exciting "willing suspension of disbelief" or pleasing illusion. Demanding a strong degree of the literal they became fixed, tyrants to the imagination rather than liberators.

While Hurd maintains that "fashion and philosophy" banished the "charmed spirit" of fable and allegory, Blackwell and others see modern philosophy as a possible counterpart to mythology. Bacon, after all, considered mythology "the wisdom of the ancients," and Fontenelle linked early philosophizing to myths. If philosophy could only turn away from extremes of rationalism and empiricism and pay more attention to the imagination, what Blackwell calls the "creative Faculty,"[54] then the charmed spirit of the poet would conflict less with the philosopher. This begins to happen in the early nineteenth century and continues throughout it.[55] By the romantic period, Blake, Keats, Goethe, Novalis—and in some moods Shelley and Wordsworth—effectively show that to philosophize in poetry *is* to create myth. Keats's *Lamia* dramatizes that struggle and sees its potentially problematic nature. The optimistic Blackwell even suggested that systems such as Descartes' and Gilbert's could serve as "modern" analogues to ancient myths. (If they were weaker it was only because they relied on but "one Principle of their own invention" rather than being an interlocking series of major principles. They were like single, centered myths rather than a body or system of mythology without a specific center.)[56] By putting mythography into contact with currents of contemporaneous philosophy and psychology Blackwell helps to revive the stature and relevance of the poet's mythmaking faculty.

Sapere aude, dare to think independently, is the famous motto Kant uses to spearhead *Was ist Aufklärung?* But this phrase from Horace's *Epistles* occurs as an intellectual battle cry in 1748. Blackwell uses it in *Letters Concerning Mythology* to promote a sympathetic and multifaceted inquiry. Regretting the "meer *historical,*" as well as the purely skeptical and religiously dogmatic uses of ancient mythology, he envisions "higher considerations." Is there one basic impulse that explains mythmaking? Blackwell feels readers can learn about themselves through a "sympathetic Intercourse" with mythology. Myths still "work," he implies; that is, they continue to fascinate us, they call on deep-seated psychological traits. As he explains it, myths engage imagination, mimesis, judgment, and the urge to philosophize all at once.[57]

Blackwell's tolerant optimism shows itself when he laughs gently at the wild syncretist Postelli, author of *Pantheosia . . . That is Universal Unity, or the Sound of the last Trumpet save one:* "The best Key to this Conduct, is to tell you, that this great Man was, at times, a little crazy, though with some lucid Intervals." Yet even in "crazy" theories Blackwell sees an affirmation that mythology is a fascinating and inevitable human pursuit. It always surfaces, its presence part of human nature, though manifested in different forms. What appears remarkable, as Vico and Herder also point out, are different manifestations and cultural identities of mythology. So Blackwell says that *"Human Life* is the veriest *Proteus* in the World."[58] This may not sound like the conclusion of the Enlightenment, for it seems to deny the immutability and consistency of universal human nature. But Blackwell's point, read on a metalevel, is that although myths and cultures are inconsistent, the fact or presence of myth is itself an ever present structure. It is found everywhere and continues to raise its protean head. Life in ancient times, he says, was equally diverse; it is only that ancient mythologies permit us to grasp that diversity imaginatively and without choking on detail. He ends *Letters Concerning Mythology* with the already famous "the lunatic, the lover, and the poet" speech of Theseus. It is the human imagination that remains present, and when it dares to think or to create independently, then the result may be Blake's *Jerusalem* or Kant's *Critiques.*

The New Poet

With every major consideration of mythology in the eighteenth century—with religion, philosophy, poetic language and diction, and with the newer ideal of originality—the poet is being asked to perform a great deal in a growing atmosphere of self-conscious critical demand. No wonder a myth of the poet as genius, seer, prophet, sage, and hero develops again, more fully than it had since classical times.[59] Such a myth is formative, yet it could weigh heavily, too. To invent modern heroes seems as hard as to be one. Coleridge, so learned and philosophically acute, balks at the attempt to finish *Christabel.* For an imaginative writer to create a new mythology generally known and influential in modern culture poses the ultimate test. Nevertheless, Keats—who according to Charles Cowden Clarke had little more than schoolboy learning of mythology—makes considerable headway in creating a series of myths about the odyssey of the individual's inner life caught in "the van of circumstance."

Schelling sees mythology as the basis for art and religion. But as Walter Jaeschke points out, Schelling concludes that older "mythology loses its binding validity in the modern world," so "in modernity the task is to develop a new mythology and, consequently, a new art, on the foundation of religion. This new mythology differs from the Greek because it has lost its binding validity. It is no longer the work of the species but of the individual, who himself has to produce his own world since it is no longer provided for him."[60] Such a program is not unique to Schelling; it is also found in Friedrich Schlegel's *Rede über die Mythologie.*

For Schelling this transformation of mythology (exemplified, we might say, by Keats's effort) separates what is "modern" from what is "ancient." This marks the continental divide of cultural experience in the West—the loss of an old, communal mythology and the attempt to create a new one, or ones, from the artist's individual effort. The problem for the modern mythmaker is a feeling that society or culture is false or deadening to myth itself, and as such myth would then need to expose or reject culture: its fine fabling would become a political or ideological act, its author fundamentally alienated or revolutionary. We see this in romantic myths, whether *Frankenstein, Faust,* or *Cain.* We see it also in Marx.[61]

As poetic creativity aspires to mythological heroism, the poet as hero—as the subject of the poetry—and the power of mythmaking, as much as any specific myth, become valued. Mythology in the romantic era often takes on the tincture of autobiography. *Don Juan, The Prelude, Faust, Prometheus Unbound, Milton,* the second *Hyperion, Lamia,* even *The Rime of the Ancient Mariner,* these all relate the poet's experience. Often they face up to Johnson's criterion of "real life" and avoid a hollow use of classical mythology. And without becoming instruments for Christian doctrine they often explore religious experience and the problem of evil. In many respects the hope fulfilled is a hope of the eighteenth century. As early as 1735 Blackwell urged that the potential poet "be indulgent . . . to his *Imagination,* which is the prime Faculty of a Mythologist. It is this, that distinguishes the *real Poet.*"[62]

PART TWO

Judgment and Values,
Literary and Social

CHAPTER 4

Non Disputandum: *Hume's Critique of Criticism*

I have the simplest of tastes . . . I am always satisfied with the best . . . I have quite a taste of my own. I am always content with the best.

OSCAR WILDE ON
SEVERAL OCCASIONS

Even a casual glance at critics from Hobbes through Coleridge reveals their search for objective principles and for an accompanying, though admittedly elusive, standard of taste. They hope to guide taste with systematic criticism and to reinform critical precepts with empirical observations. Thus the critic and the common reader ideally merge, with criticism and taste bearing somewhat the same relation to each other as tailoring and sewing. When Johnson concurs with the popular estimate of Gray's *Elegy,* "rejoice" really does describe his feeling that a professional critic such as himself could suspend "the dogmatism of learning" long enough to agree with the "common reader . . . uncorrupted with literary prejudices."[1]

Although Dryden rejected formulas and arbitrary authority, he insisted that critics acquire special knowledge. As he explains in the preface to *All for Love,* it is not enough to enjoy, "Nor is every man, who loves tragedy, a sufficient judge of it; he must understand the excellencies of it too, or he will prove a blind admirer, not a critic."[2]

The concern over principles echoed a preoccupation with the larger question of "rules of art" and the social function of literature. These issues could not, ultimately, be taken up separately—and any debate about critical principles or evaluation becomes suspect unless it is founded on assumptions about the role and reception of literature in society. During the eighteenth century an increasing suspicion of traditional, didactic rules governing artistic creativity and the formal or generic characterisitics of literature was paradoxically yoked to a growing mandate for more exact "systematic" and methodical principles of criticism. We are still living with this paradox.

"Taste" or "judgment," as used in the eighteenth century—and as generally understood since then (except when standing for idiosyncratic or subjective whim)—amount to the same thing as the abstract, latinate term "evaluation," with its overtones of academic, even demonstrable precision and dispassionate method. The more recondite "axiology" is the philosophical study of value or different types of value—religious, moral, aesthetic. Many debates in criticism, and their novelty, result from turning the semantic kaleidoscope. Taste or evaluation goes beyond the learning or intellectual *sprezzatura* brought to bear on a work; it means to judge that work according to values, which may include more than formal or stylistic ones. To evaluate, to exercise taste as an activity, urges the critic or reader to consider what values and what standards form the criteria of judgment.

Whatever worth the massive eighteenth-century attempt to clarify standards and to formulate "objective" criticism holds for us, it lies not so much in any number of specific principles we have inherited and revere, as in that century's brilliant critique of the very possibility and limits of system and principles in general. As René Wellek explains, Kant, in expounding "a theory of taste very similar to Hume's," would arrive "at an impasse." Yet Hume, in "On the Standard of Taste," first "poses the antinomies of Kant's *Critique of Judgment* and resolutely raises the problem of criticism as such. Actually it is a criticism of criticism."[3] Striving to construct or to extract "principles," Hume and other critics (including Johnson) become acutely aware of the limitations of such as enterprise. Coleridge, for example, begins his *Essay on Taste* in 1810 with a tentatively optimistic statement: "The same arguments that decide the question, whether taste has any fixed principles, may probably lead to a determination of what those principles are."[4] But he aborts the essay after three paragraphs, using it simply for lecture notes.

The eighteenth-century legacy provides at least two lessons. The first is that any system or theory built on purely formal qualities of genre, type, and kind of composition (as many neoclassical theories are) may succeed in describing a given body of literature and will even influence literary production, but its principles will not hold up under the natural variety and change that continually modify literary forms and the taste of readers, especially in a society where readership expands in pluralistic fashion. In "The Modern Mind," Eliot notes: "So our criticism, from age to age, will reflect the things that the age demands; and the criticism of no one man and of no one age can be expected to embrace the whole nature of poetry or exhaust all of its uses. Our contemporary critics, like their predecessors, are making particular responses to particular situations." The lesson seems to be that principles having a chance of succeeding beyond a generation or two are based on formal qualities in active confluence with other disciplines, and with a sense of psychology, history, and the study of language—rhetoric, linguistics, philology, and semiotics.

Neoclassic theory had, in fact, offered internally consistent rules. But Hobbes, Butler, Dryden, Addison, Pope—even Rymer—and later Johnson and Reynolds reject many of them as conventions imposed *ab extra*. Johnson praises Dryden as "the writer who first taught us to determine upon principles the merit of composition," but not according to "A dull collection of theorems." His criticism "is the criticism of a poet."[5] Samuel Butler abhorred the critic examining new plays "precisely by the rules of the ancients" as much as he detested the solipsistic "modern critic" who "is not bound to proceed but by his *own* Rules."[6]

Despite these powerful voices, the itch for critical system remained. Johnson states that by the latter part of the century Addison has lost respect as a critic because he became viewed as unstructured or "experimental," negligent of "rules" considered "scientific."[7] Explaining why Shakespeare has remained so popular despite his technical "faults," he reverts to the distinction between "principles demonstrative and scientifick" and those principles more open to experience and perception—and thus generally more applicable to literature as an imitative art. He worries that criticism in his own time is spending too much effort in the direction of method, a state of affairs expressed at its narrowest in the coffeehouse theories of Dick Minim. As minima become maxima they grow less satisfactory, and late eighteenth-century and romantic critics finally turn the principles of criticism into the principles of the imagination itself. Critics begin to equate—or, depending on the point of view, to confuse—imagination with taste, so that the two become nearly inseparable.[8] Richard Payne Knight, Alexander Gerard, Archibald Alison, and even Reynolds view taste as the product of an organizing play of mind that combines the passive perception of what Hume calls "objects, as they really stand in nature," with the active structuring of objects in a larger associational and contextual framework of yet other objects, personal experiences, sympathy, and the power of suggestion. Burke had emphatically urged the fusion of two concepts once considered different: "to cut off all pretence for cavilling," he says in the "Introduction: On Taste" to the *Enquiry,* "I mean by the word Taste no more than that faculty, or those faculties of the mind which are affected with, or which form a judgment of, the works of the imagination and the elegant arts."[9] Taste and imagination are increasingly treated as synonyms or indispensable partners, as they become in Kant. This increases the psychological element in aesthetic judgment and helps explain why Kant says such judgment "cannot be other than subjective." In the course of these developments, we commonly find statements such as Goldsmith's on Spenser: "However, with all his faults, no poet enlarges the imagination more than Spenser."[10] In a quest for the source, and end, and test of art, the principles of criticism move from nature and the ancients toward the modern artist's imagination.

Judging from a Continental perspective, it is first "in Hume," says Cassirer, that "the whole battlefront of aesthetic controversy is reformed. . . . Feeling no longer needs to justify itself before the tribunal of reason. . . . Reason not only loses its position of dominance; even in its own field, in the domain of knowledge, it has to surrender its leadership to the imagination," which "is now treated as the fundamental power of the soul."[11] As Coleridge would say, "The *rules* of the IMAGINATION are themselves the very powers of growth and production." And so it was a central object of the *Biographia* to present the "deduction of the imagination, and with it the principles of production and of genial criticism in the fine arts."[12]

One reason Coleridge wrote the *Biographia* (so he claims in the book) was not only to distinguish his view on poetry from Wordsworth's but also to refute or at least to rectify Wordsworth's critical "sentiments" by replacing them with genuine "principles."[13] Sixty years earlier in his essay on the standard of taste—which might also be referred to as an essay on the elusiveness of such a standard—Hume had also distinguished between "principles" and "sentiments." Hume's essay is one of the sharper eighteenth-century tests of the possibility and limits of objective standards in art and criticism. With the background just outlined, we can see its detail in this larger perspective of "a criticism of criticism."

A Bisociative Act

"Of the Standard of Taste," published in 1757, confronts the difficulty of establishing a standard by which to judge works that arouse our sentiment and imagination as much as they accommodate our sense of the matter-of-fact. Hume thus explores a problem that recalls Plato's charge that the poet falsifies reality. But he treats the problem with wider scope and psychological acuity: How can critics find a "standard" to be shared and understood logically, when that standard must apply to works that are imaginative and emotional (hence often "original")?

A barrier in the way of critical principles may arise from the nature of imaginative art as it addresses the whole mind. For, on one side of the psyche we tend to arrange judgment and the understanding, faculties that shape what Hume calls "opinion" or "science," and that guide us in matter-of-fact knowledge, which Hume associates with reason and the understanding. On the other side of the psyche we tend to place matters of "taste" and "sentiment," of our likes, dislikes, and feelings ("pleasure" and "pain" to use the common catchwords). These are self-referential or, as Hume says, they are—according to some—"always real" or always "right: Because no sentiment represents," or pretends to represent, "what is really in the object." No "sentiment" sees the object as it really is. The dominant faculty here is passionate imagination. As Hume resolves the dichotomy, reason "discovers objects, as they really stand in nature," and "internal sentiment" discovers those objects as they exist for us. But it is taste that "has a productive faculty, and gilding or staining all natural objects *with* the colours, borrowed from internal sentiment, raises, in a manner, a new creation." A dilemma ensues if we assign our criticism either solely to judgment and understanding or solely to sentiment and imagination (recalling Dryden's distinction between one who merely understands and one who is merely a blind admirer). In Hume's formulation, "The difference, it is said, is very wide between judgment and sentiment." Hence he believes that emphasizing one more than the other is lopsided. The belief that taste reconciles reason and sentiment persists even in the most recent, sociologically oriented views. In *Distinction: A Social Critique of the Judgment of Taste,* Pierre Bourdieu states "the judgement of taste is the supreme manifestation of the discernment which, by reconciling reason and sensibility, [that is, by reconciling] the pedant who understands without feeling and the *mondain* who enjoys without understanding, defines the accomplished individual."[14]

When romantic criticism began to base itself on sympathy and the imagination, it was, in a sense, attempting not to exclude judgment and understanding but to synthesize them with sympathy and imagination. But in doing so it could also magnify the subjective element to the extent that the personal and sentimental, either in poetry or in criticism, could become self-indulgent. This is the chief complaint Hazlitt lodges against the writing of his own day, in poetry against Byron and Wordsworth (though he recognizes both as great poets), and in criticism—while realizing his target is a living genius of English letters—against Coleridge.[15]

One crucial issue of modern poetics develops into something like the following: Is human nature (and hence experience or even truth itself) essentially divided between an inner *I am* of personal, visionary feeling and perception responsible for creating "fictions," and an equally inner *it is* fitted to understand the external claim of cause, effect, and matter-of-fact? (We might recall Blake railing against Wordsworth's "fitted and fitting.") This is one way to read Keats's question, "Do I wake or sleep?" Are these states mutually exclusive? If the poet indulges imagination, is there a danger of becoming, as Keats wondered, a fever of himself, a useless thing? Is there no third possibility, no waking dream, no willing suspension of disbelief? Is the soul or its dream vision separate from the reasonable self, or perhaps even antithetical to it—or is human nature more of a unity in which soul and self, imagination and reason, inner vision and external experience exist in *discordia concors*?[16] Moreover, because all these questions are not about the self and nature so much as about the condition of the self alone, might we not expect as many different answers as there are selves? How, in matters of taste, can there be consensus? These are the basic and persisting questions that Hume poses.[17]

His analysis anticipates many stances in which two critical faculties, one basically rational and the other nonrational, square off against each other. This occurs in Shelley's *Defence* with its split between reason and imagination, Blake's similar division, Yeats's mirror and lamp, Wallace Stevens' "fictions," Eliot's "dissociation of sensibility," and Richards' "intellectual" *versus* "emotional belief." Or are the two opposites united by a third, synthesizing element such as *Spieltrieb* in Schiller, the poetic imagination in Coleridge,

Arnold's "imaginative reason," or Newman's "illative sense"? The potential dualism, essentially one between imagination and judgment, also becomes a subject for poets themselves—Keats in *Lamia,* for instance, or Tennyson in *The Palace of Art.*

Add to this potential dualism Hume's admission that "when critics come to particulars . . . it is found that they had affixed a very different meaning to their expressions," and we see that the imprecision of language, what Berkeley calls "the delusion of words," further clouds the issue. Even "the seeming harmony in morals" found among writers may be an illusion created by "the very nature of language." Yet, despite these observations and in face of his own warning that "variety of taste" may be "still greater in reality than in appearance,"[18] Hume maintains that a standard of taste exists. He anticipates Eliot's affirmation, near the close of "The Modern Mind," that "Amongst all these demands from poetry and responses to it there is always some permanent element in common, just as there are standards of good and bad writing independent of what any of us happens to like and dislike."[19]

In his analysis, Hume's affinities rest with a line of English poet-critics including Sidney, Dryden, Johnson, Coleridge, Arnold, and Eliot. He appeals to experience, that is, to *all* experience, which includes both art and "reality," imaginative production and matter-of-fact. He concludes that the mind is not inherently cleft between the literary equivalent of right and left hemispheres. "It appears," he says, "amidst all the variety and caprice of tastes, there are certain general principles of approbation or blame, whose influence a careful eye may trace in *all* operations of the mind."[20] There exists a natural tension, much like the one separating the horses that draw Plato's chariot of the soul, but there is no unharnessed tug-of-war.

A literary physiologist might say that Hume affirms a *corpus colosum,* a connecting body, between judgment and sentiment. He explicitly states this as his overall purpose: his "intention in this essay is to mingle some light of the understanding with the feelings of sentiment."[21] Hugh Blair would later echo and amplify Hume:

> The difference between the authors who found the standard of
> Taste upon the common feelings of human nature ascertained

> by general approbation, and those who found it upon estab-
> lished principles which can be ascertained by reason, is more
> an apparent than a real difference. Like many other literary
> controversies, it turns chiefly on modes of expression. . . .
> These two systems . . . differ in reality very little from one
> another. Sentiment and Reason enter into both; and by allow-
> ing to each of these powers its due place, both systems may be
> rendered consistent.[22]

Such a mingling, not an emphasis on sentiment or understanding
alone, is Hume's critical basis.[23] When Blair refers to "general approbation" as distinguished from "principles ascertained by reason,"
it is telling that Hume's own formulation ("general principles of
approbation") not only in spirit but in vocabulary combines these
two "modes of expression." The critical act becomes a bisociative
one.

True, the object of poetry is "to please by means of the passions
and the imagination" and not by means of the understanding. But
Hume counters that "every kind of composition, even the most
poetical, is nothing but a chain of propositions and reasonings; not
always, indeed, the justest and most exact, but still plausible and
specious [able to be seen or perceived], however disguised by the
colouring of the imagination." As examples he gives the events and
characters in tragedy and epic poetry, and though his case may be
vitiated by the rise and eventual dominance of the lyric, his point
is able to embrace all genres: "It seldom, or never happens, that a
man of sense, who has experience in any art, cannot judge of its
beauty; and it is no less rare to meet with a man who has a just
taste without a sound understanding."[24] These criteria also imply
that poet-critics will both be better poets for being critics and better
critics for being poets.

Accepting criticism as a bisociative act, we see that the familiar and
much abused term "common sense" means far more than a body of
communally received ideas and tastes, one connotation of *sensus communis*. Hume wants common sense to mingle the illumination of
mirror and lamp, of "the understanding *and* the colouring of the

imagination." True *common* sense becomes the mediating ground of experience drawn from imagination and sentiment as well as from our understanding of the matter-of-fact. It is common to both and combines them.[25] This common sense is as far from naive common sense as one can get, and confusing the two leads to a shortsighted dismissal of a good deal of eighteenth-century criticism and philosophy. This is what Hume has in mind when he admits that the latitude in subjective tastes, "by passing into a proverb [*de gustibus non disputandum*], *seems* to have attained the sanction of common sense," but "there is certainly a species of common sense which opposes it, at least serves to modify and restrain it."[26] This higher sense is not the authority of a homogenous society but an appeal to reason and sentiment simultaneously.

Such an attitude had already been broached, though in a less sophisticated way, by one of Hume's acquaintances, Adam Smith. In his *Lectures on Rhetoric and Belles Lettres* delivered at the University of Glasgow in 1762–1763 (probably an expanded version of his 1748–1751 Edinburgh lectures), Smith rather bluntly asserted: "If you will attend to it, all the rules of criticism and morality, when traced to their foundation, turn out to be some principles of common sense which every one assents to."[27] More significantly, Johnson would write in his life of Gray that "by the *common sense* of readers uncorrupted by literary prejudices . . . must be finally determined all claim to poetical honours."[28] And in Gray's *Elegy,* the context in which Johnson makes this judgment, it is precisely the image-laden union of original notions with deep sentiments that he finds so appealing. It is intriguing to see Hume, the most radical skeptic in the English tradition, oppose a skeptical view of taste (of all things) in favor of a finer "species of common sense," the lineage of which is as mixed as experience itself.

"The Key with the Leathern Thong"

Hume remains troubled that sentiment and judgment rarely appear to coincide. He admits the scarcity—the genuine uncommonness—of his preferred stock of common sense. "Those finer emotions of the mind" on which art and poetry rest "are of a very tender and delicate nature, and require the concurrence of many favourable circumstances to make them play with facility and exactness, according to their general and established principles."[29] How does he imagine such a "concurrence"? There is no appeal to prevailing social custom or literary authority. The answer is suggested by his vocabulary, in which we encounter, repeatedly: "tender," "delicate," "exactness," "discrimination," "notice," "nice," "finer" and "minute qualities," "particular flavours," "particular feelings," and "delicacy of taste."

Although Hume owes a debt to Bouhours's aesthetic of *délicatesse,* the point here is not to trace influences but to see Hume's essay as a crucial first document in "the criticism of criticism." Hume stresses that repeated perusals give rise to interlocking sets of comparisons; minute particulars become connected at many interstices—we structure; judgment and feeling come together as a net work or matrix. Immersion in reading, interpreting, and appreciating art will form the organs of taste and observation until they become susceptible to all possible shades and particulars of what we read and see. Hence "nothing tends further to increase and improve this talent"—this delicacy—"than *practice* in a particular art, and the frequent survey or contemplation of a particular species of beauty." The key is experience, thorough and complete. "But allow him to acquire experience," Hume says, and like a weathervane the critic will point judgment in the right direction. "So advantageous is practice to the discernment of beauty" that every object or work of art must be repeatedly "surveyed in different lights." A work of art is a structured object, a made object or text, and we must try to see it in all its possible perspectives, not to demand that it appear in, or by, one light.[30]

Hume's example of *délicatesse* from *Don Quixote* (part I, i, chapter 13) relates how two of Sancho Panza's kinsmen taste a certain wine and pronounce it excellent. But one detects a hint of leather, the other of iron. Both men are ridiculed until the drained hogshead reveals an old key tied to a leathern thong. "The great resemblance between mental and bodily taste," says Hume, "will easily teach us to apply this story." Any standard requires *"delicacy of taste."* And to "produce these general rules or avowed patterns of composition is like finding the key with the leathern thong, which justified the verdict of Sancho's kinsmen, and confounded those pretended judges who had condemned them."[31]

One might ask, Has it ever been otherwise? Isn't Hume operating from neoclassical premises, from what he calls "general and established principles" or "avowed patterns," which he assumes his audience shares? And isn't he then simply saying that the application of these principles becomes clearer with practice and repetition?

What if two descendants of Sancho were to read Allen Ginsberg? Both might discern nuances and, comparing Ginsberg's work with others', earn minute knowledge of it. But if the premises of Sancho's kin were to differ, one might praise the poet and the other reject him. "Where these doubts occur," Hume says, "men can do no more than in other disputable questions, which are submitted to the understanding: They must produce the best arguments, that their invention suggests to them."[32] Nowhere in his essay does Hume attempt to describe what the standard of taste actually is or should be. He will only say that it *exists*. It is not based on canons, patrons, academies, or standard education. Yet he also wants to make clear that taste is not completely relative—which would be the case if there were no standard.[33] One direct result of this postulate is that some literary views are, in *fact,* better than others, but *which ones* cannot be demonstrated. (In a sense Hume demonstrates that such a demonstration cannot take place.)[34] This is analogous to Hilary Putnam's argument that we cannot prove a statement's truth a priori, but neither can we demonstrate that there are no a priori truths. The two descendants of Sancho, to use Hume's conclusion, "must acknowledge a true and decisive standard to exist somewhere, to wit, real existence and matter of fact; and they must have indulgence to such as differ from them in their appeals to this standard. It is sufficient for our present purpose if we have proved that the taste of all individuals is not upon an equal footing."[35]

The standard of taste becomes a presence that is, in a sense, an absence, what Hazlitt calls an Ideal of Taste, a fact that can no more be denied than it can be exactly determined. No one can be proved to have attained it. But in the attempt to attain such a standard, the reader must exercise empathy with the work of art itself, which, as Hume says, "in order to produce its due effect on the mind, must be surveyed in a certain point of view, and cannot be fully relished by persons, whose situation, real or imaginary, is not conformable to that which is required by the performance." Here Hume sounds like Pater or Arnold—or like Pope's *Essay on Criticism* or Johnson's life of Dryden: the reader needs to make an effort to overcome prejudices ingrained by his own time, milieu, social position, and personal experience. The "different humours of particular men," Hume remarks, and "the particular manners and opinions of our age and country," as well as speculative beliefs, especially religious ones, always distort taste.[36] Hume's ideal reader or critic does not belong to a certain class of a certain nation, but will ferret out, assess, and minimize these predilections.[37]

It is instructive to compare Hume's position—that of an atheist skeptical of the Western philosophical tradition in metaphysics—with the position of someone as recent as Jacques Derrida. Hume is saying that in matters of taste, although there is very definitely at any given time in history a center or a standard, we cannot define or find that center—at least we cannot precisely agree what it is. It is always, for us, de-centered. Yet Hume continues to uphold that such a center or standard does exist and that it is grounded on the totality and delicacy of all our experience. In what may be taken as an analogous statement, Derrida says that the "absent" center is to be interpreted *"otherwise than as loss of the center."*[38] If one were to take the radical stance that neither center nor standard exists at all, there could be no judgment whatsover, *only* pleasure or displeasure of the text, only individual or social prejudice confirming itself.

In the epigraph at the start of this chapter, Wilde claims the elusive standard of taste for himself. No logic can refute him, for, like Hume, he knows that the issue will not submit to logic or proof. All the better to express his position in a syllogistic tone. His statement becomes a virtual tautology. The implication is that Wilde knows what is best—and saying so in an entertaining fashion, we could say, is his own genius. What he does know, as a fact, is that neither he nor anyone else can ever "know" taste convincingly; taste is irreducible to certain knowledge. In Johnson's phrase, it is not "demonstrative and scientifick." Wilde's word play on taste is witty as Johnson considered wit, strength of mind galvanizing disparate realms—*discordia concors*—in this case the verbal assurance of a logically demonstrated knowledge yoked to the quintessential phantom of it. Wilde appropriates the absent center of taste ("the best") and no one can gainsay him. To argue about "the best" would be vulgar, the commonest kind of "common" sense. In another guise, less witty and serving far more practical ends, this claim of the best in taste is a lesson that antique dealers, gallery owners, and publicists practice every day. In selling art, embarrassment comes from being unsuccessful, not from bad art. The only fraud is recognized forgery, or lies about what has been sold for what price.[39] The seller will never lose an argument about taste—or lose his customers—if the argument is presented tastefully. As Wilde himself said, the only person to whom all works of art are equally valuable is the auctioneer.

Hume is far less neoclassic and rigid than he at first appears. Gerald Chapman remarks, "The conviction of mid-century critics like Burke and Kames that rules cannot be drawn from dogmatic tradition owes much to Hume's example."[40] Hume recognizes no body of authority, no defined rules or dicta. And, like Johnson in *Rambler* 3, he stakes a modest claim for the critic's power; time makes more final judgments. Yet all critics and interpretations are not equal. The realm of taste may be a democracy and its voters may be created equal, but the votes cast are not equally well informed, and the candidates vary in quality. In a critical version of Kurt Gödel's Incompleteness Theorem, all demonstrative arguments concerning taste are ultimately circular, but the radius of some is more extensive, the center more accurately plotted.

In principles of criticism, Hume and Johnson are not far apart. Both believe that literature should please and that it should also examine values of behavior and virtue that rise above changes in "local," meaning parochial, customs and manners. The good critic, well read but not merely bookish, writes a forceful and agreeable style, is informed by history, delights in language, and reads human character with charity and insight.

A Principle of Art

Hume remains skeptical about defining or demonstrating absolutes of taste because such judgments cannot be verified. Yet in turning to our actual experiences of taste he is a realist. And he is even an idealist in his insistence that a standard of taste does, in fact, exist— though it is perpetually elusive, never actually present for us to agree upon in the clear light of day. This standard represents a shifting ideal extrapolated from particulars of experience. Although belonging to a class of facts that cannot be "known" or demonstrated, it nevertheless exists as a fact. This standard is "known" or guessed at only through the traces or tracks of experience that make up our individual and necessarily incomplete views of reality, views we sharpen by more experience and reflection. It is constructed through an imaginative process. Hume's stance is a "skeptical realism," ultimately based on imagination. The critic, the reader in general, extends individual encounters with texts into fully formed taste in a manner analogous to the artist who mixes and extends colors on the palette and then onto canvas.[41]

Yet Hume assumes one essential fact or principle—and it is not, strictly speaking, a principle of criticism. In contradistinction, he calls it a "principle of art," or rather the assumed postulate that art does have "avowed principles" or purposes, that there is an end to art, that art is teleological or purposive, and that it is not hermetically sealed nor completely autonomous. "Even poets and other authors," he notes, "whose compositions are chiefly calculated to please the imagination, are yet found, from Homer down to Fénelon, to inculcate the same moral precepts and to bestow their applause and blame on the same virtues and vices."[42]

To produce "general rules" of criticism and of composition "is like finding the key with the leathern thong." This is done by showing the "bad critic" what Hume calls "an avowed principle of art" (not "of criticism"). Once we have won acceptance for such an avowed principle, we can proceed, as it were, to empty the hogshead. At that point the bad critic "must conclude, upon the whole, that the fault lies in himself, and that he wants the delicacy, which is requisite to make him sensible" of excellence. In the end, a set of "avowed" or established principles of art determines the principles of criticism and assures the existence of a standard of taste. And the first postulate or "principle of art" concerns the purpose or function of art in society and culture.[43]

If art is "autonomous," unanchored in any other valuation of experience, if art has *no* purpose—the MGM motto above the roaring lion *ars gratia artis,* or Ortega y Gasset's reductive "just art" at the end of *The Dehumanization of Art*—if art has no ends outside itself, no standard of taste can exist. The most exciting area will be an avant-garde perpetually struggling to maintain its identity while becoming absorbed and conventionalized at an ever more rapid rate. The only principle of art then becomes the imagination or "fictions" of the artist, who is judged in his own court under his own laws. Criticism will stress only how we read, not how we judge what we read.

All this helps to explain why Aristotle and Coleridge—and countless other critics and poets—define poetry, a poem, and the nature of the poet not in formalistic or linguistic terms alone (though these are always included), but in terms of their functions, and of their immediate pleasure and their eventual truth. In the simple phrasing of Tolstoy: What is art? Hume's analysis—and all such analyses or debates over principles of taste and criticism—devolve to this question about the nature and purpose of art.[44] If we feel there is no answer to Tolstoy's question, or that there are as many answers as there are authors, then all principles of criticism vanish. As Hume wrote to George Cheyne in 1734, under such conditions philosophy and criticism exhibit "little more than endless disputes, even in the most fundamental articles."[45] One of many qualities giving Keats's poetry and letters so fresh an appeal is that he never stopped asking Tolstoy's question—what should a poet do, what is poetry? Keats had answers but was unsure of them, an uncertainty that adds to his gifts, perhaps because he does not force the answers on us but invites us to consider them with him.

Although the formulation is simple, it may be overlooked. Until the critic answers—or attempts to answer—the questions What is art? and What is the function of art in society and culture? no standard of taste can operate, and the only "principles" that can exist will deal with formalistic or linguistic considerations. Objective principles seem to be the *Ding-an-sich* of criticism. Whether they exist, no one can prove with certainty, though no one can prove they do not. They are regulative, and ultimately they may constitute a social idea as much as an aesthetic one. In "The Polite Learning of England and France Incapable of Comparison," Goldsmith remarks, "Truth is a positive, taste a relative excellence."[46] Most sentiments and fashions in criticism do not last; the permanence and objectivity of any critical system or set of principles remains elusive. But such principles and the standard of taste they imply, if associated with a sense how art affects education and society, may exist as an absence that has the force of a presence, a missing capstone that serves to ventilate the smoke of provincial controversy: a vacancy at the top that cannot be filled but that, like heaven, we guess at—as Keats said—"from forth the loftiest fashion of our sleep."

Social Grounds Inescapable

Hume's essay and Kant's third *Critique* briefly touch on one issue we have so far only glimpsed: the social dimension of taste. The social status of art, the judgment of worthiness as art or not, complicates and enriches our whole discussion. In approaching works of craft or invention, the initial and crucial decision often is whether or not to regard a work as "art" in the first place. In most cases this decision seems to have been made already by institutional or cultural forces beyond individual control. Such decisions exert great force. Hume's critique and all such analyses of aesthetic taste come into play only as we direct them to a class of objects or texts judged worthy as "art," or as objects of aesthetic or "literary" contemplation. A larger prejudgment has previously been made—not on artistic worth as good, mediocre, or poor—but on the question, often more subtle and fundamental, whether a text or object qualifies for the status of art in the first place. This, in some measure, is what the formation of canons in literature addresses.

Although this decision of worthiness as art is not part of what Kant calls pure aesthetic judgment, it is another, equally important kind of aesthetic judgment. Experience (Hume's basic criterion) confirms that we constantly meet individuals who readily grant the status of art or serious literature to works they do not like or even think are "bad." At the same time those individuals enjoy and express pleasure for "trash" novels or entertainments that sometimes do not meet their own criteria for worthiness as art. Thus, we are willing to bestow on works that do not please us—even on ones we emphatically do not like—a judgment of worthy as art. We encounter friends or colleagues who say they "cannot stand" D. H. Lawrence or Gower—or Johnson or Gide—or who disdain Paul Klee, John Cage, or Schubert. But these same people grant—or even insist—that authors and artists who incur their active dislike may still belong to art, even to genius. At the same time, we pack convention bags or vacation suitcases with Ross MacDonald, Ian Fleming, Barbara Cartland, and any number of writers widely enjoyed but often not considered serious artists.

This does not contradict Kant's analysis, for he clearly distinguishes between pleasure and pure aesthetic judgment. But as Kant himself points out—though he does not follow up his note with a separate, full-blown social critique, "Judgments of taste . . . do not in themselves establish any interest. Only in society is it *interesting* to have taste." And in that context, in the context of social institutions, ideology, and culture, pure aesthetic judgment cannot exist, for in a social context all aesthetic judgment *is* interesting. In society the status of art may at first seem chaotic or pluralistic, but we sense that the status of art is not as completely bewildering or as varied as would be all personal tastes taken at equal par value. It follows that worthiness as art—what is sometimes loosely referred to as "canonization"—is largely a social and institutional judgment.

We as individuals are implicated in this prejudgment, though reserving the right to call particular works good or bad. To question the assumptions of art worthiness requires a theoretical perspective that society at large does not encourage.

We may agree with or acquiesce in those cultural and social judgments of "worthiness as art" as long as we can preserve and satisfy our private preferences, our right to disagree, by registering a personal response. Yet what is or is not "art," if it is a collective and social judgment bestowed over time, stands relatively immune from individual challenge, unless one is able to champion a particular reappraisal or new movement. Even then success may be limited. The modern system of the fine arts is a set of assumptions with long social and cultural pedigrees. As M. H. Abrams notes, the sociology of modern aesthetics took shape during the eighteenth century when it gradually became established that "the condition and status of being a work of art, in accordance with the standard definition of art-as-such, is not an inherent fact but an institutional [social] fact."[47]

What is or is not art may be influenced by a set of critics and custodians, an élite who can "push" or "dump" a particular writer or artist. For instance, J. J. Hunsecker in the famous depiction of the New York theater world, *Sweet Smell of Success,* falls on the ghastly side of such brokers. College reading lists are another and potentially more liberating and disinterested way to influence social patterns of reading. These lists have commercial aspects, but stronger economic interests move outside the academy: buyers of hard-cover fiction for major book chains state that, "Merit has a lot to do with certain books," but "most of the time it's not the most important consideration." This particular buyer goes on to say that "people often write novels because they want to tell a story, and how a book sells isn't their number one consideration." Authors may write excellently and sell well, but modern publishing, as one writer for *The New Yorker* puts it, has introduced "what may be new" in the practice of a bottom-line ethos of pure commercialism in publishing, that is, "the elevation of this practice into a principle."[48]

Wordsworth, in the *Essay Supplementary,* identifies the "public" as a body of critics, opinion makers, and seekers. By contrast, the "people," whose judgment and reverence he trusted, are at the root of lasting value and continued popularity: "lamentable is his error, who can believe that there is any thing of divine infallibility in the clamour of that small though loud portion of the community, ever governed by factitious influence, which, under the name of the PUBLIC, passes itself, upon the unthinking, for the PEOPLE."[49] Directly related to Wordsworth's appeal to a broader "people" rather than "the name of the public," is the difference between what is "mass" or "popular" and what is avant-garde, difficult, obscure, studied, or, to use Ortega's characterization, consciously "anti-popular." In other words, art can become, by definition, what shuns the people, what seeks to avoid mass popularity. Near the end of the seventeenth century the determining factors elevating individuals above the mass, and hence conferring artistic judgment, were largely birth, wealth, and social position or power. But in the next century the sociology of art changes significantly, particularly if we are looking at the reading audience in England. John Dennis could speak with some confidence of "the Taste" as a single entity. But by the early 1800s Hazlitt sees a splintered, shifting audience. The arbiters of select fields in art had become connoisseurs, specialists and critics, individuals whose learning, education, critical skill, and, as Bacon observes in *The Advancement of Learning*, whose pretense and "vanities of learning" all begin to establish specialized criteria for worthiness as art. Francis Jeffrey, apparently less disturbed by these developments than Hazlitt, observes that "The great multitude, even of the reading world, must necessarily be uninstructed and injudicious. . . . the poetry which appears most perfect to a very refined taste, will not often turn out to be very popular poetry."[50] In *Distinction,* Pierre Bourdieu concludes, with more bitterness, that today cultivated pleasure in art and criticism is basically a matter of exclusion—of keeping the vulgar or uninitiated out, of addressing only those who can follow the game and its allusions.[51]

Kant never intends his model of pure aesthetic judgment to describe the activity of taste and aesthetic judgment in society. He recognizes that in the social context many other factors are at work, including those of moral and cultural values. We thus find, as Kant himself clearly points out, that his model of disinterested pure aesthetic judgment is inadequate to explain our complex reaction to art as both a social and individual phenomenon calling on many responses and attitudes. As Schiller says, in the context of addressing social and ideological issues in the *Aesthetic Letters,* art ultimately calls on the "whole" individual, not merely on pure aesthetic judgment.

Addison and Kames, among others, suggest that a certain class of reader and appreciator determines taste. To acquire this judgment, Addison recommends in *Spectator* 409 reading the finest of polite authors and critical writers. Kames stresses the upper-class tinge of criticism: a day laborer cannot turn to literature with acumen. Hume, in contrast, simply prefers someone who reads, studies, and compares a broad variety of material with diligence. While these opinions are being stated, the new leisure pursuit of art in the eighteenth century seeks to bring the populace "up" to the level of art, to "improve" individuals—not to level art "down" to address the newly literate. However, neither Hume nor Kames—in fact, very few eighteenth-century critics—closely examine new, essentially sociological assumptions about the nature of art. Yet this status of art as a leisure activity of apparently disinterested aesthetic contemplation and enjoyment (under whose aegis we still live) emerges in the eighteenth century. "In sum," M. H. Abrams states, "during the span of less than one hundred years, an extensive institutional revolution had been effected, with the result that, by the latter eighteenth century, the cultural situation in England (as, to various degrees, in Germany and other countries) was recognizably the present one, with a large, primarily middle-class public for literature, together with public theaters, public concerts of music, and public galleries and museums of painting and sculpture."[52]

Today, as in the eighteenth century, it is problematic to point to a theoretical middle class, or "the canon," and leave the matter there. In what way does social role correlate with taste? The question is

not meant to establish a hierarchy, but to examine the socially determined factors that create variety in taste. Observations about so-
cioeconomic, educational, and professional distinctions in the judgment of art, observations which have been empirically and
exhaustively verified by sociologists of taste such as Bourdieu, deny
any purely philosophical basis of evaluation and aesthetic judgment.
Such a purely philosophical basis has its modern touchstone in
Kant's third *Critique,* the apex of eighteenth-century aesthetic theory. Yet ironically such a critique became possible only because of
sociological changes in the eighteenth century itself, only because
art became viewed at that time, institutionally and sociologically,
as an arena for disinterested contemplation. Kant realizes in his brief
glance that taste in society cannot be disinterested (it becomes "interesting"), nor is the aesthetic judgment of art in society ever pure.
But he does not analyze the very changes that have permitted and
prompted his own "philosophical critique." This leads Pierre Bourdieu to conclude: "In short, the philosophical sense of distinction is
another form of the visceral disgust at vulgarity[, a vulgarity] which
defines pure taste as an internalized social relationship, a social relationship made flesh; and a philosophically distinguished reading
of the *Critique of Judgement* cannot be expected to uncover the social
relationship of distinction at the heart of a work that is rightly
regarded as the very symbol of philosophical distinction."[53]
   It is the shift in social relationships and cultural activity during
the eighteenth century that permits the Kantian analysis, the
widely known model of "pure aesthetic judgment," to develop in
the first place. Yet that model, understood exclusively, as Kant
himself is the first to recognize, fails to take into account those very
changes in the relation of social context to aesthetic judgment.
These changes proliferate today and have become the subjects of
critical theories. In this light, we can return to Hume's wise suggestion that societies, institutions, and speculative beliefs (religions
and ideologies) all be understood and taken into account in the act
of criticism. He insists on this even as art—and the critical judgment of what is worthy as art—is ironically becoming a new kind
of social institution in its own right. For Hume, the issue of taste

reveals that even attempts at disinterested contemplation and pure aesthetic judgment cannot sever art from the interests of society, culture, or ideology, which constitute the ground and conditions of its existence and production. To recognize this, and then to argue against parochialism while avoiding pure relativism, is Hume's metacritical achievement, his subtle and brilliant contribution to a criticism of criticism.

CHAPTER 5

Estrangement: The Problem of Ethics and Aesthetics

Although literature is one thing and morality a quite different thing, at the heart of the aesthetic imperative we discern the moral imperative.

SARTRE, *What Is Literature?*

While composing *The Death of Virgil* (1945), Hermann Broch became convinced that when culture and the world enter an age of decline, writing poetry becomes an immoral act. Broch devoted his last years to social psychology and politics. Because of the immense trust—or at least hope—placed in the liberating, "uplifting" vision of poetry and art throughout the nineteenth century, a hope expressed repeatedly in romantic theory and spread by cultural critics and church spokesmen, it is little wonder that the generation eviscerated by World War I felt art and "humanism" had betrayed their aims and ideals. Perhaps it was more consoling to conclude that art never could fulfill them in the first place—that culture emancipation and a bourgeois worship of "high art" and high seriousness amounted to what T. E. Hulme called "spilt religion," a thin, messy liquid unable to infuse hard, indifferent technology or to penetrate new economic and political ideologies. To use Emerson's simple word with its manifold implications, "experience" soon tempers every speculation about the saving power of art, which becomes, as Ortega wryly remarked, "just art."

With the intriguing exceptions of overtly ideological criticism such as feminism and Marxism, some structuralist thought—particularly on the Continent—and a handful of humanists envisioning literature as a potentially formative influence on human character, most critics since the First World War have hesitated to adduce moral or ethical claims for literature. This holds particularly true for the imaginative literature dominating the canon assigned in schools, and which some, more by habit than conscious decision, have come to regard as constituting "serious" literature. That narrowed conception of literature began, as Raymond Williams and countless others have pointed out, with an increased refinement and specialization of *belles lettres* in the eighteenth century.[1] Certainly the ethical claims of literature have not stood in the first rank. The New Criticism, concerned mostly with poetry, either dismisses moral concerns as "unliterary" or detours cautiously around them. Confidence dips in any ethically positive (or negative) role played by reading and studying literary texts. Aside from literary criticism, intellectual and ideological prose is underrated and underrepresented in most systematic literary study. Rather, criticism, especially the scholarly and academic sort, has for decades retreated from the kinds of positions articulated (often shrilly, but sometimes with tough pragmatism) by F. R. Leavis, Lionel Trilling, Arnold, Shelley, and Sidney.

Two Old Camps

Near the beginning of a long and distinguished English tradition, John of Salisbury stresses moral philosophy and literature together, "that he who reads may become better in himself." What we read is useless if not directed to "the conduct of life" (*afferunt aliquod adminiculum vitae*), a foreshadowing of Emerson and of Arnold's definition of poetry as, at bottom, a criticism of life. Later, in the Dedicatory Epistle to *Volpone,* Jonson speaks of "the impossibility of any mans being the good Poët without first being a good Man," a view now generally considered naive, but cherished by many Renaissance critics, including J. C. Scaliger and Minturno.[2] Jonson

claims the poet strives "to inform men in the best reason of living."
Even the comic poet attempts "to imitate justice and instruct to
life—or stir up gentle affections." In *Timber* Jonson says the study
of poetry, "if we trust *Aristotle,* offers to mankind a certain rule and
pattern of living well and happily, disposing us to all civil offices
of society." In the eighteenth century Vico inherits and elaborates
on poetic wisdom as the foundation of all civil societies, a doctrine
strongly informing Shelley's *Defence* as well.

Sir Richard Blackmore provides the dogmatic formulation in his
preface to *Prince Arthur,* a poem understandably ignored even by
specialists: "To give Men right and just Conceptions of *Religion* and
Virtue, to aid their Reason in restraining their Exorbitant Appetites
and Impetuous Passions, and to bring their Lives under the Rules
and Guidance of true Wisdom, and thereby to promote the publick
Good of Mankind, is undoubtedly the End of all Poetry." He admits
"one End of Poetry is to give Men Pleasure and Delight; but this is
but a subordinate, subaltern End, which is it self a Means to the
greater and *ultimate* one before mention'd."[3] The emphasis on "publick Good" carries even into Johnson's Preface to Shakespeare,
where, in famous lines summing up Shakespeare's "faults," Johnson
says: "He sacrifices virtue to convenience, and is so much more
careful to please than to instruct, that he seems to write without
any moral purpose. From his writings indeed a system of social duty
may be selected, for he that thinks reasonably must think morally;
but his precepts and axioms drop casually from him; he makes no
just distribution of good or evil." Johnson goes on to forestall a
common reply to his common observation: "This fault the barbarity
of his age cannot extenuate; for it is always a writer's duty to make
the world better."[4] The didactic imperative of literature rarely had
a more succinct defender, one who sees not only personal enlightenment but "a system of social duty" at stake.

These ideas of the function of literature are representative as far
as they go, but only for one side of the question. Stressing the moral
duty of a writer, they do not offer a critical consensus. (It is typical
of Johnson that we will see him again, on the other side.) By the

eighteenth century an impressive pedigree of critics could be cited to deny that poetry should or even could be a vehicle for moral values. Early in this century Joel Spingarn identified Robert Wolsey's preface to Rochester's *Valentinian* (1685) as "the most interesting of all discussions of poetry in its relation to morals" during the English seventeenth century. Addressing the issue with intelligence and rhetorical skill, Wolsey produces "the first attempt approaching adequacy since the *Verato Secondo* of Guarini." And he argues the total independence of moral and poetic spheres. Criticism adulterates itself with moral scruples. The idea of poetry divorced from moral philosophy had already flourished in Castelvetro, Bruno, Tasso, Marino, and especially Guarini.[5]

Fifty years earlier than Wolsey, Henry Reynolds' *Mythomystes* (1632) concedes that ancient poets mix morals with verses. But he believes poetry answers a higher calling to unveil nature. The proper medium of moral instruction—the one Reynolds believes that Spenser should have used for the *Faerie Queene*—is prose.[6] (In the twentieth century, Sartre also believes that prose bears the moral imperative.) Though writing the *Lives of the Poets* with the intention of promoting piety, Johnson's views on poetry and virtue have mellowed from his selective censure of Shakespeare fifteen years before. Discussing Gray's *Progress of Poesy,* he criticizes the antistrophe of its second part, where "the conclusion will not rise from the premises. The caverns of the North and the plains of Chili are not the residences of 'Glory' and 'generous Shame.' But that Poetry and Virtue go always together is an opinion so *pleasing* that I can forgive him who resolves to think it true."[7] The stanza concludes with "The unconquerable mind, and Freedom's holy flame" (echoed in Wordsworth's sonnet to Toussaint L'Overture). In other words, Johnson suggests that since literature must please, it might please more if it also transmits virtue—to the moral imagination pleasure will be yoked to considerations of virtue. He recognizes that pleasure may be a mixed mode derived from varied appeals to the reader. But because of the cardinal importance of pleasure, he disbelieves that poetry and virtue must go together.

From this tangled situation we may look back with either nostalgia or a sense of achieved sophistication to locate a unity of aesthetic and ethical principles in earlier literary theory and criticism. But we do not find an undisputed unity. It was never there. Memorizing Horace's injunction about pleasing and instructing can be a reductionistic step, especially when the problem of translating it simply as please *and* instruct is overlooked. Neoclassical critics by no means accept a secure marriage between a socially approved moral life and life's aesthetic perception in the production of literature. And we condescend to earlier literature and criticism by assuming that it always follows a "classical" injunction to teach virtue, an assumption too frequently made about the eighteenth century, perhaps because of the ethical inclinations of leading writers—Pope, Swift, Young, Richardson, Johnson, Fielding. But the young Voltaire remarks that the only way to exist sanely in a world of sorrow and injustice is to throw oneself with abandon into the arms of pleasure. So he did for five years, then ceased when he learned that sensual pleasure, like instruction, fails to banish boredom. And boredom, not vice —even according to Johnson—is, of all literary faults, the most fatal.

As noted earlier, even critics with moral outlooks as broad as Johnson, Dryden, Corneille, and Sidney, or as relatively constricted as Rymer, emphasize that intellectual pleasure—what today we might call entertainment (or even Barthes's more specialized *jouissance*)—remains the primary object of artistic and literary attention. While assuming the potentially formative influence of poetry, all believe pleasure comes first. As Sidney says, "moving is of a higher degree than teaching, and it may by this appear, that it is well nigh the cause and the effect of teaching." That is, the emotions are charged and excited, which is the essential and special province of poetry. Sidney may derive this idea directly from the Italian humanist Minturno, who added "moving" to Horace's delight and instruction. Beattie stresses a similar point in his early essay "Of the End of Poetical Composition" in *Essays on Poetry and Music, as They Affect the Mind* (1776). To instruct is fine but, as Leonard Welsted said in his *Dissertation On the English Language,* "Does not Poetry instruct . . . much more powerfully, through its *superior* charm of pleasing?"[8] In "The Idea of Universal Poetry," Hurd sets Eratosthenes against Strabo to make the point. Eratosthenes says, "*the poet's aim is to please, not to instruct,*" and although Hurd allows that instruction may be one means of pleasing, "pleasure *is still the ultimate end and scope* of the poet's art; and *instruction* itself is, in his hands, only one of the *means,* by which he would effect it."[9]

Many eighteenth-century critics remark that instruction is desirable, but unlike pleasure it cannot stand alone; instruction is neither sufficient nor necessary. Hume stresses the primary role of enjoyment in contemplating art and developing taste. He notes that critics and authors supposedly agree about the nature of virtue, but undercuts this "*seeming* harmony in morals" by suggesting that it is a mirage created by similar vocabulary. On close observation, different circumstances and imprecision in "the very nature of language" vitiate any concord. In "Truth and Lie in the Extra-Moral Sense," Nietzsche would choose the word "honest" as an example of that apparent agreement foisted on us by linguistic and social convention. And so we become the "honest herd."

True, if we look at criticism of the arts as a whole, not only in the eighteenth century but at almost every juncture from Homer and Hesiod through Dante, Sidney, Vico, Yeats, and Frye, we sense a constant reference to some enlarging and shaping power of literature to create a more liberal—meaning a more informed and generous—soul. For these writers a world without art would not only be less beautiful but less just. But how to achieve that moral power is never, and can never be, explicitly formulated. Hume admits that works of imaginative literature examine ethical motives and propound moral lessons, but he refuses to establish these as conditions of their creation or success. He implies that it depends on a tradition of public morality—from which a generation later Byron recoils and thus ironically enjoys his great public success.

It is *not* in the eighteenth century, then, that we encounter either a consensus on ethics and aesthetics or any breakdown of the classical ideal of their unity. That "breakdown" is as old as the idea itself. But in the eighteenth century we do begin to encounter a potential reversal—an opposition—of aesthetic pleasure and received notions of virtue in "a system of social duty," and the magnitude of this opposition is new. It is based on increased dissatisfaction with the concept of authority in general. Byron's heroes—family, social and religious outcasts—become strikingly popular in print.

New Forces

A relatively fresh argument is brought to bear in the eighteenth century. Addressing social change and moral authority, it strikes at the heart of the issue. The new argument, further weakening any commonly accepted moral function of poetry, goes like this: as society matures, the first civilizing function of poetry, admittedly moral and formative, will have been completed; other institutions and traditions begin to take over the duties and teaching once assumed by poetry, which becomes increasingly marginalized, Peacock's "rattle to amuse a child." Poetry and art need no longer be "moral." Literature as an institution need no longer bow to that god and can actually feel liberated—even be a liberator. As early as Elizabeth's reign, the premise of this argument receives glancing attention from William Webb. "Besides the great and profitable fruites contained in Poetry, for the instruction of manners and precepts of good life (for that *was* cheefly respected in the *first* age of Poetry) . . . Kings and Princes . . . did euer encourage, mayntaine, and reward Poets."[10] In other words, once society refines itself out of the "barbarity" attributed to Shakespeare's age by both Dryden and Johnson, poetry will have performed its historical duty of moral education once and for all. The task set by Addison and Steele in *The Spectator* will not go on indefinitely. (Interestingly, philosophers and moral essayists now increasingly write in prose, as Henry Reynolds recommended. Pope is the last major exception.) The first age will close, and then something else beyond "instruction of manners and precepts of good life" will occupy poetry as its chief end. A general refinement in society and its institutions reduces the need for basic moral instruction through the medium of poetry. To a reader already well-versed (once an apt phrase), poetry becomes an intellectual pleasure, not an authoritative guide.

Further splitting poetry apart from moral instruction, as distinct from subjects of conceivable moral interest, is the new and heightened interest in a science or system of aesthetics. Its modern growth begins with Italian and French critics, Baumgarten's *Aesthetica* (1739), Burke's *Enquiry* (1757) and attitudes fostered by virtuosi and connoisseurs. "What defines a work of art" in this changed view, M. H. Abrams notes, "is its status as an object to be 'contemplated,' and contemplated 'disinterestedly'—that is, attended to 'as such,' for its own sake, without regard to the personal interests or the possessiveness or the desires of the perceiver, and without reference to its truth or its utility or its morality."[11]

Yet this stress on pure aesthetic contemplation finally returns to its estranged partner. Even if one accepts anything like pure aesthetic judgment in practical criticism, Kant himself drops hints in that difficult section of the *Critique of Judgment,* "Beauty as the symbol of morality," that somehow (he is not explicit how), "taste" and "imagination" create or function as an analogy between beauty as the object of aesthetic judgment and law as the foundation of moral judgment. There are differences, of course. Moral judgment can be cognitive and conceptualized. Aesthetic judgment, by definition, cannot be other than subjective and therefore has no concepts or "logic" as such. It is undemonstrable in the "objective" or systematic sense. Yet both kinds of judgment are finalized by their *ideal* nature, by the fact they do not refer purely to real, sensual experience. Hence, Schiller's "On the Sublime" carries this analogy into a realm of the moral sublime. In positing the analogy in the first place, Kant says we attribute to aesthetic beauty in nature certain moral qualities, as when we speak of an "innocent" color, a "noble" mountain, a "majestic" tree. (Coleridge, citing similar lines in Shakespeare, calls this the power of "humanizing nature," a basic trope

of romantic literature.) Our aesthetic sensations, devoid of self interest and of cognitive understanding, nevertheless contain, according to Kant, "something analogous to the consciousness of the state
of mind brought about by moral judgments." The rhetorical figure
of personification, of "humanizing nature," will eventually involve
all that characterizes human nature, including morality and the debate over it. Kant specifically says that "If the beautiful arts are not
brought into more or less combination with moral ideas, which
alone bring with them a self-sufficing satisfaction," the fate of art
will be eventually to leave the mind "discontented . . . and pee-
vish."[12] We may speak of a Kantian model of pure aesthetic judgment, but that model is only one analytical part of Kant's view of
the total experience that art represents, and within that totality he
includes the expression, even the necessity, of moral ideas. There is
a hint, or more than a hint of this when Wordsworth says, in the
1800 Preface, that even though he may not begin to compose with
a purpose in mind, and while all poetry must operate through pleasure, as he contemplates the forms of nature the arousal of associated
passions involved with describing those objects "will be found to
carry along with them a *purpose*." The emphasis is his.

Both Kant and Hume specifically designate "taste" as an analogizing activity of imagination mediating between the ideal touchstones of pure aesthetic judgment, pleasure and displeasure, and the
ideal concepts of moral judgment, right and wrong. Taste thus
takes on its shoulders the immensely difficult task of reconciling—
somehow (again, Kant is not specific how)—the aesthetic and the
ethical. As Hume noted, taste deals in a higher common sense, one
in which elements of the rational and the sensual are mutually referred to one analogizing activity. It involves taste and imagination
but seems a complex interworking of them, along with both sensuous and "objective principles." This analogy "is not nature, nor
yet freedom, but still is connected with the ground of the latter,
that is, the supersensible—a something in which the theoretical
faculty gets bound up into unity with the practical *in an intimate
and obscure manner*."[13] This analysis does not equate ethics and aesthetics but posits an analogy between them, an analogy Kant se-

cures in the name of a symbol. And the nature of this analogy and its symbol-making power depends to some extent on our ethical concepts and on their associations with sensory experience. Coleridge in *On Poesy or Art*—an "essay" published posthumously and drawn from a long Notebook entry and lecture notes in part based on Schelling's "Über das Verhältnis der bildenden Künste zu der Natur" (1807)—says art is "the power of humanizing nature, of infusing the thoughts and passions of man into everything which is the object of his contemplation; color, form, motion, and sound, are the elements which it combines, and it stamps them into unity in the mould of a moral idea."

The ideal of pure aesthetic judgment and the ideal of pure moral judgment are not for Kant identical—aesthetic ends are not determinate. Unlike moral ends they are subjective and cannot be *understood* "by means of a universal concept." However, because of a shared characteristic of "the idealism of finality" operating in both aesthetic and moral ideas, they do enjoy an inescapable relation or association. We might here recall that "pure aesthetic judgment," like "pure reason," is a construct intended to permit the isolation and analysis of circumscribed mental and emotional operations— that in actual experience we may, by an act of will, treat our experience, including whatever we read, under a mixed heading of many categories. Thus, Coleridge and Schelling, Schiller and Shelley, each say art calls on the "whole" human being. Schelling says it is necessary for art to complete, to unify, and to symbolize philosophy. And so Schiller (and earlier Herder) protest Kant's mode of analysis. However brilliant, it splits apart a sense of lived experience, particularly in the mouths of lesser commentators. Sick and tired of those commentators, Fichte said imagination cannot be analyzed—it must be possessed inwardly and intuitively, a view Kant tacitly accepted when he earlier called imagination "an obscure power hidden within the depths of the soul."

Kant's parallel or analogy between aesthetic harmony and moral conduct is not new as such (though his careful formulation is). It is voiced earlier in the century, first by Shaftesbury. Keats will debate it in the context of interpreting art, quoting Shaftesbury's terse for-

mulation in a new context of aesthetic object and historical actual-
ity, "Beauty is truth and truth beauty." Addison notes the analogy
in *Spectator* 62: "*Bouhours,* whom I look upon to be the most penetrating of all the *French* Criticks, has taken Pains to show, that it is
impossible for any Thought to be beautiful which is not just, and
has not its Foundation in the Nature of things: That the Basis of
all Wit is Truth; and that no Thought can be valuable, of which
good Sense is not the Ground-work. . . . This is that natural Way
of writing, that beautiful Simplicity, which we so much admire in
the Compositions of the Ancients."[14] The moral/aesthetic analogy
enters theories of rhetoric and literature as a common proposition.
According to William Melmoth's *Letters of Sir Thomas Fitzosborne,* a
taste that relishes "fine style" can be considered "as an evidence, in
some degree, of the moral rectitude of its constitution; as it is a
proof of its retaining some relish at least of harmony and order."[15]
But even here qualifications forshadow Keats's open, dialectical
symbolization of the question through the presence and voice of the
Grecian Urn (which echoes Addison's and many others' admiration
of Greek art for its union of beauty and truth.) A "fine style" is only
one evidence "in some degree," a proof of "some relish at least."

However inexact, analogies remain powerful and suggestive. Although he could not have had Kant's *Critique of Judgment* in mind
when he wrote the *Reflections on the Revolution in France,* Burke clearly
sees the same analogy at work. Commenting on a new intellectual
"cabal" feeding the French revolutionary mind, he notes: "I will
venture to say that this narrow exclusive spirit has not been less
prejudicial to literature and to taste than to morals and true philosophy," exactly because, for Burke, a connection, indefinite but in-
eluctable, exists between them.[16]

Instruction or Exploration

We enter a new dimension if we assume that poetry explores and
discovers the individual or inner life and may largely turn away from
society and social norms because it no longer finds its moral vision
there. Society's moral cohesiveness expressed in art is at stake. And

that is where the real estrangement enters. The eighteenth century exerts a powerful critique against social institutions, against revealed religion and received truths. Poetry (and soon romances such as *Frankenstein*) begin to take on personal voices of moral vision, even rebellion and alienation. Poetry, rather than being an instrument of socially moral instruction and didacticism patronized by external authority, becomes a vehicle for inward moral reflection, doubt, and debate. When Keats says no one likes poetry with a design upon us, he is essentially stating Blake's credo that we must create our own systems or be enslaved by those of others. The estrangement of aesthetics and ethics grows more acute not only because of the idea of "pure" aesthetic judgment, or because poetry has already accomplished its civilizing process in previous ages, but because trust in moral social authority as a whole is fraying. Weaker bonds link author and aristocrat, and less trust is placed in authoritative rules of aesthetic theory and the primacy of didactically oriented genres. Didactic motives influence genre theory more heavily in the first half of the eighteenth century, for instance, than in the second. Ralph Cohen sees a generic hierarchy inherited from the Renaissance altered during the "Augustan Age" in "terms of the elevation of the longer didactic forms: the georgic, the epistle, and satire." Here Cohen uses the "Augustan Age" presumably to establish a somewhat earlier time frame than the whole of the eighteenth century.[17] Joseph Warton's general stance regarding Pope and satire, as distinguished from more "imaginative" poetry (noted in "What Is Poetry?" Chapter 9), leads Alastair Fowler to see a shift from the earlier eighteenth century, when "didactic poetry rose to the very highest level of estimation," to the "late eighteenth century," when "the didactic genres were no longer quite on this height."[18]

Although the analogy of which Kant spoke may be valid in outline form, the specific causes and effects of moral and aesthetic values are now so much debated that the analogy produces only more debate. The erosion of a shared social taste represents a collapse of consensus, more specifically of *sensus communis,* the common sense or "taste" that negotiates between moral and aesthetic life, the good and the beautiful. That this happens over the course of the late eighteenth and nineteenth centuries is the very premise from which Tolstoy begins *What Is Art?*

Swift already recognizes this shift, and his conservative impulses react vigorously. We see his backlash, particularly regarding religion, in the "Letter of Advice to a Young Poet" (a fascinating subgenre with social, moral, and literary crosshatchings). The advice drips with irony:

> But although I cannot recommend religion upon the practice of some of our most eminent English poets, yet I can justly advise you, from their example, to be conversant in the Scriptures, and, if possible, to make yourself entirely master of them: In which, however, I intend nothing less than imposing upon you a task of piety. Far be it from me to desire you to believe them, or lay any great stress upon their *authority,* (in that you may do as you think fit) but to read them as a piece of necessary furniture for a wit and a poet. . . . For I have made it my observation, that *the greatest wits have been the best textuaries.* Our modern poets are, all to a man, almost as well read in the Scriptures as some of our divines. . . . They have read them historically, critically, musically, comically, poetically, and every other way except religiously. . . . For the Scriptures are undoubtedly a fund of wit, and a subject for wit. You may, according to the modern practice, be witty upon them or out of them. And to speak the truth, but for them I know not what our playwrights would do for images, allusions, similitudes, examples, or even language itself. Shut up the sacred books, and I would be bound our wit would run down like an alarm, or fall as the stocks did, and ruin half the poets in these kingdoms.

Swift concludes with what would soon become more of an issue, and finally an obvious condition of modern literature, even one of its hallmarks: "I am not yet convinced, that it is at all necessary for a modern poet to believe in God, or have any serious sense of religion."

Here is a brilliantly phrased but nevertheless ironically moral point of view: "For poetry, as it has been managed for some years past, by such as make a business of it, (and of such only I speak here; for I do not call him a poet that writes for his diversion, any more than that gentleman a fiddler, who amuses himself with a violin) I say our poetry of late has been altogether disengaged from the narrow notions of virtue and piety, because it has been found by experience of our professors, that the smallest quantity of religion, like a single drop of malt liquor in claret, will muddy and discompose the brightest poetical genius."[19]

One can say that whether one attacks or defends the *sensus communis,* its breakdown must produce, as it does in Swift's advice, irony. No author can count on even a basic moral sympathy of the reader, and often assumes in the audience a moral antipathy or opacity. Satire is thus not based on an objective, commonly received set of moral values. It is more appropriately based on a felt absence or betrayal of that commonality, and satirists, like Byronic heroes, feel themselves outsiders. Insofar as the concepts of moral justice are institutionalized and are conditioned, as Hume notes, by the social compact of common language, they form a given. But if one disagrees with them, if there is no community, or if one's own imagination cannot square aesthetic values with socially given moral concepts, irony results. We encounter a difference between the morals of social authority and those of individual character (suggested by Fichte's *Moralität* versus *Sittenheit.*)

In this light, what we call romantic irony (a better term may be modern irony) is the rhetorical reflection of a breakdown in *sensus communis* with its accompanying estrangement of aesthetic and moral judgments. (The concurrent romantic stress on sympathy and love may be seen as an attempt to bind up these disintegrations.) Even Jane Austen's irony, while not "romantic," is nevertheless not based on a set of classical notions shared by *all* of society. Her work represents a tension between selective approval of (or submission to) social convention and an equally selective disapproval when the heroine's personal integrity rebels against society's morally myopic practice and assumptions. Or, to take an extreme example, Hardy's *Tess,* subtitled "a pure woman faithfully presented," was viciously attacked as immoral, presumably by those of like mind with Angel Clare's family. In the book, and in its reception, irony reaches a tragic level. The deeper estrangement is now between society at large and a personal, even alienated moral vision of the author and protagonist, who can no longer be a hero but in modernist literature becomes an antihero.

When the estrangment of ethics and aesthetics involves questioning or rejecting social standards, there is no particular way to restore the marriage. Moral concepts and aesthetic concepts are not, Kant reminds us, actually found in nature but in a final ideality in the subject. We create them. For instance, if unity of moral and aesthetic concerns does not hold in characters, the fascination turns to energy and power. Goldsmith, reviewing Home's *Tragedy of Douglas,* speaks of "this tragedy's want of moral, which should be the ground-work of every fable," that is, of every plot or narrative. But Goldsmith goes on to say that this and many other faults "we could easily pardon, did poetic fire, elegance, or the heightenings of pathetic distress afford adequate compensation."[20] So Lamb, in "The Tragedies of Shakespeare," admits: "The truth is, the Characters of Shakespeare are so much the objects of meditation rather than of interest or curiosity as to their actions, that while we are reading any of his great criminal characters,—Macbeth, Richard, even Iago,—we think not so much of the crimes which they commit, as of the ambition, the aspiring spirit, the intellectual activity, which prompts them to overleap those moral fences."[21]

From here it is little distance to Wilde's effective repudiation of social ethics in art: "The artistic critic, like the mystic, is an antinomian always. To be good, according to the vulgar standard of goodness, is obviously quite easy. It merely requires a certain . . . lack of imaginative thought, and a certain low passion for middle-class respectability. Aesthetics are higher than ethics. They belong to a more spiritual sphere. . . . Even a colour-sense is more important, in the development of an individual, than a sense of right and wrong."[22] The great inheritor of Restoration wit, itself emerging out of social turmoil and sudden shifts in ethical sympathies and authority, is hard on the heels of Victorian respectability. (As an aside, a good case can be made that Restoration wit, especially on the stage, derives from a suspicion and suspension of authority, its backdrop a supposedly authoritarian social ethic which is perforated and violated by sectarian and private practice at every intersection. No system or "enthusiasm" can dominate. Wit, in its contest of opposites, becomes a proving ground for alternate opinions. Butler, Rochester, Wycherley, Congreve, Farquhar, and later Sheridan— the line of wit Wilde revives—while having their differences, all portray the subversion or hypocrisy of respectable authority in social, religious, and political conventions. Pope's sympathies lie elsewhere, and his wit is essentially of a different kind.) Wilde even manages to equate all ethics with that respectability. He hates English "puritanism" and "practicality" (what Shaw in *Pygmalion* calls "slum prudery"), and regards any plea for morality in art as an easy cover for propagating thoughtless conformity and moral tyranny. Johnson, however different from Wilde, expresses similar sympathies by reacting against children's moral primers designed to inculcate social respectability. They do nothing to enlarge a young imagination (Johnson would have preferred Wilde's fairy tales). Challenged and reminded how well *Goody Two Shoes* sold, how popular it was, Johnson scoffs yes, it had. But the parents, driven by social pressure, bought it, not the children.

Wilde is not attacking the presentation of moral issues in art, a point often blurred over. The preface to *The Picture of Dorian Gray* contains fine aphorisms: "There is no such thing as a moral or an immoral book. Books are well written, or badly written. That is all." Aesthetics seems to have gained the upper hand with little room for appeal. But when Wilde calls "an ethical sympathy in an artist . . . an unpardonable mannerism of style" and says, "There is no sin except stupidity," he is using the language of morality and religion in the service of another god. He is preaching to his audience an unexpected sermon, but not the total divorce of art and moral issues. Like Heine and Nietzsche, he wants desperately to shrug off the monkey of conformity to social codes, and that in itself is an ethical sympathy, though Wilde expresses it with such irony that it *becomes* and graces his style. We can recall his interesting, never quoted qualification, that while "the morality of art consists in the perfect use of an imperfect medium," we still see that "The moral life . . . forms part of the subject-matter of the artist." All Wilde's works exert a moral, the one calculated to challenge and delight his audience. To make the reader feel uncomfortable or disoriented is a hallmark of the irony we have been discussing.[23]

Generic Determinations

Another fruitful way to look at the larger subject is from the standpoint of genre. The novel and the drama, seen as the most direct imitators of "real life," "life and manners," or "morals and manners" (phrases increasingly common in eighteenth-century criticism), are saddled with the greatest expectation of didactic choice and presentation. They are also—an important point with social implications—popular genres and, in the public eye, open to young readers, often women. Other genres less imitative of real life—ode, lyric, the prose romance (Gothic)—are more exempt from ethical claims. In fact, one could begin to remove poetry as a whole, as Henry Reynolds had, and to place the burden of ethical involvement on prose, either intellectual or narrative. A growing correlation exists between ethical expectations and the mimesis of day-to-day experience encountered in "real life," the phrase repeatedly used and already prominent in Johnson's *Rambler* 4 on modern fiction. Hence Austen, Crabbe, Fielding, Burney, and Richardson, by the material of their representations, are generally regarded by critics under one sort of ethical expectation, while lyric poetry (Chatterton, Burns) and less realistic prose narrative *(Ossian, Castle of Otranto, The Monk, Vathek)* roam on a longer tether.

Genre is a powerful stimulus to ethical expectation. Rymer states: "Some would blame me for insisting and examining only what is apt to *please,* without a word of what might profit." He then orders three principles. First, that "the end of all Poetry is to *please.* Second, that "some sorts of Poetry please without profiting," but, third, that "I am confident whoever writes a *Tragedy* cannot please but must also profit; 'tis the Physick of the mind that he makes palatable."[24] John Newbery, in *Art of Poetry on a New Plan* (1762), admits that "poetry has a language peculiar to itself, which is in many respects very different from that of prose." But even though "the poet's design is principally to please," and so affords him "greater latitude of language," the goal of the epic or heroic poem, where the poet "has now left the borders of fairy land, and is got into real life, where his imagination must be always bounded by nature," is still "to inspire the soul with noble and sublime sentiments," to "inflame the mind with the love of virtue."[25]

In works written about and for the new larger audiences outside of court and gentry, we most often hear the moral strain in earnest tones. The prologue to Lillo's *London Merchant* perfectly states the idea of inculcating acceptable, age-old truths. Here again, social morality informs the work:

> We hope your taste is not so high to scorn
> A moral tale, esteem'd ere you were born.

The address to the audience concludes with the kind of argument soon formulaic in prefaces to popular novels, that even "Tho' art be wanting, and our numbers fail, / Indulge the attempt, in justice to the tale!" There is a gendered as well as a generic side to all this. In such plays and novels the audience is increasingly more female, and numerous women, probably more than men, were writing novels. Male critics, if they address the issue at all, generally condescend to woman's supposed need for greater moral guidance, and male reviewers often pardon women novelists for loose writing if the morals are not.

Larger minds make fun of that tradition and play with it ironically. Sheridan spoofs it in his epilogue to *The Rivals:*

> Ladies, for *you*—I heard our poet say—
> He'd try to coax some *moral* from his play.

But the whole notion of socially determined morality taught through literary production becomes newly irreverent (and also, at all social levels, a revelatory phenomenon in its wild popularity) in *The Beggar's Opera.*[26] There conventional social expectation is turned upside down:

Player: But, honest friend, I hope you don't intend that Macheath shall be really executed.

Beggar: Most certainly, Sir. To make the piece perfect, I was for doing strict poetical justice. Macheath is to be hanged; and for the other personages of the drama, the audience must have supposed they were all either hanged or transported.

Player: Why then, friend, this is a downright deep tragedy. The catastrophe is manifestly wrong, for an opera must end happily.

Beggar: Your objection, Sir, is very just and is easily removed. For you must allow that in this kind of drama 'tis no matter how absurdly things are brought about.—So—you rabble there— run and cry a reprieve!—let the prisoner be brought back to his wives in triumph.

Player: All this we must do, to comply with the taste of the town.

Beggar: Through the whole piece you may observe such a similitude of manners in high and low life, that it is difficult to determine whether (in the fashionable vices) the fine gentlemen imitate the gentlemen of the road, or the gentlemen of the road the fine gentlemen. Had the play remained as I at first intended, it would have carried a most excellent moral. 'Twould have shown that the lower sort of people have their vices in a degree as well as the rich; and that they are punished for them.

(III, xvi, penultimate scene of the play)

Here Gay succeeds in satirizing political, social, and class morality, and the social expectation ("the taste of the town") of what "tragedy" should present in the way of poetical justice—no matter how absurd and unlikely its action in relation to real life. And in doing so, as Johnson later notes, Gay creates, as he had to, a new genre.

Inexact Freedom

What we miss in all the arguments about ethics and aesthetics is any argument about precisely what literature should convey by instruction, if indeed it instructs in any sense. In what does its "virtue" consist? Interestingly, Rymer, Hume, Johnson, Fielding, and others intentionally keep the sense of virtue represented in literature on a general or situational level. Otherwise virtue becomes dogmatic or fossilized. Shaftesbury, Hobbes, Hume, Johnson, Hazlitt, Byron, even Coleridge, all place poetry and *mores* together but regard that union rather as a possibility, a potential to be explored by individual genius. None of these critics supports the aesthetic-ethic claim with rigorous, concrete principles. None cares to. Hobbes cannot wrestle ethics into a clear system; Shaftesbury's attempt seems vague and shaky. Hume makes acute observations but admits he can prove nothing demonstrably. The subject won't admit it. Johnson wishes poetry to present some belief either to be imitated or declined; there is no sense of a rote lesson.[27] The concept of virtue or moral instruction cannot be delimited, for that would delimit each possible act of literary creation. The eighteenth-century emphasis on "general" here means what is undogmatic, not parochially formulated—not determined simply by social convention, which is local and transient. It can be a way of gaining liberality and free play, not, as many have supposed, an assertion of hierarchy or authority. Literature offers the concrete and particular, but any theoretical injunction to virtue, unless a particular work is before us, must be general in order to be valid.

Even though Rymer makes an exception to his stress on pleasure and insists that tragedy profit morally, he is inexact and says only that "something must stick by observing that constant order, that harmony and beauty of Providence, that necessary relation and chain, whereby the causes and the effects, the vertues and rewards, the vices and their punishments are proportion'd and link'd together; how deep and dark soever are laid the Springs and however intricate and involv'd are their operations." He does resort to a great chain of moral order reminiscent of Ulysses' speech (adding a religious emphasis), yet when the reader asks for something exact, Rymer concludes his principle of moral profit in tragedy with the disclaimer that "these enquiries I leave to men of more flegm and consideration."[28] The disclaimer seems wise. Coleridge himself admitted that the *Rime of the Ancient Mariner* had too much of a moral appended. Virtuous action requires a context or narrative experience, which no speculation or theory provides.

Ironically, even criticism that discusses moral issues is not a particularly good conveyor of moral values unless it contains a dramatic context and narrative. (This is, for example, Fielding's contention in the opening paragraphs of *Joseph Andrews,* and again in the chapter that begins the third book of that novel.) Otherwise, it is often too abstract, and as a secular voice lacks the weight of—or fails to excite the opposition toward—religious teaching. A moral critic like Johnson—if he is not addressing particular works, as he often does in the *Lives of the Poets,* or refuting a particular hypothesis, as in the review of Soame Jenyns—will constantly have recourse to fact, history, and biography, as in *The Vanity of Human Wishes.* "We are affected only as we believe," or as we willingly suspend our disbelief. Johnson particularizes his own fiction with concrete narrative incident; *Rasselas* is a story where moral speculation is commented upon by the interruption of specific events. *The Rambler* often attains moral specificity from letters or discussions of domestic incidents, themselves short narratives. William Law's *Serious Call* and Richard Savage, his life and poetry, are in this regard formative influences on Johnson. Part of the test of literature is not the repetition of virtue or its fruit sweetened with sugar (despite what Sidney said), but the exploration of virtue and the attempt to articulate it in character and in experience—in "life and manners"—to make us use our freedom to *see,* as Conrad said he wished to do, and not to repeat injunctions or transliterate maxims as dialogue. The goal becomes an active search through specific individuals and their stories.

From the Italian humanists into the nineteenth century, the social expectation of morality in art resides primarily in mimetically realistic and popular genres, drama and the novel (or long, realistic verse narratives). But literary theory exerts renewed stress on pleasure and what might be called the privatization of poetry. And whenever there is talk of virtue, the refusal to be specific about it in the more flexible critics and writers unconcerned with parroting social conformity is intentional and considered, based also on a suspicion of language to carry exact representations of moral qualities. (This is why Henry James nuances his prose almost endlessly.) Few specific, abstract virtues or specific systems are emphasized. Rather the enlarging of experience, the going out of one's nature, becomes the quest. It may have a bitter end—Marlowe discovers Kurtz in the act of *his* horrible discovery—but nevertheless it is a quest, a commentary on civilization and the individual that may be called moral and ethical. The eighteenth and early nineteenth centuries at times direct a sharp initial critique at authority in religion, morals, politics, and personal conduct. Seen from this perspective, the question ever since has hinged between institutionalized authorities and individual freedom, thus art in the modern world has become more than ever an emblem of liberty and revolt. Even ideological critics such as Marxists, who espouse a specific political system, do so in opposition to a previously established tyranny of the bourgeoisie. It involves, after all, a perennial revolution.

The attitude tends away from authority, and romantic irony is one result. There authority becomes totally suspended. Romantic irony is many things, but among them it is a strategy to deal with the estrangement of aesthetics and ethics. With romantic irony one could still maintain a humanly created moral system in the face of an open, chaotic, and morally indifferent or even despotic cosmos (or an immoral, suffocating society). And yet one could continually question any moral system, especially the received social system, since it was, like all things human, subject to decay and flaw. *Faust* and *Don Juan* supremely exhibit this irony. These great myths of the modern, postclassical world exemplify how, in that world, the burden of morality in art cannot be fully and genuinely addressed *other than ironically,* in the spirit of subversion and opposition. Blake recognizes this; his moral vision of the cosmos is ironic in the sense that, as Northrop Frye and others point out, his universe is inverted. Rejecting public morality and official authority, all true morality flows out of personal, imaginative freedom.

One way to look at the question is to say that literature is primarily the exercise of imagination: with the provocation and assistance of texts we re-create for ourselves various narratives, situations, images, and characters that otherwise we would not encounter in our experience as such. So the moral uses of literature are simply as multiple—as vague, as difficult to define—but nevertheless as potent and rich as the uses of individual imagination, its ability to get us out of ourselves, to become disinterested or fiercely partisan.

In the eighteenth century the issue of ethics and aesthetics becomes newly unsettled, nuanced, and provocative. Forget the easy generalization that criticism of this time assumes literature is didactic and presents a moral agenda of eternal truths to inculcate. One can always find people saying that, but most critics who draw a connection between literature and morality do so intentionally, with the hope of establishing general, not eternally revealed truths. And between the two lies a significant difference, for general truths admit flexibility and actually require an active, participatory application on the reader's part. Poetry becomes a way to explore and discover the inner moral life, rather than a way to illustrate or decorate a catechism of social duties. This exploration is Arnold's praise of Wordsworth. And it is part of what Coleridge means when he claims that Wordsworth is capable of writing the first genuine philosophic poem in English—one could "do philosophy" rather than repeat received values. In his growing admiration for Wordsworth, Keats begins to understand the task of philosophy in this light and wonders if poetry affords it a home.

In this debate I am tempted to paraphrase the remark of a historian, that the only thing new in criticism is the history we do not know. But that would be facile and suffocating. The issue remains for each generation to face in a new way. For instance, the growth of literacy since the eighteenth century has become complicated in the twentieth by the relative marginalization of "serious" literature, its proportional loss of audience, the split between popular and sophisticated art, and the increased examination of ethics in relation to situational problems in the professions and politics. The danger lies in seeing no issue, in feeling it has either been settled or no longer exists, that we have "outgrown" it, or that its terms are too elusive to bother about. The issue fluctuates over time and responds to social expectations. Often criticism stretches or rejects the social standard and becomes an instrument of change. That explains why Arnold calls for a current of fresh ideas, not a defense of the status quo in social values. We have seen how new positions are articulated and advanced, yet the issue as a whole is never—*can* never be— solved or resolved except by individual conscience and taste. Or, at the other end of the political spectrum, by a "community standard" (*sensus communis* in modern dress) that initiates legal action at a threshold of censorship.

The terms and questions so often used to frame the issue of "morality and art" are worse than useless. Debates on the subject begin with a weary order to "round up the usual suspects." Is art moral, should it be?—and so forth. Lacking nuance and discrimination, those terms and formulations cause harm. They simplify and separate what is complex and alloyed. To ask whether literature is or ought to be "moral" fails utterly to pose an adequate or appropriate question. It misleads and sets up shaky assumptions; it implies that all literature should be treated in light of this question; it places a priority on the purposes and motives of writing; it lumps together moral instruction and precept transmitted by social authority with moral reflection, doubt, and conviction gained through personal experience, including the experience of literature; it is fundamentally naive. Such a question assumes a blanket purpose of writing and a shared sense of specific moral values. It ignores genre and tends to focus exclusively on imaginative literature. Yet especially in teaching literature, the question is repeatedly handled in this clumsy way as either a desperate or dismissive shortcut. A more sensitive approach would be to ask what potential does literature have for sharpening our observations, enlarging ethical views and nuancing choices, how it permits us to exercise or to test an ethical life rather than handing to us clear aphorisms (interestingly, Blake's aphorisms or proverbs are rarely clear and unambiguous, but often unsettling and challenge interpretation). Here theoretical debate must turn to specific works for illumination.[29]

By the same token, to deny any moral effect of literature is equally naive. It is as if we said that experience itself, conversations with other people, events we encounter, look forward to with anxiety, and remember with remorse in fitful nights serve only to entertain or to establish a pattern of shifting signifiers whose "differences" and deferrals constitute their own *raison d'être*. Both our experience and our language, Wilde's admittedly "imperfect medium," a medium not "worked through" and hence constantly deferring its own end, can still give local habitation and a name to objects, ideas, and actions we articulate, however imprecisely, in order to communicate, to suggest, and to reveal. One power of literature is to open problematic moral perspectives, areas with unclear or debatable answers, where justification is not only difficult but also not assured; precisely where no authority is universally accepted, in controversial situations where ethics and truth are forged rather than reflected. As with each of literature's multiple powers, its moral dimension resides in potential. And its actualization is something outside the text, for it depends on different readings that the work half creates, but half receives.

CHAPTER 6

Kinds, Canons, and Readers

As trade is now carried on by subordinate hands, men in
trade have as much leisure as others, and now learning itself
is a trade. A man goes to a bookseller and gets what he can.
We have done with patronage. . . . An author leaves the
great and applies to the multitude.

JOHNSON ON THE TOUR

Addison advises his "fair readers to be in a particular manner careful
how they meddle with romances, Chocolates, novels, and like inflamers." His warning—and the curious juxtaposition of food with
literary genres—suddenly comes alive when we recall how widely
the eighteenth-century shopgoer accepted what had been common
knowledge among the Aztecs, who first cultivated and brewed the
cocoa bean: chocolate acts as a quick, effective aphrodisiac. Giving
a box on Valentine's Day has an ulterior motive. (Modern science
has discovered that chocolate contains phenylethylamine, a natural
chemical in the brain that neurologists speculate increases with—
or causes—erotic thoughts and fantasies.) Addison's gentle advice
indicates that genre or literary kind may be determined not only by
formal considerations and conventions of subject, style, and language, but even more appropriately by the values and nature of
experiences associated with a particular genre (its "ideology"), what

it can arouse, and the prevailing objects of its imitative power. As novels and romances act as such "inflamers," at least potentially, they are of all nondramatic genres held most accountable to social standards of virtuous conduct.[1]

Neoclassical and earlier eighteenth-century criticism directly continues a Renaissance stress on a theoretical primacy accorded to genre.[2] Systematic study of literature must properly—if not first— be approached in taxonomic fashion. The so-called rules, or any principles of criticism, would mean little unless applied to specific kinds of literature. The rules rely on an initial naming of kinds. Much criticism, especially routine theory down to the mid eighteenth century, centers on genre. But in this area criticism lags behind the actual practice and production of literary works. The heroic and epic, pastoral and tragedy, the sublime and the beautiful, all receive extended treatment, but many or even most successful poems and works appear as new genres, or newly derived and transformed, mixed, or sometimes recreated as antigenres.[3] In a real sense these "mixed," transformed, or countergenres are the most vital. We might include in them the loco-descriptive or geographical poem, various meditative verse forms mingling pastoral, elements of eclogue, and even panegyric, also the mock-heroic, and individual poems immensely difficult to classify—over which debate continues—such as *Absalom and Achitophel* and Cowper's *Task*. Sometimes it is worth asking to what genre *The Rape of the Lock, Windsor Forest, Eloisa to Abelard,* Gray's *Elegy, The Deserted Village,* or *The Parish Register* belong, simply because the answers become complex and enlightening. We leave the arid debate of taxonomy and engage questions of reception and interpretation, where genre is helpful as a way to think, not merely to name. "By mid-century," as Ralph Cohen states, "the combination or mixtures of forms and parts of forms had come to be taken for granted."[4]

In drama the greatest successes also tend to appear in new or altered genres: Gay's ballad opera, middle class tragedy such as Lillo's *The London Merchant* (itself a transformation of the early seventeenth-century "Excellent Ballad of George Barnwel"), and Sheridan's metamorphosis of Restoration wit. Pastoral undergoes broad transformation, with more intelligence attacking than defending it, until it finally cleaves, in Wordsworth's *Michael* (subtitled "A Pastoral"), to the sense of real country life that Johnson two decades before declared was hypocritically absent from it. The novel, easily the most important major new genre to emerge, generates comparatively little theoretical criticism or description. In the arena of kinds its great strength is a self-proclaimed "variety," its ability to overstep rules, to meld, to extend already defined generic patterns. Fielding allies it to the comic epic romance, already a genre with highly varied individual works. Defoe, Fielding, and Austen, among others, plea eleoquently not so much for a new genre as for a new nongenre, a form of writing that defies generic prescriptions in order to imitate the totality and variety of human nature, life, and manners.[5]

Difficulty and irritation accompany the problem of naming this new kind not a kind at all. Richard Hurd, familiar with genre theory, and recognizing that writers may "mix and confound" different kinds, nevertheless is exasperated:

> For instance, what are we to think of those *novels* or *romances,* as they are called . . . which have been so current, of late through all Europe? . . . As they are wholly destitute of measured sounds (to say nothing of their other numberless defects) they can, at most, be considered but as hasty, imperfect, and abortive poems; whether spawned from the dramatic, or narrative species, it may be hard to say. . . . But whatever may be the temporary success of these things . . . good sense will acknowledge no work of art but such as is composed according to the laws of its *kind.* These KINDS, as arbitrary things as we account them (for I neither forget nor dispute what our best philosophy teaches concerning *kinds and sorts*), have yet so far their foundation in nature and the reason of things, that it will not be allowed us to multiply, or vary them, at pleasure. We may, indeed, mix and confound them,

if we will. . . . But true taste requires chaste, severe, and simple pleasures.[6]

Beginning in the late 1700s and continuing through the Romantic period, the sense of genre, however stable it may appear in some writers, leans on a weak reed when it repairs to older, more static notions. For a period of eight or nine decades we have rapid metamorphosis, an experimentation that continues through the nineteenth and twentieth centuries. Generic transformation had always occured, but now it intensifies and accelerates. And it culminates in the modernist and especially postmodernist tendency of all genres to become more mixed, less purified, either less identifiable as a specific genre, or self-consciously using genre as an expectation to be subverted. In general, the later the first appearance of a genre, the later its modern "newness" or reincarnation appears. Poetic genres are already transformed quite radically by the Romantic period. We encounter increasing reliance on rapid shifts and transitions, a greater spread in acceptable subject matter and "poetic diction," until nothing is exempt, including the baby crap, hissing potatoes, and cut thumb that demand our attention in Sylvia Plath. The essays of Montaigne, Bacon, and Cowley mutate into early eighteenth-century periodicals, and into something yet again through the familiar essays of Hazlitt and Lamb—or into the personal and philosophical kinds pursued by Emerson, who will "essay to be." In the novel, the appropriation of techniques once reserved for verse begin to characterize increasingly sophisticated narrative forms. But the novel, as its name implies, is a relatively new genre; the "experimental novel" and *nouveau roman* will not emerge until the twentieth century. Only recently can the novel use intentional generic atavism as a strategy, as with John Fowles' statement, by way of that all-important generic marker, the title, that he has not written a novel but *A Maggot,* the action of which significantly takes place in the later seventeenth century, just before the novel arrives on the literary scene. "Autobiography" does not enter the language as a word until the 1820s or 1830s, and we have yet to see its

rebirth in a substantially new form or antigenre, though Malraux's
Antimémoires makes the gesture.

Those eighteenth-century critics who are also practicing writers
of merit become suspicious not so much of genre per se, as of constructing a system of criticism on genre. Genre is already becoming
removed from any unchanging foundation of literary criticism and
establishing itself as a perennial yet changing topic. Genre criticism
remains but genres change (a fact that eventually permits genre
criticism to take on new life in interpretation and literary history,
particularly in the last generation or two). Classification and types
will always be necessary, but now they alter so rapidly, or are seen
as participating in the literary process rather than dictating it, that
generic criticism can no longer be a predominant foundation for
critical theory as a whole. Perhaps the first writer and critic to notice
this, somewhat uncomfortably, is Dryden. While he possesses an
excellent and informed sense of genre—his observations everywhere
illuminated by it—he ultimately rejects kinds of literature as the
critical basis for his judgment. For him, genre changes with literary
development, shifting and adjusting to separate nations and languages. His comparative instincts lead him finally to reject traditional generic prescriptions and to alter them in more flexible, tem-
porary relations accommodating the context and processes of
writing literature in a given tradition at a given time. (This discovery is later appreciated by Eliot.) Johnson is perfectly aware of genre
or kinds; he could cite the origin and expectations of each type of
literature almost verbatim from critical sources and early classical
examples. But he distrusts criticism fixed on genre and vigorously
attacks its static incarnation.[7] He seeks out the metamorphosis of
genre—in Thomson's *Seasons,* Gay's *Beggar's Opera,* or Pope's *Eloisa
to Abelard* as new attempts.

There must be literary classification, a tool critics find themselves
constantly defending with varying degrees of enthusiasm.[8] But
during the eighteenth century, in England and Germany more than
in France, even as Linnaeus produces his great work, it becomes
evident that literary classification can no longer be Linnaean: each

literary work presupposes at least a minor mutation. An airtight taxonomy becomes impossible, like Casaubon's Key to All Mythologies. What today is thought of one way, may in a generation be considered under a new heading, for works that follow upon each other will alter the sense of tradition and genre they first seem to establish or continue. As kinds metamorphose quickly, classifications struggle to keep up. In the later nineteenth century notions of evolution derived from Darwin, though indirectly and often distorting the original theory he set down, continue to exert residual effect on the nature of genre and narrative.[9]

Pope's argument is a strong one, an empirical case that has continued to dominate much Anglophone criticism: the real rules of genre never come from critics in the first place, but from the original poets themselves. The rules are empirically derived only from practice; theory had its birth in practice, and, according to Pope, always should. If one combines this argument with the increasing pressure for originality, the case made by Edward Young in his *Conjectures on Original Composition* (which Johnson said repeated, in 1759, ideas commonly received), the sense of stable genres is further eroded. Young and others stress not the imitation of earlier forms but the capturing of a creative force or spirit. After all, Rousseau announces that his *Confessions* have neither precedent, nor would they have an imitator; they are *sui generis* as, in a sense, each "original" work must be.[10] And part of the impetus to weaken generic boundaries and preoccupations comes in a carom from Longinus. In the simplistic, yet influential and famous, opposition of Aristotle and Longinus, we see that as Longinian elements gain ascendency, the weight of genre diminishes.

Classical models still exert vast pressure in the eighteenth century, but new interest in establishing an English or British literature (Gray, Collins, Beattie, and others)—a drive for "Northern" forms and nationalistic strengths—introduces new generic expectations and models. With Shakespeare and Jonson behind him, Dryden recognizes this in the theater; it soon becomes a force in landscape poetry and narrative. As the idea of *imitatio* declines, Roman or Greek models grow less crucial to an understanding of the English original. Johnson's *Vanity of Human Wishes* is basically a classical imitation, one of the last major ones. Even he is not imitating very closely. Gray's twin odes are Pindaric, as is Wordsworth's later *Intimations Ode,* but Gray—and Wordsworth—present whole new subject matters. The more one tries to grasp the Pindaric style, the more elusive it becomes. What starts as a critical attempt to define the Pindaric in terms of form and genre ends by praising its fire, spirit, and rapidity of mind. In addition, as literacy grows in the eighteenth century, a large segment of the reading population finds it cannot handle the classics in the original. Most schools fail to provide that level of mastery. Common translations are now indispensable for most readers, and tuition schools spring up where those translations are assigned. Theaters grow in size until, in the early nineteenth century, two thousand is not an uncommon audience. As both Hazlitt and Coleridge observe, not only size but spread-out seating, and popular taste make it difficult to perform serious classical tragedy. The best romantic drama becomes, to use Byron's term, "mental theater," itself a new genre. Goldsmith and Hazlitt claim that because of the pressure of popular taste (nothing new, but now exerted in mass at large theaters), comedy declines to sentiment and tragedy to melodrama.

To sum up, English neoclassical genre theory to about 1770 tends to be fairly rigid, and often considerably more inflexible than the actual practice of writers. Genres had always changed, but in literary practice the shift now becomes accentuated and speeds up, while genre theory ironically experiences a drive toward relative purity and immutability, all with a new, more didactic coloring. Genre theory lags behind until, somewhere in the middle of the century, it begins to broaden. During the second half of the century we hear a new refusal to consider genres as either particularly well defined or at all immutably based on nature.[11] Ralph Cohen makes a determined effort to show how ideas of genre in neoclassical criticism emphasize mixed and interrelated aspects, and that any hierarchy of genres is to some degree subsumptive and therefore not rigidly compartmentalized: that it is "mistaken" to assume neoclassical genre theory holds genres to be definite, lasting, and separate.

This is all true, and gains greater relief if we look at practice in both poetry and prose. But we are facing a matter of emphasis, not of absolute contraries. The idea of pure, totally distinct and timeless genres is an extreme not widely held, perhaps never held at all. Theoretical interest in "mixture" begins in the Renaissance, or long before. Hence no argument here can be pushed to the wall. However, at the same time, the "mixed" and "interrelated" qualities recognized in neoclassical theory are ultimately based on a sense of temporal stability in the concepts and definitions of the greater genres, a sense of stability *comparatively* greater than it would be after the advent of high neoclassicism, and certainly stronger than at any time since. We can recall what Hurd said above about kinds being anchored in "nature and the reason of things," a view also espoused by John Newbery in his *Art of Poetry* (1762). Newbery proposes to expand and alter the genres he sees as acceptable, but his proposed "alterations" are to be based on "truth and right reason."[12] As Fowler ventures (somewhat overstating a case worth stating), this is the "belief that the genres are timelessly immutable," a "delusion, which almost all the Augustan critics shared."[13]

The relative sense of temporal stability weakens, largely from the pressure of admixtures successfully created. The fundamental assumptions and superstructure of all generic criticism and theory shift. The idea of genre as reliable taxonomy and primary theory is cast into doubt during the late eighteenth century. The place of genre in literary theory undergoes its largest single modern change until well into the twentieth century, where Fredric Jameson even posits that genre criticism is "thoroughly discredited by modern literary theory and practice."[14] Uses of genre aside from taxonomy—for literary history, interpretation, and analyzing the processes and cultural contexts of literary production—remain relatively dormant in Victorian and early modern criticism but have reawakened in the last generation.[15]

At the time of Newbery and Hurd, several other strong models were presenting themselves as a basis for criticism. We can speak of competing methodologies or orientations in a new, more complex way. The sense of a rich and long British heritage, with its own changing types of poetry, is one. Here, significantly, imitation of the past relies more heavily on style or stanzaic form than on genre. Not all Miltonic imitations are epics, in fact very few are. And certainly not all Spenserian imitations follow the kind of romance Spenser wrote. Is Shenstone's *Schoolmistress* the same genre as *The Faerie Queene?* As Thomson says in his headnote to *The Castle of Indolence* (certainly more Spenserian in nature), his intention is only to write in the "manner" and "style" of Spenser; he does not inquire deeply into definitions of genre or kind. New interest in Chaucer further complicates notions of older English genres; no dependable nomenclature exists to discuss the separate tales or "fables" and their generic origin in English or Continental writers. The rhetorics of the last four decades of the century analyze grammar, figures of speech, and phrasing, but pay less attention to genre. When they do, they exhibit new flexibility.

Increased interest in the psychological origins of the poetic or literary process—an "inner sense"; the association of ideas; the "origin" of aesthetic ideas such as beauty; the interest in "creative imagination," a phrase heard as early as the 1730s—these all provide, in a way that the four humors, five senses, and "wit" never did, a groundwork for studying literary works. (Wit itself, what Johnson calls "strength of mind," is not associated with a particular set of genres, but can appear in almost any kind of writing, including the tragic. Hazlitt and others stress the lack of synonymity between wit and humor.) The *Lyrical Ballads* are a new "experiment" in ballad revival, considered a "northern" or ancient British genre, but later are grouped according to mental faculties. Coleridge finally decides that the study of poetry should be based not only on poetic grammar and logic but also on knowledge of the faculties of the mind relative to each other, their separate functions, inner relations, and comparative importance. This he believes is the theoretical primacy of contemporaneous German criticism, its foundation not in literary kinds or abstract rules but in human faculties and their distinctions, such as reason, understanding, the will, fancy, and imagination. Latter day psychological theories of literature—Freudian, Jungian, Lacan-ian—reflect a similar desire to understand literary processes through models of psychic development. In the eighteenth century the stress is on analysis of characters in drama and, to some degree, on the nature of the creative process in individual authors. Thus, as more models for understanding the basic form and processes of literature accumulate, and as the importance of classical precedents in genre wane, the enterprise of a criticism based on kinds is squeezed and becomes one of many competing, though often complimentary, theoretical orientations—no single one of which may be considered more essential.

Readers and Canons

Before the eighteenth century there was no common reader. Perhaps we could say there were "gentle readers," which itself implies a social standing, but not the "multitudinous public" about which Coleridge expresses skepticism. Naturally, the "common reader" is a mental construct. Pope insisted that the various printings of his poems be handled to reflect the different intended audiences: in some versions names might be supplied and words italicized; in others the reader was trusted to know the individuals and supply proper emphasis. Coleridge whimsically differentiates common readers as sieves, sponges, fountains, or oysters, the last preferable for their ability to take a piece of grit and over time create a pearl. But the mere fact that Johnson can speak of his criticism directed at "readers uncorrupted with literary prejudices" indicates a shift in readers and critical discourse. Although I will not examine the growth of literacy or the specific impact of new institutions on readership (circulating libraries, an increasing number of printers, more available translations, the waning of patronage, or the explosion and competition of periodicals, among others),[16] this section will outline some implications of what all agree, though not always in the same terms, is a changing and vastly changed readership from Dryden through Wordsworth.

As late as 1762, in *The Elements of Criticism,* Kames was indicating social—or, more accurately, economic rank—as a favorable precondition to cultivating taste, which "goes hand in hand with the moral sense." This cultivation—in effect the development of critical faculties—"especially is the duty of the opulent," Kames says, "who have leisure to improve their minds and their feelings." Like many social critics, he fails to realize that events have overtaken him. Not only the opulent but the newly leisured classes who, if they chose to, can specialize in criticism, have sufficient time for refinement and scholarship. Malone, Burke, Coleridge, Hazlitt, none of them is opulent. The point is: not only does the new literacy and changing social order actively alter the content and forms of imaginative literature, it opens up criticism and critical debate to new audiences. Criticism is not immune from the rise in literacy or the "rise of the middle class" (however troublesome "middle class" may be as a term). Periodical criticism alone, the sale of critical histories and anthologies with critical introductions, the general success of treatises on aesthetics, instruction in grammar, rhetoric, and elocution—all this reflects a reading public that is not only reading more but reading more criticism too. While many novels and poems might enjoy only one or two printings, a number of substantial critical works go through edition after edition—Reynolds' *Discourses,* Hogarth's *Analysis,* Burke's *Inquiry,* Addison and Johnson's critical essays, Kames's *Elements* itself, not to mention the works of the New Rhetoricians, many of which become textbooks in universities and secondary education.

Some efforts aim to educate or inculcate the new reading populace, to teach them established and correct "taste." There is a degree of deferentiality, and a portion of the popular audience never gets beyond chapbooks.[17] But taste itself, including literary taste, registers social pressure. The paradox of refinement, discussed near the beginning of this book, grows more acute in a society that considers itself becoming more refined, yet in artistic matters realizes that it is, slowly yet inexorably, escaping the direct sway of hierarchical social authority, the court, and aristocratic patronage. And as literature becomes more of a commercial proposition, so does criticism. Many critical efforts and editions achieve excellent market success.

Readers are actively considered as responding to and helping to create the work and its effects. This is nothing new, but it can now be seen in light of a rich, fairly systematic, and current body of critical material available to them. Of course, we must keep in mind that an interpretation is often implied, its direction suggested or adumbrated by the author or text. But we also need to abolish the cliché that eighteenth-century criticism (and authors) expect one, univocal interpretation because the text is expected to be explicit and clear. For reasons too complicated to enter into here, that view has been the peculiar fate which much eighteenth-century criticism and literature has suffered. One reason much eighteenth-century criticism stresses clarity of language is its immense and keenly felt distrust of language, the realization—acutely observed by Bacon and then particularly by Locke—that significations of words and especially of rhetorical figures are highly imperfect and open to abuse both in creating discourse and in its interpretation. Allusion itself, working suggestively and not as mechanical memory, evokes a response not fully predictable or channeled. Only with high modernism do we find again a poetic idiom where allusion is so richly used to stimulate response and to enhance compression.[18] Narratives, even by supposedly the most "authoritarian" of critics, Johnson, call on a sympathetic and open response. What else could one say about *The Life of Savage* or *Rasselas,* where the conclusion concludes nothing?[19]

The literary canon is certainly not a fixed canon in the eighteenth century. The general conception of literature includes more than than it does now. Moreover, there was less to read. Any sense of canon in the eighteenth century carries with it more the sense of relative importance within a whole body of known literature than a judgment on which works should be read and discussed, and which might never be picked up. As always, some traditional reputations remain strong, others grow or erode. Cowley falls into relative disrepute or obscurity. Shakespeare becomes idolized, and Rowe enjoys a vogue. Satiric and didactic modes wane after mid-century, with concomitant effects on Pope and Edward Young, though they are still judged significant writers and reprinted many times. Collins and the Wartons, in the 1740s, try to revive the sublimity and splendor of Milton and Spenser. Wordsworth, fifty years later, attempts to reduce the artificiality and the sensationalism of what people read. The star of Erasmus Darwin shoots and fades with a meteoric glitter appropriate to the shimmering surface of his verse. The novel gains a vast readership, as do many forms of history considered by their audience to be just as much literature as the latest play or wildest ode. No one can unravel the skein of influences on canon formation with certitude.

The canon is to a significant extent determined by popularity. While canons and popularity differ, the eighteenth century does witness a new phenomenon: the direct effect of an expanding readership—and of the new social place of literature—on the past and present canon. Since Horace or earlier, one test of a classic had been the sheer survival of a work, usually past a century. (Pope uses this test ironically in his *Epistle to Augustus* and Johnson's *Preface to Shakespeare* echoes it: "he has long outlived his century.") As more people read, as literature becomes, if we allow the term its general connotation, "consumed," the canon responds to popular pressure. Johnson does not canonize Shakespeare, but feels he must explain that canonization. Aside from five poets Johnson wished to add to his prefatory *Lives,* the thirty-six booksellers and publishers involved in the joint scheme had already selected the other forty-seven poets on grounds that were largely commercial and popular. They had, incredibly, excluded James Thomson, whose reputation and popularity were still high. (Coleridge would later say fame was a well-worn copy of *The Seasons* found at a country inn.) The omission may have been because Thomson was a Scot and the publishers were competing for the poetry market against Apollo Press of Edinburgh, already selling a collection of English poets that would eventually run to 109 volumes.[20]

Often the impression of canon formation during this period is that "authorities" such as Dryden, Addison, and Johnson establish a canon through coffeehouse comments or published criticism. A little truth inheres in this; but as a complete view it is seriously flawed. It does, however, indicate that future generations reading those critics must grapple with and confront their strong, well-informed criticism. In that sense they have had a much stronger influence on twentieth-century readers and on students enrolled in formal courses than on their own contemporaries. And it is to some degree by the lasting popularity or controversy of their critical writing that they themselves have entered the canon.

Thinking about canons involves many questions, two of which are simple to formulate but hard to resolve. First, what is, or is not, literature? Second, what is good or worthy literature, worthy of "the" canon or "the" tradition (if there are such exclusive entities)? The first question is not much addressed in the eighteenth century; the system of the arts and of imaginative literature as distinct from other literature, and literature in general as distinct from other discursive writing, is not yet established with strong self-consciousness. It might be said that a social expectation is kept up concerning what an educated gentleman should know. But when we turn to the actual criticism, theory and practice, of the century, this kind of social or educational canon is not prominent and often seems to disappear, as it virtually does in Johnson's criticism.

Furthermore, English literature is not yet regularly taught in schools or universities, and would not be so, in a modern sense, until the mid nineteenth century or later. That curriculum change has continued to affect and to institutionalize canon formation as much as any other single social or literary force or event. In the eighteenth century the canonical texts are the classics, and even there reputations bob up and down. Furthermore, no English Academy or institution establishes canonical English texts; to a large extent this is done by the reading public and by critics whose existence depends on selling criticism to the public. Also the canon changes, as does acceptance of certain genres, as the reading audience changes. Fowler acutely observes that "A kind is doomed altogether when the education of its fit audience ceases."[21] In this sense it is clear that both canons and genres within them have a direct relation to education, to social values, and to the audience that buys literature for pleasure or studies it systematically in the academy. Finally, these last two distinctions, that of pleasure and of systematic study, produce their own canons.

A few instances are fascinating. In poetry, the novel, and nonfictional prose, those eighteenth-century works held in high critical esteem near the end of the century remain the ones that are read, anthologized, and assigned in schools. It has been said that the eighteenth century canonized itself. If this is true, and to some extent it appears to be (though certainly not in terms of what was taught in schools near the end of the eighteenth century), it may be a function of a relatively expanding reading audience and means of publication coupled with a relatively small number of actual books published (compared with the nineteenth and twentieth centuries). In addition, the later nineteenth century did not scrutinize Augustan and late-eighteenth-century literature with a changing, active eye. The attitudes established in 1830 are close to those of 1930. Only in the past fifty years of scholarship has the eighteenth-century canon been reopened more significantly (to scholars, at least). Perhaps canons constantly and significantly revised are a postromantic phenomenon, and some interesting recent shifts occur in the eighteenth-century canon. In the last two decades the prose of Addison and Steele has suffered tremendously on reading lists in colleges and universities.[22] This decline of once standard authors may be related to the social values and manners implicit in their essays, values that are associated, however crudely, with a bourgeois power structure, with weak intellectual "politeness" and polish. Or it may be that the essays require a strong historical imagination and are fundamentally impervious to many techniques and terms of the New Criticism. At any rate, these essays will reenter the academic canon as literary theory turns to social and political issues of ideology and to discourse in the public sphere as a key element in the sociology of literature.

The idea of a canon (though not called by that name) was an aid to establishing a national British literature. The idea of a "northern" set of inherent literary forms, voices, myths, writers and their works—in contrast to what was southern or Mediterranean—provoked interest in recording older ballads, in searching out minstrelsy and folk traditions. *Ossian* enjoys instant canonization and almost instant controversy. And, as one striking connection, Walt Whitman's marginalia to Sir Walter Scott's poems indicate the American poet's strong interest primarily in Scott's border minstrelsy as songs of the people, voices of the native inhabitants.[23] Indeed, in the United States, the formal study of English Literature could be said to start with a recanonization of the native English and Scottish ballads by Francis James Child.

Kinds of Criticism

When considering kinds of literature, we often forget that there are kinds of criticism too. Since the inception of systematic criticism, the literary judgments and commentary the vast majority of readers usually consult appear primarily in periodicals. Academic book publishing tends to obscure the fact that most—and almost all popular—criticism falls in the category of the *periodical.* Who can cast a secure judgment against the critical literature that originally appears in magazines and reviews and journals, as opposed to that criticism which finds its way into a book, or because it addresses a subject already contained in other books?

Every week hundreds of thousands of readers dip into reviews and essays. They may scan, in bulk, almost as much critical prose as other kinds. And, curiously, the criticism they read lends a further cachet to the book because such criticism is aimed predominantly at reviewing books. How many reviews or essays address themselves to single poems, other essays, lectures, or one short story? "Review" is almost synonymous with "book review." Furthermore, it is difficult to write an engaging *long* piece of criticism. Virtually none exist in any language. If we look at lasting works of criticism in any tradition, length seems a liability. The *Poetics, On the Sublime,* James's prefaces, Keats's letters, Johnson's essays, Coleridge's lectures, Goethe's remarks, Rilke's letters, Woolf's essays, or Barthes' studies—almost any influential twentieth-century critical statement: these suggest that criticism is a genre that does not invite length. A few classics are book-length, *The Lives of the Poets* and

Biographia Literaria. Yet these exhibit segmenting features: editors cut and anthologize them, with a loss, but not a debilitating one. To write books of criticism is a task with relatively few predecessors outside the areas of rhetoric and poetics (unless we consider line-by-line commentary and interpretation of a classic). In the modern academy "professionals" read and write books of criticism, but most other readers read criticism in essays, reviews, and articles.

Today the task of book-length criticism is largely performed in the academy (and reviewed in limited-circulation learned journals). Although reviewing in mass periodicals may be done for the same motive as in learned journals, it is more often done out of a desire to get paid, or to bring public attention to the work reviewed, or to oneself. Writing a book of criticism implies a specialized audience.

The relations between periodical literature, criticism, and the "book" begin in the Enlightenment, at least in the forms we recognize today. Johnson's "epidemical conspiracy for the destruction of paper" refers in large part to the criticism and commentary of the Grub Street presses for which he worked as a younger man. Most of the figures of literature and criticism we remember were involved in periodical criticism or essays: Voltaire, Addison, Johnson, Smollett, Coleridge, Lessing, Hazlitt, De Quincey, Goethe, and the Schlegels. Even Henry James, speaking from his own experience, called periodical literature "a huge, open mouth which has to be fed." Much of his criticism, outside the prefaces, comes in periodical form—more than two thousand pages of it, some republished only after a century or more. Taking the pragmatic view, one could say that the institution of modern criticism develops when the reader no longer can digest all the books being published and needs a guide to help judge and sift beforehand. In this sense modern criticism is a product of mass culture. Hence this criticism begins not as a specialized or specifically "literary" criticism, and not as a product of academic research, but as criticism in general, with a sense of literature at its core, but with major cultural issues—such as religion, economics, and politics—on the stage too, or in the wings. Criticism on a large scale in the eighteenth century presents itself to a broad enough leisured social audience to make it commercially feasible. One image of its spread and cultural significance is Cowper's description in *The Task* of the rural byway, its inhabitants anticipating, then immediately animated by, the arrival of the newspaper.[24]

Critics who have written in periodicals tend to veer away from the theoretical or dogmatic, at least in their periodical work. James said of Sainte-Beuve that the "very horror of dogmas, moulds, formulas" made him "one of the least doctrinal of critics." So an interesting set of relationships develops between literary theory and the form of criticism. Periodical criticism, the kind that most readers in a mass society—most generally educated readers—turn to, is not theoretical in essence. It never can be, unless it is also theoretical in a way that connects literary and cultural issues, as does Barthes. (Who, incidentally, rarely made the mistake of extending his critical books, especially his later ones, past the length one could absorb in an evening.) Theory appears in books or in academic journals, but in mass periodical form it appears almost exclusively in reviews of books that contain theory in the first place, or through essays written by interpreters or annotators of theory.

The eighteenth century sees, for the first time, what has become an entrenched phenomenon throughout the world of modern literature—a discrepancy, even an essential discrepancy, between books of criticism, books about "literature"—and shorter, more popular critical forms: single essays, reviews, and commentary in periodicals. It is fascinating to note that Johnson, Addison, Goldsmith, Smollett, Reynolds, Coleridge, Hazlitt, and Jeffrey all write periodical criticism and lectures, but comparatively little criticism—next to none—in a form conceived by them originally as a separate book. As the periodical work of Poe and Henry James is republished, we approach them in a new light, as more substantial critics. Those in the eighteenth century who do write books of criticism tend to be academicians, New Rhetoricians, members of philosophical societies, and professors of literature or moral philosophy. But what is particularly fruitful is the mutual communication and awareness—the intellectual crossings—established between periodical critics and essayists and their book-length counterparts working within the universities.

At present we are living with a range of critical discourse first introduced and permanently established in the eighteenth century. I am speaking here not about approach or methods of criticism—which have changed even as they continue to return to perennial issues—but about the forms in which criticism appears in print, the kinds of criticism. We are likely to continue with this range of discourse, for it seems entrenched. But perhaps the difference between the kinds of criticism and their audiences is also now more decided, with the result that academic books are more specialized and perforce carry less direct cultural implications of interest to readers outside the field. The types or subgenres of critical discourse established two or two hundred and fifty years ago remain with us as determining factors, often overlooked, in the nature of criticism as a large enterprise. The kinds of criticism erect crucial signposts in the relation between critic and readers—the critic's own audience. On one end of this spectrum of critical discourse we find the notice or squib, often simply announcing a publication (usually anonymously, presumably because no judgment or opinion is offered). We ascend to the periodical review with its familiar assignment of 750 words (or less). From there we continue to the review essay, a longer, more learned exploration with a book or books either as its centerpiece or as the excuse for writing a long essay on the subject matter of the books. Then we have the essay or chapter of a book, often transplanted from a journal appearance, and finally the scholarly book concentrating on one subject or author, parts of which may appear as articles or chapters in books elsewhere. The range is fluid, and one might ask whether it makes sense to delineate types: the kinds in which criticism appears are varied enough in length, tone, and audience. But there is a reciprocal relation between form, length, style, and intended audience on one hand, and the critical discourse and its boundaries on the other. Until these issues are more widely delineated, the roles played by criticism in society, education, and culture will be confused and made targets for easy generalization.

Such distinctions in critical discourse are highlighted in reviews of the late eighteenth and early nineteenth centuries. For example, Francis Jeffrey draws an implicit comparison between certain kinds of book-length scholarship (describing them in terms that could still be employed) and another kind of criticism that Hazlitt practices in his *Characters of Shakespeare's Plays*: "This is not a book of black-letter learning, or historical elucidation;—neither is it a metaphysical dissertation, full of wise perplexities and elaborate reconcilements. It is, in truth, rather an encomium on Shakespeare, than a commentary or critique on him—and is written, more to show extraordinary love, than extraordinary knowledge of his productions. Nevertheless, it is a very pleasing book—and, we do not hesitate to say, a book of very considerable originality and genius."[25]

It would be futile to develop extensive categories of criticism in the way Genette develops them for literary genres, or to expect that one type of criticism necessarily determines its content or insight. Generally speaking, it is the quality of mind, the observations and insights, the ability to arrest attention and make a text or idea come alive, that remain important. But the establishment of kinds of criticism, and the kinds of audiences served by them, helps to explain the varied functions of criticism. It suggests that certain forms—and hence certain styles of writing—are more congenial to one function of criticism than another. We see a sociology of critical forms, just as there is a sociology of kinds of literature in general. The sociology, though inexact, is worth examination. We can see too that gifted critics—Addison, Johnson, Hazlitt, even Coleridge, Arnold, Wilde, James, Eliot, Barthes—often succeed in using popular and accessible critical kinds.

The realization that literature is a business "and now learning itself is a trade" comes with a bold stroke in the eighteenth century. The twilight of patronage encourages the commercial institution. Johnson says as much in the offhanded judgment quoted at the beginning of this chapter (something, by then, Johnson took for granted from his own experience, starting the day he arrived in London). His phrase the "manufacturers of literature" resonates with his images of commerce in the *Lives*. Eighteenth-century criticism, like the rest of literature, becomes a commercial enterprise.

In the twentieth century we see an academization of much critical effort, and a potential breakdown in the fluidity between critical forms. As Barbara Lewalski has shown—using the case of *Paradise Regained*—the specific genre label of a work predetermines, in large measure, the kind of criticism aimed at that work. In like manner, a given kind of criticism largely predetermines its audience, effect, and reception. The academic book or article are examples. They also highlight the question of refinement and specialization in criticism, the differences and mergings of scholarship and criticism, esoteric theory, and "journalistic" comment. Where do they enrich each other and combine, and where does refinement begin to encounter diminishing returns? In the eighteenth century, the richness and interplay of various kinds of criticism, and their supporting institutions, reveal new social and economic infrastructures for both the production and the self-conscious examination of literature. Kinds, canons, and readers—and kinds of criticism too—remain intrinsically bound up in these larger structures and institutions today.

PART THREE

Methods and Aims

CHAPTER 7

Johnson and the Contraries of Criticism

He would often say the exact opposite of what he had said on a previous occasion, yet both would be right. He liked to talk and he talked well.

> PLATON KARATAYEV DESCRIBED IN
> *WAR AND PEACE*

Without contraries is no progression. Attraction and Repulsion, Reason and Energy, Love and Hate are necessary to Human existence.

> BLAKE, *THE MARRIAGE OF HEAVEN AND HELL*

In Johnson's criticism we see several motives at work—strong judgment, moral depth, an urge for reformation, a quarrel with authority or submission to it—all caught by powerful, compact phrasing directed at his fellow readers, not learned critics. Whatever the motives, one thing is clear. Johnson's positions do not stem from a constrained or rigid system, nor from a code of maxims built on fear of the practices of others simply because those practices are different. There is rarely anything narrow or self-righteous about his positions and their strictures. His actions and words are the product of thinking always alert to the opposite implication of whatever is being forcefully presented at the moment.

We rarely think of Johnson contradicting himself or being contradicted in conversation, something that seems as unimaginable as defeating Socrates in debate. It usually seems the other way around. After hearing an innocent remark by Thomas Barnard, later Bishop of Limerick, that it became impossible for a man to improve much after forty-five, Johnson tartly called out, "I differ with you sir. A man may improve; and you yourself have great room for improvement."[1]

Johnson seems always in possession of himself, a writer who has monumental strength of expression, certain and positive in holding the values he cherishes. But along with his habit of rapid composition, of conversation (in Ozias Humphry's words) "as correct as a second edition," he kept a habit of talking for victory, even of espousing, alternately, both sides of the same question, so that one came away believing him twice as opinionated as anyone else. Boswell notes that one could catch Johnson "varying from himself in talk." As Johnson frequently contradicted others, he also contradicted himself, a phenomenon nutured from early days with Cornelius Ford at Stourbridge and later with Gilbert Walmesley at Lichfield, when Johnson would debate both sides of a question, talking pro and con on any issue, each time inhibiting in himself the ability to strike out the alternate conclusion with equal vigor. He temporarily entertains and expresses more forcefully an opinion he finally rejects than most of his opponents express the opinions they continually embrace. The side Johnson was willing to have contradicted cannot be explained merely by psychologizing it, by considering inner fears and internal struggles (though those play a part). It is evidence of a larger dialectical play of mind true to experience, a willingness to entertain contraries or opposites to a strong degree, an open readiness to be honest and, ultimately, undogmatic; to achieve a doubled stream of thought that defies common notions of common sense. This tendency informs both his conversation and criticism. "Inconsistencies," says Imlac in *Rasselas,* "may not both be right, but imputed to man they may both be true."

This is why, as T. S. Eliot remarks, Johnson is a dangerous man with whom to disagree, the essence of which is not only that Eliot thinks Johnson is often right but that he knows Johnson can win critical debates by authoritative, forceful performances in argument that express more than others perceive. This commanding tone, yoked to a large surview of mind, can lead us, however well we know his writing, to respond almost automatically to Johnson as a critical monolith. Eliot publicly revised the tendency to view himself in the same way. In "The Music of Poetry," he admits a painful need to modify his early militancy. Some of it remains, but much does not: "I can never re-read any of my own prose writings without acute embarrassment . . . I may often repeat what I have said before, and I may often contradict myself." We may recognize shifts in his career (if only pointed out by Eliot himself) and analogous shifts in the careers of other critics as diverse as Dryden and Roland Barthes. But for many, Johnson unfortunately remains a critic who, like a statue, was cast. The youthful Swinburne, writing an Oxford essay he chose not to publish, reacts to Johnson's vigor of statement with an objection still common: "As Johnson grew older his character appears scarcely to have undergone any change. Right or wrong, his opinions never modified. . . . There was no hesitation about him, either in forming an opinion or in expressing it. This plan seems to have succeeded admirably. . . . At least, how seldom do we read of anything like a contradiction."[2]

Johnson's ability to see the contrary, even to act it out, must have puzzled less imaginative minds. For example, how could Boswell square Johnson's advice on refinement? Once Boswell had argued that refinement of taste is a disadvantage, for those who possess it must be less easily pleased than those who lack close discrimination. But Johnson denies this: "Nay, Sir; that is a paltry notion. Endeavour to be as perfect as you can in every respect." In other words, refine. But another time, Johnson bluntly advises Boswell not to refine the education of his children. "Life (said he) will not bear refinement: you must do as other people do."[3]

The Character of Criticism

Johnson's criticism contains striking examples of contraries, even of attitudes that may seem odd and, at worst, cranky or smacking of censorship. He chides Shakespeare for swear words. "There are laws of higher authority," he says, "than those of criticism"—a declaration that today puzzles or annoys some in the academy, where critics are their own highest authority or else, in an outflanking maneuver, deny that any criticism carries claim to authority at all. Nevertheless, Johnson's condemnation remains odd to most of us. Who would strike *Lycidas* from the library because it is "polluted with . . . irreverent combinations" of the classical and Christian? We tend to skip the admonitory remarks that do not square with our more elastic standards. Johnson specifically attacks *The Dunciad* for "the grossness of its images," and follows that censure with a general comment that "Pope and Swift had an unnatural delight in ideas physically impure . . . of which every ear shrinks from the mention." If Pope and Swift, like Lazarus and the dead man who touched the bones of Elisha, had come back from the grave, I wonder what satiric portrait of Johnson they would have added to their works.

No writer seems immune from Johnson on this point of propriety. Dryden is an author who might safely be put into the hands of any adolescent; unfortunately something not done often enough. However, even "In Dryden," retorts Johnson, are "*many* passages, which, with all the allowance that can be made for characters and occasions, are such as piety would not have admitted, and such as may vitiate light and unprincipled minds."[4] And we come to actual censorship if we believe Boswell's report that Johnson specifically wished George Steevens to "castrate" Rochester's verse for the edition of poets to which the *Lives* are prefixed.[5] Rochester remained castrated until the 1960s, when the U.S. courts shed their own inhibitions. The lost parts, privately printed before, were then restored to the public.

The larger question here is one of poetic justice. Not a single reader takes up the *Preface to Shakespeare* without noticing an inconsistency between Johnson's praise of Shakespeare's realism, its truth to nature, and his condemnation of Shakespeare for not following through on occasions where he might polish virtue bright and leave vice tarnished. We hardly consider this one of Shakespeare's faults. The subject, as far as Johnson's criticism is concerned, is rarely pursued. It is briefly explained, usually in context of prevailing morality. But something larger may be at work.

What is the list of writers whom Johnson calls to task for improper language, lack of poetic justice, and deviation from piety? It is an impressive one of distinctly popular English literary genius: Shakespeare, Milton, Fielding, Pope, Swift, and Dryden. It includes the great and widely read, authors whose formative influence in society could be expected to be deeper than any others' or perhaps all others' combined—and writers Johnson admired in many other contexts. The more estimable the writer, the harder Johnson could tax what he detected as slips of rectitude. (He seldom bothers to lash out at the openly bawdy or pornographic.) Johnson's inhibition about certain aspects of these writers stems not so much from personal shock—he would not be shocked in that sense—but from his ready awareness that literature can, in fact does, have a formative effect, especially on the young. He was, after all, criticizing the most popular and widespread medium of mass communication, self-education, and popular entertainment—reading.

There remain academic critics who deny any imitative connection between literature and life or between language and representation, and declare that art does not form character, or shape or damage human conduct. Yet these same people are often outraged by violence on television and in the movies, scurrying to guard their children from it; the next day in the classroom they tell other people's children that literature is an enclosed, self-referential system with no behavioral consequences.

Johnson knew that free moral speculation always has a place, but that its place may not be everywhere. Talking with Boswell and Anna Seward's father, Johnson is asked by the latter: "Would you restrain private conversation, Sir?" And Johnson counters: "Why, Sir, it is difficult to say where private conversation begins, and where it ends. If we three should discuss even the great question concerning the existence of a Supreme Being by ourselves, we should not be restrained; for that would be to put an end to all improvement. But if we should discuss it in the presence of ten boarding-school girls, and as many boys, I think the magistrate would do well to put us in the stocks, to finish the debate there."[6] The example may seem extreme, but before anyone thinks that it implies a banning of inquiry or an insulating of students, we should remember that the children mentioned here are very young and the children of others. Johnson's point is that literary and intellectual education does not consist in a facile assumption that one's subject has no ethical bearing on the young or on anyone else, an assumption which, if granted, would make one's job infinitely easier and less confusing.

Johnson at times seems an authoritarian figure, and even one who relished the idea of authority.[7] Yet he struggles with the authorities and in general distrusts canonized criticism primarily because it is canonized. The motto of *The Rambler* is that of the Royal Society, "*nullius in verbis magistri,*" nothing is to be judged by dicta—"We judge nothing by authority." (The motto derives from an old Latin phrase *Nullius addictus iurare in verba magistri,* used by Horace in his first Epistle.) As with Dryden, Johnson's later criticism becomes more flexible, less rooted in convention. But in 1765 his hesitancy to contradict critical authority of several centuries is so profound as to produce a written apology. It is informed not so much by an agressive humility as by a genuine minority voice, even an outsider's voice. In the *Preface to Shakespeare,* Johnson questions the unities of time and place, the prohibition against tragicomedy, and the prescriptive decorum of type in character. He then feels compelled to offer an apology, as if he had violated a canonical curfew of taste, which for many he had:

> When I speak thus slightly of dramatick rules, I cannot but
> recollect how much wit and learning may be produced against

me; before such authorities I am afraid to stand . . . because
it is to be suspected, that these precepts have not been so easily
received but for better reasons than I have yet been able to
find. . . .

Perhaps what I have here not dogmatically but deliberately
written, may recal the principles of the drama to a new examination. I am almost frighted at my own temerity; and
when I estimate the fame and the strength of those that maintain the contrary opinion, am ready to sink down in reverential
silence.[8]

This is no assumed modesty. Johnson, writing this, had produced little literary criticism in any systematic form, virtually none
between hard covers published as a book; and much that he had
published was anonymous. He had published less criticism than
Dryden, Addison, Dennis, or Rymer; the *Lives* were fifteen years
away. Although the unities had been questioned or even dismissed
before, successful playwrights of the ensuing decade, Goldsmith
and Sheridan, would continue to craft their work according to the
rules. John Newbery's *Art of Poetry* (1762) steadfastly defends the
unities, "because they are correspondent with nature, and,' the more
they are observed, the more perfect will be the Play."[9] Johnson's
preface seems to be arguing consciously against Newbery's specific
attributes of the unities as they add to the real psychological deception of the audience. (Johnson knew Newbery well enough to have
borrowed £2 from him in 1751.) French theater would follow the
unities for another fifty-five years. Byron seems to have had this in
mind as he wrote his preface to *Sardanapalus*. There we find a protest on behalf of the unities, according to what "was, till lately, the
law of literature throughout the world, and is still so, in the more
civilized parts of it." Francis Jeffrey, reviewing Byron's play, notes
that "Dr. Johnson, we conceive, has pretty well settled this question." Hazlitt was of the same opinion. But the issue was contested
over a long period of time. In his *Dissertations Moral and Critical*,
almost twenty years after Johnson's *Preface*, James Beattie was still
arguing at length the case against the unities of time and place as

"mechanical rules of composition."[10] Johnson's defense of Shake-speare's irregularity may itself derive from the complete shift in his own attitude toward regularized neoclassical tragedy. Though his first bid for literary recognition, predictable for an aspiring writer in the 1730s or 1740s, was the writing of a regular, formal tragedy such as *Irene,* W. J. Bate notices that Johnson "was to develop what amounted to nothing less than an obsession against the kind of play that he was writing."[11] Here again Johnson's critical opinions, seemingly set in stone, altered considerably.

There are many instances of an inherent tension or dialectic in Johnson's criticism, its internal contradictory play or, to use a less accurate word, its "balanced" nature. Yet it is never the shopworn, false dialectic of massing simplistically interpreted concepts one against another—classic versus romantic, English versus French, ancient versus modern.[12] Some examples of the strenuous quality of recognized opposites held both in solution can be given staccato:

—Johnson's revival of the metaphysical poets in the *Life of Cowley* contains both admiration and censure, respect coupled with reservation. After all, he chose to spend time discussing Cowley and a race of poets who, in many respects, occupied a neglected margin of English poetic tradition. When Eliot revived the metaphysicals in the twentieth century, he was echoing, though in a more positive tone and for other purposes connected with his own verse, Johnson's assessment.

—Approval of modern fiction as distinguished from older romance literature (especially in *Rambler* 4), yet with the qualification that the new fiction still fulfill what Johnson conceives to be general aims of literature. His choice to write on this subject can be seen too in the context of his own obsession with romances, insatiable at times, and so great that the language and vocabulary of romance literature colors his own writing, for example, in *The Vanity of Human Wishes.* Yet he tried to deny or inhibit this urge in his own taste, and warned others against similar reading habits.

—If we compare *Rambler* 4 with what Johnson says about *Clarissa* in one of his earlier letters to Richardson, we can see that he has changed his mind.[13]

—Of the *Lives,* the one devoted to Milton is perhaps the least sympathetic. Johnson felt antipathy on the crucial subjects of government and religion. But we might remember, when Johnson was traveling in France he delivered to the Abbé Roffette at the Benedictine Library in Rouen "a long eulogium upon Milton with so much ardour, eloquence, and ingenuity, that the Abbé rose from his seat and embraced him." The eulogy, entirely ex tempore, was delivered in Latin.[14]

—At a time when the pull of conventional wisdom was still toward criticism of the greater epic and dramatic genres, how much effort does Johnson devote to them? Comparatively little, and in this sense he is again fighting against prevailing currents.

—Like Dryden (and with Dryden in mind), Johnson becomes more flexible as his career advances. The *Lives* in their totality convey most his sense of dialectic.

—In his own verse Johnson leaves imperial tragedy and the imitations of Horace, Addison, Juvenal, and Pope; in his later years he strikes out modestly but definitely in a different poetic idiom. This reflects a changed attitude in critical judgment and values, a sense, if nothing else, that time is passing, and that what was once practiced will no longer wear. Again, the sense of being "cast" seems inadequate.

For all his change and even contradiction in critical attitudes, change that is realized over time, Johnson, like Dryden and Coleridge, does not overturn what he sees as the basic premises or ends of literature. (For instance, Coleridge conceived of the general functions of literature in 1830 much as he did in 1795, but his late poetry differs greatly from imitations of Bowles's sonnets and kind

words for Erasmus Darwin's couplets.) In fact, Johnson's critical
career can be seen as a struggle to free those views on the general
function of literature from the snakeskin of old convention or authority, to bring them into the notice of readers by changing the
emphasis on the means and processes entailed by the production of
literary works. As Joshua Reynolds noted from his own experience,
Johnson wants the reader not to think "properly," but with independence and strength of mind.

Johnson's judgment is always aware of another, more powerful
and lasting force—that of the public, the common reader, what
Coleridge calls the "multitudinous public." Boswell reports that
Johnson accepted "without a murmur" the judgment of the public
on *Irene*. "He had, indeed, upon all occasions, a great deference for
the general opinion: 'A man (said he) who writes a book, thinks
himself wiser or wittier than the rest of mankind; he supposes that
he can instruct or amuse them, and the publick to whom he appeals, must after all, be the judge of his pretensions.'"[15]

Reading over Johnson's works, and especially comparing remarks in
the *Lives* to statements made twenty or thirty years earlier, we can
see a critical *pentimento*. The general nature of the landscape has not
changed, but details, perspectives, and certain inclusions or exclu-
sions have been retouched completely. Aided by a searching cast of
light and memory, comparison reveals erased outlines of the original
opinion.

An analogous operation occurs in Johnson's character, or in judgments on the character of others: a realization that the first sketch
was not quite right, and something quite different needs to be said.
This might be described as the *butness* of his judgments, as described
in this letter from Richard Farmer to Percy: "but he throws about
rather too much of what some *Frenchman* calls the *Essence* of BUT:
in plain *English*, he seems to have something to *except* in every man's
Character. *Hurd* for instance comes off badly, and *Shenstone* still
worse: he pitys *You* for your opinion of the latter. indeed what he
takes from *you*, he gives to your better half—Mrs Percy's judgment
is, he assures me (where there has been an equall opportunity of

information) much to be prefer'd to her husband's!"[16] One thing
that makes this passage particularly revealing is that Farmer has
launched into his qualifications with "but" himself—and therefore
is partaking (apparently without design) of Johnson's "technique."
Perhaps technique should be without quotation marks, for this sway
and juxtaposition, this oppositional movement, the dialectic of
Johnson's thought, really is a technique, a powerful method, and
rarer than its apparent simplicity indicates. Johnson's critical prose
is remarkable for its frequency of conjunctions that qualify or state
contraries: but, yet, nor, however. These sentences are not so often
quoted as the pithy, direct pronouncements, for in order to quote
them a fuller context and interplay of thought must be given. They
constitute, however, as much or more of the fabric of Johnson's style
and approach:

> But good sense alone is a sedate and quiescent quality, which
> manages its possessions well, but does not increase them. . . .
> Pope had likewise genius.

> The attention, therefore, which cannot be detained by sus-
> pense, must be excited by diversity. . . .
>   But the desire of diversity may be too much indulged.
> (*Pope*)

> His similes are less numerous and more various than those of
> his predecessors. But he does not confine himself within the
> limits of rigorous comparison: his great excellence is ampli-
> tude. (*Milton*)

> He is . . . sometimes verbose in his transitions and connec-
> tions, and sometimes descends too much to the language of
> conversation: yet if his language had been less idiomatical it
> might have lost somewhat of its genuine Anglicism.
> (*Addison*)

> Oppression is, in the Abissinian dominions, neither frequent
> nor tolerated; but no form of government has been yet discov-
> ered, by which cruelty can be wholly prevented. (*Rasselas*)

That this is a practice contrary to the rules of criticism will be readily allowed; but there is always an appeal open from criticism to nature . . .   (*Preface to Shakespeare*)

It is indeed true, that there is seldom any necessity of looking far, or enquiring long for a proper subject. . . . But it often happens, that the judgment is distracted with boundless multiplicity, the imagination ranges from one design to another.   (*Rambler* 184, on essay-writing)

We can even see a similar dialectic or structure of contrary natures in *The Vanity of Human Wishes,* where, at key transitional points in the poem, verse paragraphs begin with "But," "Yet," or "Nor"— seven times. And in the last verse paragraph the vain oppositions of the meditation make their final turn to religion with the same turning:

> Enquirer, cease, petitions *yet* remain,
> Which heav'n may hear, *nor* deem religion vain.
> Still raise for good the supplicating voice,
> *But* leave to heav'n the measure and the choice.

Although Johnson's critical discourse (and poetry) is rational, sane, and full of control—especially in the *Preface to Shakespeare*— his principles and judgment, the larger sweep of his thought taken over paragraphs rather than in individual sentences, reveal a mind unconvinced that literature or life can be forced into a settled, rational system. There is always a tension between clear-sighted statement and the realization that one is walking on a sheet of ice, poking holes through to a world inhabited by other creatures fathoms below. In Johnson's writing, paradox or opposition is not revealed by paradoxical turns within a single phrase. He delivers it by a *tone* of dogmatic rationality alternating over longer stretches— often a balance of two phrases or even two paragraphs—which, for the mind with scope, is perhaps all the more powerful.[17]

Hazlitt called Johnson "a complete balance-master in the topics of morality. He never encourages hope but he counteracts it by fear;

he never elicits a truth, but he suggests some objection in answer to it."[18] Yet if we delete the adjective "balance" and its connotation of circuslike lack of commitment, and then read it as "a master in the topics of morality," the remainder of the description catches Johnson's restive insight into the restless imaginings of the moral life, itself riddled with contraries and conflict.

Henry James remarks, "Just in proportion as he is sentient and restless, just in proportion as he reacts and reciprocates and penetrates, is the critic a valuable instrument." This emphasis on feeling, even turbulent feeling, on saturation, on the reactive quality of intellect (akin to Johnson's "butness"), and on the way the critical mind reciprocates, penetrates—analyzes, seeks motives, means and ends—this is what makes criticism an instrumentality. It is interesting to recall Henry James's remark in *A Small Boy and Others,* that for the children of Henry James, Sr., "the literal played in our education as small a part as it perhaps ever played in any, and we wholesomely breathed inconsistency and ate and drank contradictions." James the novelist is clear too that the critical mind becomes "a valuable instrument," not an end in itself. Its instrumentality penetrates the human, it puzzles and broods; it enjoys dramatic experience, not just literary questions and forms. Johnson would agree that criticism is not an end in itself, but an instrumental activity that mediates, what in *Rambler* 208 he calls a subservient activity.

A degree of Johnson's contrariness or shifts can be attributed to the critical habit, prevalent in the seventeenth and eighteenth centuries, of scoring up the pluses and minuses of a work, its faults and beauties. Coleridge keeps up this practice in his famous critique of Wordsworth in the second volume of the *Biographia.* The *Preface to Shakespeare* adheres to that skeletal formula. But in Johnson a larger awareness operates, more than just a balancing of merits and defects. He must explain, as in the case of Shakespeare, why several generations of readers have reacted to the writing in the way they do. He knows that all writing involves choices, that style is not an absolute good or goal but a solution of qualities where doing one desirable thing may well hinder or prevent doing another desirable thing.[19] He does not dwell at length on the faults of a work—he more likely will be dismissive. And abrupt dismissals earn him a reputation for being curt and negative. (What is the use of criticizing what will never be read, he says of Akenside's odes; or he calls Gray's twin *Odes* "hothouse cucumbers.") But the bulk of Johnson's criticism dwells on positive achievement—or how one positive achievement can preclude another; not all that is desirable can be gained at once or in one author. As Nekayah reminds her brother Rasselas, "Nature sets her gifts on the right hand and on the left." Johnson's discussion of *Paradise Lost* is one example of this—the way he praises it but has reservations. We think of his quip that no one ever wished it longer, but may minimize the implication of his final statement that it is not the greatest of epics only because it is not the first. For any long poem written after Homer there is no higher praise.

In Dryden we find a similar desire not to be rigidly consistent, perhaps first put succinctly by Samuel Derrick in his introduction to Dryden's *Miscellaneous Works* (1760). Derrick remarks that "In his prefaces, indeed, we find him sometimes a deserter, and opposing his own arguments in a manner to which Dryden only was equal; he has appeared unanswerable till he answered himself." It is this very quality that pulls Johnson to admire Dryden's critical response, his "principles" that are not rigidly frozen as "theorems."[20]

A Criticism of Experience

Johnson, however strong in his own opinions, nevertheless felt wary about a prescriptive or dictatorial role for the critic. (Yet none could have provided one better—and was even expected to do so.) Literature might have as one of its functions a didactic, ethical role, but the critic could not pretend to define and establish the boundaries within which literature ought to flow. Once respected or even enshrined, it was too easy for the critic to become worshiped, but equally easy, Johnson also knew, for the critic to close off possibilities, to grow petrified, short-sighted or narrow-minded in judgment. In the pursuit of special distinctions, the critic might forget obvious concerns confronting the mass of general readers in other professions and walks of life. Literature was meant for readers without pretension to professional criticism. He might have been thinking of Pope's critics "For ever reading, never to be read," when "He declared that the perpetual task of reading was as bad as the slavery of the mine, or the labour of the oar." A friend reported that "He did not always give his opinion unconditionally of the pieces he had even perused and was competent to decide on. He did not choose to have his sentiments generally known; for there was a great eagerness, especially in those who had not the pole-star of judgment to direct them, to be taught what to think or to say on literary performances."[21]

As with fashion or religion (how quickly Swift had coupled the two in satirizing the abuses of both), and as with the arts in general, or even politics—pursuits in which informed opinions rather than uniform facts emerge as pivotal—the free mind needs to fend off threats of demagoguery. Although Johnson knew that opinions could be well or ill informed, there was little room—over the centuries or even over the decades—to set up as arbiter of particular literary judgments. After all, critics finally withstood the test of time not so much for their specific pronouncements but for their ideas, their play of mind, the ways they thought about literature, all of which become guides to the spirit and intellect, not dicta to repeat.

Johnson's powerful sense of contraries in criticism is bound up and acts in concert with an equally powerful side of his character, his rather surprising ability to contradict himself, to throttle back his own inclinations or temptations—in short, to inhibit himself in order to reach a greater sense of balance or correction, a fairer view of things.[22] His outspokenness, along with his personal and critical inhibitions, his measured reverence for authority accompanied by his bridling against it—this strong dialectic, which he describes as "not dogmatically but deliberately followed"—help give his conversation and criticism its unpredictable, refreshing quality. For this reason if for no other, as Johnson said of Shakespeare, "He has long outlived his century." We say Johnson distrusted literary and philosophical systems. I think this is in large part because systems do not readily allow of internal contradiction; systems are internally uninhibited constructs. They do not readily permit the progress of contraries, and hence they often do not allow for experience itself. Johnson's distrust of systems does not come from an "unsystematic" mind nor from such a strong sense of empirical evidence and induction that no larger, coherent generalizations can be made. He is always making generalizations. Rather, the distrust of system seems similar to that voiced by Auden as he closes the foreward to *The Dyer's Hand:* "A poem must be a closed system, but there is something, in my opinion, lifeless, even false, about systematic criticism. In going over my critical pieces, I have reduced them, when possible, to sets of notes because, as a reader, I prefer a critic's notebooks to his treatises."[23] Auden deliberately says "false," as if the very idea of system violates that vital imaginative freedom—by definition unsystematic—which wrests the "closed system" of an individual poem from the chaos and silent confusions of experience.

Finally, there is a special inhibition or prohibition in Johnson's criticism, a barrier that to today's refined and settled methods of proceeding in universities and journals seems almost unthinkable. We are all implicated. On the Tour in Scotland, Johnson observes "how common it was for people to talk from books, to retail the sentiments of others, and not their own; in short, to converse without originality of thinking. . . . I do not talk from books."[24] This is true, but it is astonishingly true of Johnson's criticism as well (and an emphasis Hazlitt too later stresses). Aside from the works of an author whom he may be writing about at the time, Johnson's criticism is amazingly sparse in reference to other books. Yet he knows the other books; he has distilled his reading, this man who knew more books than perhaps anyone else in Great Britain, more perhaps than anyone else in Europe and the New World. At least Adam Smith thought so. But Johnson's criticism is, even by standards of his own day, radically accessible, "uncorrupted with literary prejudices," as he remarks in the *Life of Gray,* which may be paraphrased as protected against excesses and vanities of learning inherent in criticism as an academic profession. Johnson many times stated his strong inhibition against mere bookishness. And yet no one could have indulged it more triumphantly.

If Johnson does not espouse a system, he is also *not* the preeminent critic of common sense as commonly understood. In "Of the Standard of Taste," Hume says, "there is certainly a species of common sense that opposes" whatever is merely proverbial or rooted in naive realism; "at least," he continues, this higher common sense serves "to modify and restrain" such tendencies. The higher mode "opposes" or inhibits what we usually think of as the rather one-sided, unimaginative passivity of common sense. Johnson's intellect and criticism belong to this higher species of common sense. It is common sense uncommonly and untraditionally received, a cast of mind constantly thinking how to reconcile the conflicting claims that life and art place before us, claims to which we find ourselves embarrassingly permeable.

This has been to some extent an exercise in biographical criticism, with "biography" taken in the sense of personal development and habitual operation of character as they shape thought and judgment. For no matter how "objective" (or purely ideological) one strives to be, no critic is free of the intrinsic connections between character and voice; character imprinted in the psyche holds a mysterious yet actual relation to characters on the page. The more one strives to "purify" criticism of character, the more it seems to come into play. When Shaftesbury titled his major work *Characteristics* (1711), he had in mind the widest application of that phrase to "men and morals and manners" in thought, literature, and philosophy. Johnson's own *Lives* do not sharply separate factual biography from intellectual character, nor character from its work. None determines any other; they are connected—not by formula, but by individual consideration given each writer, each work. In Johnson the bond between critical thought and character in the most capacious sense of character—which includes intellectual style—is strong and direct, virtually seamless. The self-examination of his life becomes alert and open to contraries; his criticism reveals the same. But

Johnson himself warns against expecting an author to live like his writings and be as wise as his words. This he knew not as a rote maxim, but through protracted struggles to rescue himself from what he considered his own "vain scruples" and debilitating inertia of rest.

I hope this view of connections between character, cast of mind, and criticism has not offended any who cherish Johnson as single-minded, always clear, and very nearly always right. But perhaps we should not be discomforted if we allow ourselves to disturb that construct of Johnson as solidly monolithic and unilateral, either in his combative dismissiveness or his sympathetic affirmations. His original attitude makes him one of our least dogmatic and, surprisingly, even one of our least authoritarian critics. When the political and social philosopher Graham Wallas was debating George Bernard Shaw, he read out loud two contradictory statements from Shaw's criticism. Wallas then beamed with triumph, remarking how Shaw seemed to be at least two different men. But Shaw leapt up and to the delight of the audience shouted, "What, *only* two!?"

A larger philosophical issue is at stake, as large as the elusive nature of truth. In literary studies it has been outlined in one instance by Peter Thorslev's learned book *Romantic Contraries.* But the issue surfaces everywhere, even in modern science. For example, Niels Bohr relates that when he and other "young physicists from various countries came together for discussions, we used, when in trouble, often to comfort ourselves with jokes, among them the old saying of the two kinds of truth. To the one kind belong statements so simple and clear that the opposite assertion obviously could not be defended. The other kind, the so-called 'deep truths,' are statements in which the opposite also contains deep truth." In the active process of discovery, in the intermediate steps of thinking critically, "deep truth prevails." There "the work is really exciting and inspires the imagination to search for a firmer hold."[25]

"The greatest error on earth," says Nietzsche, is the unwillingness to be contradicted. Or, he remarks elsewhere, "What is incapable of contradiction proves an impotent flatulency, not a truth. . . . The highest . . . would embody in himself most forcefully the contradictory character of existence."[26] It seems at first an odd leap from Nietzsche back to Gough Square or Bolt Court. Would Johnson accept such a challenge to his judgments? I think so. Consider *Adventurer* 107, with its gentle, self-conscious warning that "he who differs from us, does not always contradict us," for we "have less reason to be surprised or offended when we find others differ from us in opinion, because we very often differ from ourselves." As for his own proclivity to lock the page of critical judgment with a firm finality of phrase, he noted, speaking of hours typically passed in tavern conversation, "[When] I dogmatise," then I "am contradicted, and in this conflict of opinions and sentiments I find delight."[27] And delight, after all, is what literature—even literary criticism—can offer.

CHAPTER 8

The New Rhetoricians: Semiotics, Theory, and Psychology

. . . the third branch [of the sciences] may be called Semeiotica, or *the doctrine of signs*; the most usual whereof being words, it is aptly enough termed also Logika, *logic*.

they often suppose the *words to stand also for the reality of things*. . . . [it] brings unavoidable obscurity and confusion into their signification, whenever we make them stand for anything but those ideas we have in our own minds. . . . [Words] . . . come to excite in men certain ideas so constantly and readily, that they are apt to suppose a natural connexion between them. But that they signify only men's peculiar ideas, and that *by a perfect arbitrary imposition,* is evident.

LOCKE, *AN ESSAY CONCERNING HUMAN UNDERSTANDING*

The subject of rhetoric seems from the beginning to have flourished under what Johnson calls "the shelter of academick bowers," and those studying it have come largely from schools and pulpits. Most poets learn rhetoric from other poets. This is the short cut Longinus recommends when he says that Plato shows a way to attain the sublime without systematic analysis of figures of speech: "And what, and what manner of way, may that be? It is the imitation and emulation of previous great poets and writers. . . . For many men are carried away by the spirit of others as if inspired . . . from the great natures of the men of old are borne in upon the souls of them who emulate them . . . what we may describe as effluences."[1] In *The Minstrel* (I, stanza 43) James Beattie pictures his young genius seduced by the art of an aged, female bard, not by university lectures:

> Then, as instructed by tradition hoar,
>   Her legend when the Beldame 'gan impart,
>   Or chant the old heroic ditty o'er,
>   Wonder and joy ran thrilling to his heart;
> Much he the tale admired, but more the tuneful art.

Yet from 1750 through the 1780s a group of professors and divines—many of them Scottish and none of them particularly good poets, with the possible exception of Beattie himself—completely renovated the study of rhetoric and applied it to contemporary English literature. These critics, who might be called the New Rhetoricians to distinguish them from their more classical formalist counterparts in the Renaissance and earlier eighteenth century, altered the course of British letters and provided a basis for the romantic veneration of the expressive and emotional power of figurative, "natural" language. The New Rhetoricians, properly considered a unified movement, are, prior to the twentieth century, the most important and cohesive group of critics in English. The appeal of their lectures and volumes, often used as texts on both sides of the Atlantic, lasted into Queen Victoria's reign.

Depending how large a net is cast, the New Rhetoricians encompass anywhere from a half-dozen to scores of lecturers, ministers, and educators—anyone who wrote an essay on syntax or a how-to book on style and elocution. But the important names are few, though some transcend the group through other activities: Adam Smith, George Campbell, Joseph Priestley, Hugh Blair, James Beattie, and, if we stretch a bit, Thomas Gibbons, Lord Kames,

Thomas Sheridan, and Robert Lowth.[2] It was a great day for Scotland. Not until the mid-twentieth century would a group of English-speaking critics study, in so thorough and systematic a fashion, the psychological, semiotic, and linguistic foundations of literature.

Considering language as a series of signs and significations, time-honored terms they use with frequency and care, the New Rhetoricians became the first British critics to mount a collective effort to explain literature and literary form in the light of semiotics and the structure of language. Specifically championing the idea of "theory," they develop, to borrow the title of George Campbell's important work of 1776, a "philosophy of rhetoric." (I. A. Richards would consciously revive this phrase for the title of his 1936 volume, part of a larger attempt to resurrect principles of the New Rhetoric as a basis for modern critical study.) The last major rhetorics of the old stock appeared in the late 1750s, John Lawson's *Lectures Concerning Oratory* (1758) and John Ward's *System of Oratory* (1759).[3] The New Rhetoricians deserve their epithet, if only because their books are no longer handbooks, and they consistently refute Samuel Butler's charge of jargon and mere classification (*Hudibras* I. i. 89–90):

> For all a rhetorician's rules
> Teach nothing but to name his tools.

And although they draw on classical rhetoricians, they subordinate formal divisions, long lists of terms, and rote strategies in favor of a robust psychological approach, natural style, and a firm linguistic and grammatological foundation. Adam Smith, in his *Lectures on Rhetoric and Belles Lettres* (1762–63, but delivered as early as 1748) sets the fresh tone when he asserts that it was from "Figures, and divisions and sub-divisions of them, that so many systems of rhetoric, both ancient and modern, have been formed. They are generally a very silly set of books and not at all instructive." The new rhetorics—beginning with Smith's own *Lectures* and including principally George Campbell's *Philosophy of Rhetoric* (1776), Hugh Blair's *Lectures on Rhetoric and Belles Lettres* (1783), Joseph Priestley's *Lectures on Oratory and Criticism* (1777, but delivered first in 1762), James Beattie's *Essays on Poetry and Music As They Affect the Mind* (1776), and, to a lesser degree, Lowth's *Poesi Sacra Hebraeorum* (1753), Kames's *Elements of Criticism* (1762), Thomas Sheridan's *Elocution* (1762), and Thomas Gibbons' *Rhetoric* (1767)—remain useful explorations in the theory and practice of literature. Echoing their emphases, Jonathan Culler has said that the labels of rhetoric are "a sterile and ancillary activity. . . . But a semiological or structuralist theory of reading enables us simply to reverse the perspective and to think of training as a way of providing the student with a set of formal models which he can use in interpreting literary works."[4] Insofar as a single statement could suffice, this virtually summarizes the New Rhetoricians' program.

In its wider sense rhetoric means the power of language, and the art of rhetoric analyzes the means by which that power may be obtained. But the New Rhetoric was intended as both a complete system of criticism and a guide to improving style and taste. The New Rhetoricians invoke Aristotle, Dionysus of Halicarnassus, Longinus, Cicero, and Quintilian, but they wish primarily to establish the "radical principles" of language and literature.[5] And the literature they examined was by and large not ancient but emphatically contemporary. Rhetoric, they decided, derives from rigorous close reading, observation, and the study of the actual practice of writers. It goes beyond analysis and interpretation; it shows the structure of language in interplay with the process of composition, as well as how effective writing may be reinforced and faults avoided. The goal is improved understanding and improved praxis. Rhetoric begins with practice, proceeds through theory, and returns to the original acts of speaking and writing. Its procedure shifts between the descriptive and prescriptive.

Blair, in his *Lectures on Rhetoric and Belles Lettres* (1783), claims that criticism, taste, and rhetoric are nearly synonymous.[6] In academic papers we may indulge the luxury of separating them in a rarified atmosphere. As readers in the world at large we cannot. This fundamental message, which stands behind the best eighteenth-century criticism—coupled with an unwillingness to simplify or play down to readers—attracted Saintsbury so much that he based his history of criticism on the stance taken by the New Rhetoricians. For "the Criticism or modified Rhetoric," of which his book "attempts to give a history, is pretty much the same thing as the reasoned exercise of Literary Taste." This is not positivistic literary history at all. If Rhetoric avoids "the disease of technical jargon," which severs it from the generally educated public, then it can become "the Literary Criticism that it ought to be."[7] This is the ideal of the New Rhetoricians: to identify taste with criticism, not to separate the two. Blair "is to be very particulalry commended," says Saintsbury, "for accepting to the full the important truth that 'Rhetoric' in modern times really means 'Criticism.'" The New Rhetoric is nothing less than "the Art of Literature, or in other words Criticism."[8]

The revitalization of rhetoric flourished in the very places, the Scottish universities and learned societies, where the most interesting vibrant philosophical debates were being contested. Philosophy and rhetoric, philosophy and poetry, have been hot and cold lovers. The special purpose of rhetoric is not to instruct or to convey truth (though Bacon and some others thought it should),[9] but to persuade, to please, and to join those two effects in the most irresistible way. But if philosophy suspects the artfulness of rhetoric, it can hardly refrain from embracing it. One could, along with Quintilian, insist that the ideal orator and rhetorician be moral and honest, "such as to have a genuine title to the name of philosopher,"[10] but there could be no guarantees. Iago is a persuasive fellow, clever with words. Seen in a larger framework, rhetoric essentially cleaves to the worth of inventive, powerful language and, more broadly, the value of imaginative art. Rhetoric, so conceived, places literature in the context of our most pressing questions of learning, faith, and action. In an "information" culture devoted increasingly to the visual image and to quantification, and at a time when the approaches to literary study are scattered, it is salutary to return to this basic concept of rhetoric.[11]

The Psycho-Logic of Language

Even while pursuing elaborate systems and theory, the New Rhetoricians profess an empirical bias. Their theories derive from wide reading and return to specific, formative examples. At the outset of his *Lectures on Rhetoric and Belles Lettres,* Blair expresses the group spirit: "The rules of Criticism are not formed by any induction, *à priori* . . . that is, they are not formed by a train of abstract reasoning, independent of facts and observations. Criticism is an art founded wholly on experience." Hume, in "Of the Standard of Taste" (1757), likewise remarked that the basis for "rules" of art "is the same with that of all the practical sciences, experience." This "humble *à posteriori* method" is the one Saintsbury claims for his *History.*[12]

Later in his *Lectures* Blair affirms that "All science"—and by this he includes systematic criticism—"arises from observations on practice."[13] The method, then, is indeed "scientific," but Blair, Johnson, and others also consider criticism an art. Can it be both art and science at once? The answer apparently is yes, and the implication is that we waste our breath trying to decide the difference. As with many human affairs subject to general principles and relying for their expression primarily upon language, criticism, like politics, is at once a science and an art. It is a science but not an exact one.[14] It is an art, but not a fictive one. Aristotle begins his "Art of Rhetoric" by saying that his topic deals with matters of general interest "not confined to any *special* science," but that rhetoric is more than a knack and "can be reduced to a system . . . and such an examination admits it to be the function of an art."[15] George Campbell, like Northrop Frye, compares criticism to mathematics, but confesses that critical principles never attain the clarity and perfection of mathematical axioms. Some leeway, which is the essence of critical judgment, always persists.[16]

"Pure logic," Campbell says, cannot govern criticism, because logic "regards only the subject" or work at hand, "which is examined solely for the sake of information." Criticism must mediate. It is concerned with broader communication and effects. It considers not only the subject but "the speaker and the hearers, and both the subject and the speaker for the sake of the hearers, or rather for the sake of the effect intended to be produced in them."[17] Though some terms the New Rhetoricians employ are not now current (having been forgotten, and new ones invented or selectively revived), they pay considerable attention to aspects of "reader response."

The general claim is that any critic who understands both a text and responses to it must possess two kinds of knowledge: a command of interpretation and the possible significance of a text; and, in order to gauge the purpose and success of that text in rousing its audience and communicating with it, a psychological acuity—the critic must know the mind and the passions, intellect and emotion, as expressed not just in literature but in experience at large.

The New Rhetoricians are among the most perceptive psychologists of their time. If close reading was one leg of the stiff twin compass they used to measure literature, then the other leg was nothing less than knowledge of human nature—not as some steady and unchanging construct, but through personal observation, reflection, and study. One modern psychologist remarks that any of his colleagues working on anything other than language "is just wasting his time."[18] The critic becomes a psychologist in order to help the student of rhetoric become one too. In this sense at least the rhetorician is a humanist and a moralist—not a preceptor of moral rules, but one who studies mores. Quintilian made this connection centuries ago.[19] Its fundamental truth resurfaces in the university titles of several New Rhetoricians: they are professors of moral philosophy. To emulate great poetry requires an open approach to mores—to "life and manners," that key phrase informing so many pieces of criticism from Dryden through Hazlitt, and repeated by Johnson in his *Preface to Shakespeare*. This openness to experience is part of the reason Johnson readily forgives Shakespeare's mingled drama as "a practice contrary to the rules of criticism," for "there is always an appeal open from criticism to nature." We approach nearer "to the appearance of life." This is not so much a hot pursuit of some vaguely defined eighteenth-century image of permanent human nature as it is an attempt to bond together thinking about language and thinking about behavior. Priestley, who confirms that a person must be "in some sense, a *logician* before he be an orator," qualifies this statement immediately: "More especially is it of consequence . . . to be well acquainted with *human nature,*" with the "passions, prejudices, interests and views" of the audience—in short, with "principles of human actions."[20]

As schoolboys, most New Rhetoricians were whipped into mastering difficult Greek and Latin texts. They took careful reading as a matter of course. What they add is an insistence on the means by which passions, emotions, and human motives are portrayed through the use of language, especially figures. Riding the crest of the Scottish Common Sense School and the associationists' approach, Lord Kames begins *Elements of Criticism* (1762) with a rough introduction to psychology. Campbell's *Philosophy of Rhetoric,* first delivered to "a private literary society" in 1757, commences with "a tolerable sketch of the human mind," for only with this in hand, he says, can we "ascertain, with greater precision, the radical principles of that art, whose object it is, by the use of language, to operate on the soul of the hearer." The origin of poetry and of those imitative arts aimed at "internal tastes," and the "springs" by which these arts "can be regulated, must be sought for in the nature of the human mind, and more especially in the principles of the imagination."[21] This is a profound connection, a critical view that, perhaps more than any other single one, has shaped European and American literature of the last two hundred years: the principles of criticism become nothing less than the principles of imagination itself. As Coleridge would say in the *Biographia,* "The *rules* of the IMAGINATION are themselves the very powers of growth and production."[22]

Although we now recognize this as the main critical stance developing in the middle and late century, Campbell goes further and claims that not only is criticism based on psychology, particularly on the imagination, but the converse: psychology may best be understood through criticism. Would Freud or Lacan be quick to disagree? "In this view," rhetoric "is perhaps the surest and the shortest, as well as the pleasantest way of arriving at the science of the human mind."[23] Hans Aarsleff explains Condillac's importance for linguistics in a similar vein. Condillac realizes that "with the use of artificial signs, language puts thought in control of itself."[24] Grasped and followed to its source, the taxonomy of rhetoric does more than name or reflect, it analyzes states of consciousness and psychological phenomena. Linguistic tools belong to the workshop of the mind. The link between states of mind and figures of speech, between psychology and stylistics, was hinted at in English as early as John Hoskins' *Directions for Speech and Style* (composed 1599–1600), where Hoskins admits that, "though all metaphors go beyond the signification of things, yet they are requisite to match the compassing sweetness of men's minds, that are not content to fix themselves upon one thing but they must wander."[25] The mind will be delighted with its own activity, and will direct it, through the exercise of metaphor and invention.

Emphasis on psychology, rudimentary at first, matured rapidly. Above all, it meant, as Thomas Gibbons phrased it, that "Rhetoric is by no means restrained to the truth and precision of Logic."[26] It is not strictly logical because we are not. The passions are involved, and they are essential. No wonder language deconstructs itself. "So far therefore it is from being an unfair method of persuasion to move the passions," says Campbell, "that there is not persuasion without moving them."[27] Hazlitt, who studied under Priestley, imbibed this principle and John Mahoney has called Hazlitt's criticism *The Logic of Passion*. Its godparents are the New Rhetoricians. Unless wild and genuinely out of control—today we would say verging on the psychotic—passion strengthens all acts of the psyche, and its language. "When in such a degree as to rouse and kindle the mind, without throwing it out of the possession of itself," Blair claims, passion "is universally found to exalt all the human powers. It renders the mind infinitely more enlightened, more penetrating, more vigorous and masterly, than it is in its calm moments."[28] The idea of passion as the enemy of reason had been generally debunked by this time. Campbell desires the orator to engage "all . . . powers of the mind, the imagination, the memory, and the passions. These are not the supplanters of reason, or even rivals in her sway; they are her handmaids."[29] From here it is a short step to Wordsworth's concept of imagination as "Reason in her most exalted mood."

Every trope or figure may be grasped as the specific "sign" or "vehicle" of a feeling or emotion. Wordplay is mind play—or a play of passions—and at its best associates all our sensibilities. A particular trope or figure does not always represent the same feeling, but certain passions may be more closely linked with certain figures. A simple metaphor may show love or hate; asyndeton may express the excitement of anger or joy. What is crucial is that the mind is thrown into emotional activity and, guided by the meanings of individual words, interprets the figure in a way that heightens all feeling and perception. Blair sees the key to metaphor as abridged resemblance that creates a self-aware intuition: "The mind . . . is exercised without being fatigued; and is gratified with the consciousness of its own ingenuity." All figures are "prompted either by the imagination or by the passions."[30]

This attitude emerged into a science of psychology, and critics like Thomas Sheridan, father of the playwright and politician, decried the wide difference in "principles" and "definition or descriptions" contained in the "variety of treatises which have lately been published on the passions."[31] But Sheridan and others saw that inasmuch as rhetorical language was based on passion rather than "pure logic," it was foolish to expect it to communicate precisely, or to transmit exactly what an author intended. It is a "common delusion," Sheridan says, "that by the help of words alone" we can "communicate all that passes" in our minds. We need to recall that "the passion and the fancy have a language of their own, utterly independent of words, by which only their *exertions* can be manifested and communicated."[32] No human language operates like the binary code of a computer, a set of ones and zeroes, on or off. Our language is an almost infinite series of differences. As such, both in spite of and because of its flexible variety and richness, it cannot delineate a pure passion exactly; it will never be totally objective; it never offers perfected communication.

With the new psychological interest, perceptions of both nature and what it meant to imitate nature through the medium of language changed. "Truth to nature" became something of a complicated, if not stale, injunction. Nature may be external but once we perceive it, and especially when we express it in words, it is twined with the psyche.[33] We give it human reference—we humanize it. Nature is an endless text read with all our senses. Art ceases to imitate or describe nature and begins instead to imitate our experience of nature. Nature is unemotional; we bring to it our passion and express our feelings to others; we imitate states of consciousness not only by the meditative language of reflection but also through the text of nature as we inscribe nature in a psychologically attuned language. The New Rhetoricians establish a critical theory that becomes the spine of romantic poetics and criticism.[34] In many ways the New Rhetoricians have more in common with Hazlitt, Coleridge, and Wordsworth than with Johnson, Goldsmith, or Reynolds—though the changing emphasis of his *Discourses* (1769–1791) derives in part from Reynolds' acquaintance with the new rhetorics.

The stance of the New Rhetoricians produced immediate repercussions. As rhetorical language is used by the poet to animate nature—to express the peculiar interaction of Psyche and Pan—we find ourselves "humanizing nature," a gift Coleridge claimed for Shakespeare. The New Rhetoricians also anticipate Hazlitt's concept of "gusto," and what Keats called the "greeting of the spirit." In poetic language, the ideal of sympathy or sympathetic identification of poet with subject depends on similitudes, on figures of speech, if only simple metaphors. As Beattie tersely put it, "The philosophy of Sympathy ought always to form a part of the science of Criticism."[35] Character criticism, such as Maurice Morgann's *Essay on Falstaff* (1777), grew in interest and acuity.

Personification Reexamined and a New Criticism

In conjunction with the psychological approach to rhetoric and nature, at least three other ideas emerged. First, personification or prosopopeia was analyzed so that it hinged on the verb rather than on an adjective or noun. The more a human motive or feeling is attributed to a natural form or, more intensely, to an action of that form, the more effective. Blair marks three levels of personification. The "obscure degree" comes buried in common adjectives: "a raging storm, a deceitful disease." A higher level tends to personify substantive nouns (Johnson's Wolsey with "Law in his Voice and Fortune in his Hand") or natural objects as they act in sympathy with us. Blair cites Homer, Shakespeare, and Milton for this excellence, as when Eve:

> So saying, her rash hand in evil hour
> Forth reaching to the fruit, she pluck'd, she eat;
> Earth felt the wound; and nature, from her seat
> Sighing through all her works gave signs of woe,
> That all was lost.
> *(Paradise Lost,* IX, 780–784)

But in the highest personification objective nature and subjective humankind act as one. The forms of nature "are introduced, not only as feeling and acting, but as speaking to us, or hearing and listening when we address ourselves to them." This boldest use, so many instances of which are found in Wordsworth, is, according to Blair, "the style of strong passion only." So Eve, on quitting Eden:

> Must I thus leave thee, Paradise? thus leave
> Thee, native soil, these happy walks, and shades,
> Fit haunt of Gods? where I had hope to spend
> Quiet, though sad, the respite of that day,
> Which must be mortal to us both. O flowers!
> That never will in other climate grow . . .
> (XI, 269–274)

In sum, personification works effectively when it avoids abstractions, substantives, stasis, and mere description; it succeeds when it involves the actions and passions of nature and psyche together, breaking down the barrier between them until nature becomes a human cosmos.[36] Thomas Gibbons gives a similar example, the "case when Milton tells us, that *nature sighed,* and *the sky wept some sad drops* upon our first parents eating the forbidden fruit."[37]

Second, the New Rhetoricians reexamined the relation of poetry and truth (or "reality") under the headings of Kames's "ideal presence" or "waking dream," Blair's "pleasing illusion," Trapp's "wide difference between falsehood and fiction," and Campbell's "fiction of the mind" or "of the imagination."[38] All these, however interpreted, look ahead to Coleridge's "willing suspension of disbelief" or "negative faith," or even farther ahead to Oscar Wilde's "lying" and farther back to Sidney's "feigning," where the poet neither lies nor tells the truth.

What is the upshot of this concept of illusion or presence, this fiction or dream, and is anything added to its presentation by Dryden, Johnson, and Hume? (The topic is often slanted toward stage illusion.) Carried to its extreme, the position of the New Rhetoricians yields a remarkable conclusion: the pleasure or delight caused by the arousal and chemical-like mixing of our passions is produced by style, by a mysterious power or impression (*stylus*) of words as they cohere and create; all truth in literature is symbolic in nature because words are themelves purely relational and symbolic. Language can make contradictions to experience consistent, "disagreeables" can "evaporate," for a new mode of experience—an imitation of mind experiencing nature, not a copy of nature—is created.

Third, the New Rhetoricians became aestheticians by defining aesthetic values in terms of emotionally charged figures of speech that imitate perceived nature and percipient mind in interplay. The pathetic, the marvelous, the sublime, and especially the beautiful are to a large degree constructs of words as symbols as well as objects in and of themselves. Metaphoric language brings the sensuous within the bounds of intellectual communication. Without such language, without rhetoric, the aesthetic sense would be mute, even undeveloped. The dream of Kames or Keats awakes in "the fine spell of words," in poetry which "alone can save / Imagination from the sable charm / And dumb enchantment." Aesthetics and rhetoric are intimate allies, actually interdependent, a point stressed by Beattie's *Essays on Poetry and Music As They Affect the Mind* (1776).

Although I am not dealing primarily with aesthetic theory, we should note that the Rhetoricians looked with acuity at the verbal definitions and embodiments of aesthetic values. There were great obstacles to overcome: "no word in the language is used in a more vague signification than Beauty," remarks Blair. The word was never adequately defined and, by the late nineteenth century, began to lose currency as a critical term with any theoretical weight. Moreover, nature or experience as much as language may be the source of aesthetic feelings, but language is the only possible means of naming and analyzing those feelings and, as such, *any* science of aesthetics becomes bound up in significations of words.[39]

As long as rhetoric flourished, the beneficial effects of what we call the New Criticism flourished also. The New Critic is a species of rhetorician. Leo Damrosch has noted that Ned Softly, the character in Addison's *Tatler* 163, is actually "A New Critic striving to be born."[40] It is dangerous to equate "close reading" (in whatever context) with the New Criticism, but the two overlap. Critical examples and passages given by the New Rhetoricians are often exercises in close reading. Blair's last five *Lectures* (XX-XXIV) examine, paper by paper—even sentence by sentence—several *Spectators* (nos. 411–414) on the pleasures of the imagination, and Swift's letter to the Earl of Oxford. Blair's close reading, often done with real literary imagination, can also gauge rhetoric and stylistics with a micrometric vengeance. In one section he devotes almost a full page to the fact that Addison does not repeat the article *the* when he writes, "Our sight is the most perfect, and most delightful of all our senses."[41]

Many examples given by the New Rhetoricians are found later in the practical criticism and commentary of romantic poets. Wordsworth, in his note to *The Thorn,* cites the song of Deborah to show that "repetition and apparent tautology are frequently beauties of the highest kind." Coleridge, at the end of chapter 17 of the *Biographia,* cites Wordsworth, to show that "Such repetitions I admit to be a beauty of the highest kind." When Thomas Gibbons analyzes the passionate repetition of a word or phrase as *epanaphora,* from the Greek meaning "I repeat," he quotes as one example Deborah's "triumphal ode, where she describes the death of Sisera by Jael, *Judg.* v.27. 'At her feet he bowed, he fell, he lay down; at her feet he bowed, he fell: where he bowed, there he fell down dead.'"[42] These are the very words Coleridge uses to close his chapter. And when Wordsworth, in his 1815 Preface, commends Milton for describing Satan in flight as "*hanging in the clouds* like a fleet far off at sea," he echoes Beattie's praise that "Satan flying among the stars is said by Milton to '*Sail* between worlds and worlds:' which has an elegance and force far superior to the proper word *Fly*."[43]

Beattie makes it clear that rhetoric should bend language—especially the language of poetry—toward the *less* artificial, but also away from the merely commonplace. This principle informs his claim that "the utility of figurative expression" lies "in making language more *pleasing* and more *natural*"; or, "that by tropes and figures language may be made more natural and pleasing, than it could be without them. It follows that tropes and figures are more necessary to poetry, than to any other mode of writing." The poet, in quest of "sympathies he would communicate to others," speaks a natural language and "addresses himself to the passions and sympathies of mankind."[44] Wordsworth's 1800 Preface—in which the poet is a man prompted by the spontaneous overflow of powerful feelings, speaking the real language of men to men—is a short distance away. Almost forty—perhaps as much as fifty—years earlier, Adam Smith told his students that "the perfection of style consists in express[ing] in the most concise, proper, and precise manner the thought of the author, and that in the manner which best conveys the sentiment, passion, or affection with which it affects—or he pretends it does affect—him, and which he designs to communicate to his reader."[45] Smith was not specifically discussing poetry, but that is also to the point, for, like Wordsworth, he saw no essential difference between the language of prose and poetry. Smith is already supporting a natural rhetoric based on sympathy and affect: "When the sentiment of the speaker is expressed in a neat, clear, plain, and clever manner, and the passion or affection he is possessed of and intends, *by sympathy,* to communicate to his hearer, is plainly and cleverly hit off, then and then only the expression has all the force and beauty that language can give it. It matters not the least whether the figures of speech are introduced or not." They of course can be, and are particularly effective, "as they happen to be the just and natural forms of expressing that sentiment."[46]

Semioticians

Jacques Derrida begins a short essay that connects Rousseau with recent linguistic theory by stating, "Linguistics are becoming more and more interested in the genealogy of linguistics."[47] Several of his other points recapitulate what André Joly said ten years earlier (1972) in his foreword to a reprint of the 1796 French translation of James Harris' *Hermes* (1751), concerned, among other things, with the possibility of a universal grammar. Joly begins, "La linguistique, lentement, découvre son passé." And this discovery is not a retooling of literary history but a realization that critical theory has sometimes been narrower in context and background, more historically and philosophically naive than it might. Critics will increasingly find similarities and connections between twentieth-century theory and studies from the mid-1600s through the early 1800s. Derrida himself, in commenting on a "history of writing" in *De la Grammatologie,* notes the "extent to which the eighteenth century . . . is too often ignored or underestimated."[48]

The justified appeal and seeming novelty of semiotics results in part from a collective shift (or amnesia, as Morton Bloomfield contended) in linguistic study beginning in the early 1800s and extending as far as the middle 1900s. The ascendent historical and comparative methods did not emphasize the study of language as psychological. Jonathan Culler notes that, "Rejecting the link between language and mind, the nineteenth century lost interest in the word as a sign or representation."[49] In a longer summary, which Culler cites, Hans Aarsleff puts an open-and-shut case:

It is universally agreed that the decisive turn in lauguage study occurred when the philosophical, a priori method of the eighteenth century was abandoned in favor of the historical a posteriori method of the nineteenth. The former began with mental categories and sought their exemplification in language, as in universal grammar, and based etymologies on conjectures about the origin of language. The latter sought only facts, evidence, demonstration; it divorced the study of language from the study of mind.[50]

In other words, when the pioneer Saussure "came to take issue with his immediate predecessors, he returned," Culler says, "albeit at a different level of sophistication and in a different way, to the concerns of the eighteenth century."[51] While the New Rhetoricians claimed a posteriori methods for rhetoric and taste, their attitude toward language was a priori, and their richest exploration remains Campbell's *Philosophy of Rhetoric.*[52] The New Rhetoricians took the perennial concepts of sign, things signified, and signification and—with great flexibility—applied psychological and semiotic analyses to modern literature with an eye toward teaching effective and creative composition, all supported by a theoretically sophisticated view of the intrinsic bonds between mind and language.

Aarsleff maintains the importance of French linguistics, particularly of Condillac, in the eighteenth century. One of several corroborating evidences provided by the New Rhetoricians comes from Hugh Blair's remark that, "While the French Tongue has long been an object of attention to many able and ingenious writers of that nation . . . the Genius and Grammar of the English . . . have not been studied with equal care, or ascertained with the same precision."[53]

Many early adventures into the science of language proved ludicrous, dull, or impractical. Swift makes fun of them in Gulliver's third voyage. Rather than speak or write, and in the belief that things are truer than the inevitable deception of words, philosophers hand each other objects instead (a ready supply of which they burden themselves with by means of backpacks). Gulliver encounters a semiotic machine, a giant mechanical frame or billboard with small cubes that rotate individually and randomly to produce messages or signs. Far-fetched? The study of language relies on analysis and system, which can produce self-complicating Ptolemaic models that lose touch, however interestingly or stupidly, with the larger world. It turns out that Swift's story was not exaggerated. The pain of good satire is to realize that folly and cruelty are as bad as imagined. George Campbell avers that Swift's account "is not excessive, as I once thought it. The boasts of the academists on the prodigies performed by his frame, are far less extravagant" than Raimund Lully's magical circles of logic or Athanasius Kircher's coffer of arts, "Which in truth they very much resemble."[54]

The New Rhetoricians examine the fundamental nature of literature as symbolic communication. This rich and problematic study grasps the relations between words, ideas, and things. Locke is the seminal figure here in the English considerations. As Horne Tooke would note, it may be a mistake to call Locke's major work an essay on the Understanding; it is actually on grammar, language, and words. Hans Aarsleff asserts a pivotal role for Locke in a great shift in linguistic studies: "Locke stood on the line between past and future."[55] The discourse adopted by the New Rhetoricians—who were the "future"—sounds familiar to us and refers specifically to ideas, signs, signification, thing signified, and language as a vehicle. There is no *naturalité du signe* for the New Rhetoricians. Unanimously they reject it and, except for onomatopoetic words, declare our correspondence between sound and meaning to be "arbitrary." Campbell best sums up the position: "Language is purely a species of fashion . . . in which, by the general, but tacit consent of the people of a particular state or country, certain sounds come to be appropriated to certain things, as their signs, and certain ways of inflecting and combining those sounds come to be established, as denoting the relations which subsist among the things signified." In other words, "every smatterer in philosophy will tell us, that there can be no natural connexion between the sounds of any language, and the things signified."[56]

Combining the theoretical and practical, the New Rhetoricians conclude that communication by words must be imperfect. Words and things enjoy no intrinsic relation, as Byron laments in *Childe Harold* (3.114):

> I do believe
> Though I have found them not, that there may be
> Words which are things, hopes which will not deceive . . .

> I would also deem
> O'er others' griefs that some sincerely grieve;
> That two, or one, are almost what they seem,
> That goodness is no name, and happiness no dream.

So, although the New Rhetoricians agree that "In matters of criticism, as in the abstract sciences, it is of the utmost consequence to ascertain, with precision, the meanings of words, and . . . to make them correspond to the boundaries assigned by Nature to the things signified," they also realize that words signify not things imperfectly, but only imperfectly signify the ideas *of* things. They read Locke carefully. This is what Wordsworth refers to as the "sad incompetence of human speech," and perhaps what Shelley means when he has Demogorgon say, "the deep truth is imageless." Each phrase or sentence, even each definition of a word—let alone a long text—becomes a complex interplay of variously imperfect signs, a free play of differing signifiers.[57] All language thus proceeds by a kind of relational metalepsis (a point I shall take up in a moment). But however faulty, linguistic communication does operate within a range of conventions and saves itself from collapsing into "nonsense," where every interpretation is equally valid and itself equally interpretable into yet more interpretations. Metalepsis may be all we have, but it is clearer than obfuscation or total distrust of language. Perfect clarity or "true" communication is a mirage, a collective delusion, but at least one that keeps us walking.

Shelley briefly expresses the social and self-referential nature of language at the outset of the *Defence.* If our "social sympathies" develop and we use language to communicate what we see each do as "a social being," then "even in the infancy of society" we will "observe a certain order in . . . [our] words and actions, distinct from that of the objects and the impressions represented by them, all expression being subject to the laws of that from which it proceeds."

Metalepsis abridges the self-referential nature of language and provides a model by which words, as arbitrary signifiers, relate to each other in order to salvage sense from chaos. In metalepsis, as John Ward's *Oratory* defines it,

> two or more Tropes, and those of a different kind are contained under one word, so that gradations or intervening senses come between the word that is expressed, and the thing designed by it. The contests . . . between Sylla and Marius proved very fatal to the *Roman* state. Julius Caesar was then a young man. But Sylla, observing his aspiring genius, said of him, In one Caesar there are many Mariuses. . . . Now in this expression there is a *Metalepsis,* for the word *Marius,* by a Synecdoche or Antonomasia, is put for any ambitious or turbulent person; and this again by a Metonymy of the cause for the ill effects of such a temper to the Public. So that Sylla's meaning, divested of these Tropes, was, that Caesar would prove the most dangerous person to the *Roman* state that ever was bred in it; which afterwards proved true in the event.[58]

Inasmuch as each word in a figure, sentence, or text, side by side or in proximity with other words, signifies not only one thing or rather one idea of a thing or an action, but also may signify part of the confluence of many other words or tropes, we might extend Ward's analysis and say that all language and all texts (from *teks* meaning, among other things, to weave) proceed by a kind of metalepsis. All language is arbitrary; meaning inheres and coheres in the differences but also in the transitive identities of the signifiers. We must communicate with imperfect, self-referring signifiers or else, like Gulliver's dumb philosophers, hand each other objects. Naturally enough, many important acts in life still use ritualistic objects as well as words: water, bread, wine, rings, dust, ashes, candles, and eggs.

The New Rhetoricians see that the processes of thought and understanding proceed only by means of language of some sort, only by semiosis, and in language by the relational or generally metaleptic processes of signs and figures. We cannot think other than by signs. The mind not only communicates by images and signs, it cannot even think without them. Campbell asks pointedly, "what hath given rise to the distinction between ratiocination and imagery?"[59] Coleridge later proposed an essay on the impossibility of thinking without images! Rhetoric, which creates and employs language, not only is a vehicle, it may be viewed as part of thought itself. Words used habitually become icons of such power that they are "greater" than the nature and the ideas they signify. Campbell admits that the connection "between words and things is, in its origin, arbitrary." Yet, he goes on, "the difference in the effect is not so considerable as one would be apt to imagine. In neither case is it the matter . . . but the power of the sign that is regarded by the mind."[60] As for words that in essence become things, Childe Harold "found them not," yet later Byron in *Don Juan* (3.88) protests

> But words are things, and a small drop of ink
>   Falling like dew, upon a thought, produces
> That which makes thousands, perhaps millions, think . . .

Language is the vehicle of thought, and without it thought remains inert, not only incommunicable but perhaps unthinkable. The mind is an analogical organ and thinks by signs. Purely direct experience is signless, but it is thoughtless too. If the performance of language as a vehicle seems problematic, this is true with any medium. We do not encounter light as a particulate phenomenon also manifesting properties of a wave; it is simply a medium permitting us to see because our eyes react to it. Photons strike the retina, but it is not photons we consciously perceive. Yet, our cones and rods do react to light and not the actual pressure of objects that reflect the light. So it is with words; they become the photons of thought. Language as a "vehicle" is a premise of the new rhetoric. Emerson, brought up on the New Rhetoricians, remarks in "The Poet" that "all language is vehicular and transitive, and is good, as ferries and horses are, for conveyance, not as farms and houses are, for homestead."[61] Though Locke and Johnson use "tenor," I have not found it in the New Rhetoricians. However, "vehicle" appears abundantly in them. I. A. Richards was reading them when, discussing Kames, he (not Ransom) introduced tenor and vehicle in his own *Philosophy of Rhetoric* (1936).

Much of the new rhetoric depends on a realization that words are imperfect and slippery signifiers. This helps to explain the neoclassical and eighteenth-century obsession with clarity—not that writers and critics trusted words, but that they distrusted them and their possible abuses so much. Priestley urges, "A regard to *perspicuity* would direct us (if we would be understood) to explain distinctly the meaning of every word we use, that is of the least doubtful signification."[62] Language is a cutting edge blunted by use; it must be sharpened constantly. But the dialect of the tribe must be kept up, and for us there is only the trying. Campbell puts it succinctly: we try "to convey our sentiments into the minds of others. . . . Language is the only vehicle by which this conveyance can be made."

The New Rhetoricians glean fresh perspective on style from the general imperfection of language. This lack of ultimate precision and accuracy of language permits and encourages individual style. With perfect communication, style would be impossible. (Only "correctness" would attain—and this is the poetic value most prized when clarity of expression is at stake.) Priestley shows that by substituting and employing "other words of similar signification" in different orders and degrees of precision we arrive at a particular emphasis, rhythm, and sense. It is in the awareness and command of the elusive qualities of signifiers and significations, grammar, sound, and syntax that "the accuracy and excellency of style doth greatly consist."[63] Jonathan Culler has applied this principle to genres and figurative language: "One might say that debates about rhetoric and the appropriateness of particular expressions in specific genres are possible only because there are various ways of saying the same thing: the figure is an ornament which does not trouble the representational function of language."[64]

Ends as Well as Means

Near the beginning of the best discussion in the New Rhetoricians of language as signs and significations, "The nature and power of signs, both in speaking and in thinking," Campbell relates this anecdote of Lope de Vega:

> A certain remissness will at times seize the most attentive reader; whereas an author of discernment is supposed to have carefully digested all that he writes. It is reported of Lopez de Vega, a famous Spanish poet, that the Bishop of Beller, being in Spain, asked him to explain one of his sonnets, which he said he had often read, but never understood. Lopez took up the sonnet, and after reading it over and over several times, frankly acknowledged that he did not understand it himself; a discovery which the poet probably never made before.

> But though the general fact hath been frequently observed, I do not find that any attempt hath been yet made to account for it.[65]

This sounds like Browning's confession that when he wrote one of his poems only he and God knew what it meant, but thereafter only God. For Campbell this phenomenon leads to a whole treatment that merits extended study, but here I shall use his major points to summarize my discussion. Campbell establishes three connections through which signification and association work in a complex manner: "First, that which subsisteth among things; secondly, that which subsisteth between words and things; thirdly, that which subsisteth among words, or the different terms used in the same language."[66] The general background is Lockean, and Campbell relies on association in his analysis. The point, briefly, is that we use language so habitually and immediately that words, like living creatures, develop their own connections and associations; they form, as it were, a second nature. This nature is not identical, but analogous to our direct experience: "Now, as by the habitual use of a language . . . the signs would insensibly become connected in the imagination, wherever the things signified are connected in nature;

so by the regular [regulated] structure of a language, this connection among the signs is conceived as analogous to that which subsisteth among their archetypes." As a result of this habitual (metaleptic) activity, we do not always exercise the "leisure to give that attention to the signs which is necessary in order to form a just conception of the things signified."[67] Language begins to play with itself and become its own subject (as Novalis would proclaim in *Monolog*). We can be led down the dead end of nonsense, as Lope apparently was in his sonnet, but the same "insensibility" of the inner structural ("regular") associations of language also permits it to carry powerful meaning and feeling. Signs develop this power not because they are tyrannical or because we suppress our intentions, but because the mind, by constant association, seeks its own shortest route of communication and understanding, and that route admits language in its most symbolic or significatory mode. It is a question of mental and emotional habit and efficiency.

The New Rhetoricians establish a psychological basis for a figurative, natural language expressing the action of the mind in a state of excitement or strong emotion. More than any other group or critic, they also link our classical heritage of rhetoric, from Aristotle through the Renaissance, with modern semiology and linguistics. (Campbell's work especially demands more attention.) Yet the New Rhetoric presents no single synthesis. Ironically its insights prove inimical to systematic logic, for these critics realize that literature, conceived as rhetoric, derives its greatest power from affective expression. As Blair states, the poetry or eloquence, "which gains the admiration of mankind . . . is never found without warmth, or passion. Passion, when in such a degree as to rouse and kindle the mind, without throwing it out of the possession of itself, is universally found to exalt all the human powers. It renders the mind infinitely more enlightened, more penetrating, more vigorous and masterly, than it is in its calm moments."[68]

Some of the dullest books are those purporting to explain the methods and mysteries of great literature. The New Rhetoricians are dull at times, but they are rarely opaque. They avoid what Arnold later calls the "jargon of modern criticism." Many of them were academics, but they address the generally educated public. They assert that the *telos* of critical study is the persuasive use of language, not only as it scrutinizes our critical faculties and systems, but as it incites us to think, feel, and act. They realize that literature qua literature, as a separate discipline, is an ornament of society. But it can be thought of as a vital necessity if it furthers or is associated with other goals, cultural values, or larger concerns of human conduct.

As with all literary or critical movements that perceive literary values and styles not simply as ends in themselves but having at least the possibility of affecting human ends and needs at large, the New Rhetoricians neither subvert nor support prevailing literary taste. They prove both conservative and liberal, even radical and reactionary. They are at once scientific—that is, loosely systematic and empirical—yet their intuition rejects rigid positivism. They trust the perceptions of a developed, catholic taste and a trained ear.[69] Their major aim is to improve the practice of education and religion in general; they hardly set out to form a school of criticism, at least not self-consciously. Any one of them would first consider himself a theologian, economist, educator, moral philosopher, or public servant. One remarkable feature of their criticism taken in the gross is that we rarely encounter an explicit distinction between fiction and exposition such as essays, sermons, and speeches. (This is apparent as early as Smith's *Lectures* of 1748–1751.)[70] Literature, at least conceived from the standpoint of rhetoric, is for them one body. Many New Rhetoricians are divines who want their students to write and deliver good sermons and to read and appreciate not only the doctrine of the Bible but its beauty and poetry as well. We can say without exaggeration that one impetus for the new criticism of the later eighteenth century was religion, but certainly not with a doctrinal or moralizing streak. As Alexander Carlyle said in speaking to the General Assembly of Scotland in 1793: "There are few branches of literature in which the ministers of this church have not excelled. There are few subjects of fine writing in which they do not stand foremost in the rank of authors."

One example of this reasoned, felt use of rhetoric for the purpose of reflecting on the motives and ends of human action is Johnson's periodical writing. In *Rambler* 3—the allegory of true and false criticism—he asserts that "The task of an author is, either to teach what is not known, or to recommend known truths, by his manner of adorning them." In this same essay he asserts that there is a false and a true rhetoric. In Johnson's writing, Hoyt Trowbridge remarks, "The words and thoughts arise naturally from the intellectual and moral character of the implied speaker, and have added force because of it." This "naturally" has nothing to do with any supposed natural connection or *naturalité du signe* between words as articulated sounds and the moral values we agree that, however imprecisely, they represent. The words and thoughts, signifer and thing signified—the unit of the sign itself—arise naturally because the speaker believes those values and exemplifies them by action.[71]

The art of rhetoric brings the idea of *mimesis* full circle. As imitation may depict what Priestley (and later Hazlitt) calls the "principles of human actions," the end of rhetoric is to move readers and hearers to appreciate, to decide, and to act.[72] So conceived, literature is bound up with our every choice and experience, from polemics to simple pastimes to nursery rhymes (often first read as satires). The motives of writing and of criticism become the motives of human action at large.

CHAPTER 9

What Is Poetry?

The poetic function projects the principle of equivalence
from the axis of selection into the axis of combination.

> ROMAN JAKOBSON, "CLOSING
> STATEMENT: LINGUISTICS AND
> POETICS"

Those happy combinations of words which distinguish
poetry from prose . . .

> SAMUEL JOHNSON, *LIFE OF DRYDEN*

Eighteenth-century critics such as William Duff, Rousseau, Herder,
and their indirect heirs (including Hegel)—thought we should ask
instead what is *not* poetry. In almost all literatures and societies
poetry developed first. Prose follows as a descalation from poetry,
arguably a more specialized form developed as a by-product of civilization to facilitate more abstract and more specialized communication. According to many eighteenth-century theorists, the an-
tecedence of poetry makes it a more "natural" discourse. Thus
poetry should, to use the New Rhetoricians' phrase, embody "a
natural language of passion" with a premium on spontaneity. More
is involved than a reaction against so-called artificial diction established by neoclassical theory. Here the justification uses combined
anthropological and linguistic arguments appealing to far recesses
of time and hypotheses of human nature. Shelley summarizes de-

cades of speculation in his *Defence:* "In the infancy of society every author is necessarily a poet, because language itself is poetry. . . . Every original language near to its source is in itself the chaos of a cyclic poem: the copiousness of lexicography and the distinction of grammar are the works of a later age." Poetry attempts to erase the false refinement and discontents of civilization.

But technical or formal distinctions also pervade. French critics debated the border between prose and verse, inserting a middle term Dryden found useful: *prose mesurée.* Molière spoofs the silly side of this debate in *Le Bourgeois gentilhomme.* Roland Barthes takes it up again with his essay "Is There Any Poetic Writing?": "In the classical period" of the French tradition, he posits that "prose and poetry are quantities, their difference can be measured; they are neither more nor less separated than two different numbers, contiguous like them, but dissimilar. . . . If I use the word prose for a minimal form of speech, the most economical vehicle for thought, and if I use the letters a, b, c for certain attributes of language, which are useless but decorative, such as metre, rhyme or the ritual of images, all the linguisitic surface will be accounted for in M. Jourdain's double equation:

$$\text{Poetry} = \text{Prose} + a + b + c$$
$$\text{Prose} = \text{Poetry} - a - b - c$$

whence it clearly follows that Poetry is always different from Prose. But this difference is not one of essence, it is one of quantity. It does not, therefore, jeopardize the unity of language, which is an article of classical dogma."[1]

Later than Monsieur Jourdain and more defiantly, Wordsworth's 1800 Preface contends that the language of prose is *essentially* that of poetry. Coleridge, however, points out that by "language" Wordsworth in large measure means vocabulary or diction—individual words themselves rather than their particular combinations. This is crucial, for even putting aside the presence of meter, Wordsworth does not equate or identify verse or metrical *composition* with prose. Moreover, while fighting an already engaged battle against poetic diction, he has larger quarry in view: "Much confusion has been introduced into criticism by this contradistinction of Poetry and Prose, instead of the more philosophical one of Poetry and Matter of Fact, or Science." Poetry is the breath and finer spirit of knowledge, a belief Shelley holds too, as does Coleridge—when we remember that he defines a poem as that species of composition, unlike science, whose immediate object is not truth but pleasure. Wordsworth's primary distinction, and what is most representative about the Preface for romanticism as a whole, is not between forms of writing but forms of knowing. The difference is first a philosophical one. And for Coleridge, as I mentioned before, the first poet capable of writing a genuinely philosophical poem is, not surprisingly, Wordsworth.

In its postclassical phase poetry runs into several countervailing pressures. It becomes both more and less specialized. It revolts against poetic diction but champions poetic knowledge. Its "language" may in one sense be viewed as essentially that of prose—the doctrine of poetic diction wanes—but its function and meaning are more than ever potentially separated from fact and systematic understanding. The only way to account for an essential commonality of specific, individual words in both poetry and prose, yet a disjunction in paths to knowledge expressed through different species of composition, requires elevating combinations of words to a new level of importance, seeing figuration as no longer an ornament or embellishment of meaning but as a use of language generating new kinds of meaning and knowledge. What is being newly emphasized is not poetic language considered as isolated words, but as special structures and combinations of words embodying a more distilled, heightened form of knowledge and awareness.

We have at least one anticipation of structuralist attempts to define the poetic function of language. In "Closing Statement: Linguistics and Poetics," Roman Jakobson gives his famous definition. The poetic function "projects the principle of equivalence from the axis of selection into the axis of combination." Put another way, "similarity superimposed on contiguity imparts to poetry its thoroughgoing, symbolic, multiplex, polysemantic essence. . . . In poetry where similarity is superinduced upon contiguity, any metonymy is slightly metaphorical and any metaphor has a metonymical tint."[2] One commentator exemplifies Jakobson's statement this way: "When I say 'my car beetles along' I *select* 'beetles' from a 'storehouse' of possibilities which includes, say, 'goes,' 'hurries,' 'scurries' etc. and *combine* it with 'car' on the principle that this will make the car's movement and the insect's movement *equivalent*."[3] Structuralist poetics contains many similar examples. What Jakobson sees as an osmosis between metaphor and metonymy—the principle on which he rests the poetic function—is outlined by Johnson's definition and example. For him, metaphor is "The application of a word to an use to which, in its original import, it cannot be put: as, he *bridles* his anger." Here, "application . . . to an use to which . . . it cannot be put" replaces "projects . . . into the axis of combination." And "original import" substitutes for "axis of selection." Johnson is defining metaphor only, but implies a sense of metonymy and attains greater generality in his remark elsewhere about "Those happy combinations of words which distinguish poetry from prose." He repeats that idea in the *Life of Pope,* attributing to Isaac Watts an observation in *The Improvement of the Mind* (1741) that there "is scarcely a happy combination of words or a phrase poetically elegant . . . which Pope has not inserted into his version of Homer." (In 1802 Coleridge writes William Sotheby that poetry necessitates "some new combination of Language.") Finally, Johnson relates metaphor and simile in his last definition: "metaphor is a simile comprized in a word." For Jakobson, "Said more technically, anything sequent is a simile," including a single word.

Changes in critical concepts of poetry intensify about 1750. After that time no major poem in English directly imitates a particular classical model. *The Vanity of Human Wishes,* 1749, is basically the last. Moreover, defining poetry as "numbers" meets increasing resistance. In his essay *What Is Poetry?* (1833, published 1859) John Stuart Mill finally rejects the reply of "metrical composition" as "the vulgarest of all." The forms of poetry become less assured and less universally accepted. We see constant dissatisfaction with efforts to settle any theory of poetry on patterns in meter or rhyme, and more recourse to new definitions that stress either a philosophical import of poetry or structures of poetic language and metaphor. In other words, as we move into the later eighteenth and early nineteenth century, thinking about poetry becomes more theoretical and theory acquires new life. Philosophical and metaphysical burdens accumulate, either to be shouldered or shrugged off. "Poetry" comes to represent a new psychology, new Weltanschauungen—for some writers poetry represents nothing shy of a revolutionary view of the cosmos, a reinterpretation of the soul.[4] If poetry is the "breath and finer spirit of knowledge," as Wordsworth claims (what Shelley rephrases as "the center and circumference of knowledge"), this does not represent a feared retreat into specialism.

Yet the status of poetry is at the same time undeniably challenged, not only from within the literary sphere by the novel and prose fiction but by science and technology, by the development of history as a distinct branch of inquiry with its own ground rules and considerations, by law and ethics as separate institutionalized provinces, and by an expanding commercial and political world where detailed fact, "channels," "contacts," and professional vocabularies all proliferate. This new anatomy of learning, Arnold's "multitudinousness," could be said to specialize poetic discourse by increasing the number of discourses. "The cultivation of those sciences," Shelley says, has "enlarged the limits of the empire of man over the external world," but "for want of the poetical faculty, proportionally circumscribed those of the internal world; and man, having enslaved the elements, remains himself a slave." In the face of it all, Arnold clings to that most general definition of poetry as "at bottom, a criticism of life." He repeats the old claim that poetry and religion will eventually merge. Poetry had once swirled around the large end of the funnel of knowledge with room to wash large surfaces, taking in almost every human endeavor as related to its own expressiveness, avoiding the crushing duty of bearing a quasi-religious form of salvation, or of expressing profound experience and feeling culled and refined as "higher" and more "pure." But poetry now finds itself at the narrower end, under greater pressure, more expectation, more demand to assimilate and connect disparate events.

To deal with these pressures the high modernist critical strategy, exemplified by Eliot's earlier essays, jettisons transcendental or mystical dimensions of poetry and sponges off the taint of romanticism—what T. E. Hulme called "spilt religion." Eliot chides Arnold for clinging to large, inexact, and pious notions. In *The Metaphysical Poets* and *Tradition and the Individual Talent,* he concentrates instead on the complexity handled by a poet in connecting Spinoza, falling in love, the noise of a typewriter, the smell of cooking: how the poet keeps such elements "in suspension until the proper combination" arrives ("combination" again), "the pressure . . . under which the fusion takes place." Hence in poetry there seems now more pressure to encompass whole subject matters, yet poetic language and technique often appear at a farther remove from the varied languages and methods by which we accrue knowledge. A price is paid in order to assimilate disparate elements from many subject matters into a new, concentrated verbal work, a new way of knowing expressed through special combinations of words. Naturally, despite the critical rhetoric, many modernist poems—including several of Eliot's—are profoundly religious or mystical. The fact that his daily sensations (typing clicks and cooking smells) are prefaced by falling in love and reading Spinoza reveals something deeper, hard to articulate in any definition of wordcraft alone. What matter the poet combines (Wordsworth calls it, for shorthand, "sense"), as well as what words, remains vital but appears harder to speak about theoretically with any satisfaction.

Shelley believes that meter, however effective, is only one way to achieve the harmony required for verse, and that "Nothing can be equally well expressed in prose that is not tedious and supererogatory in verse." This attitude makes it difficult for didactic, political, scientific, or even satiric verse to survive. *Peter Bell the Third* parodies what Shelley considered Wordsworth's pedestrian side. But an exclusivity or rarified nature of subject creates new demands. We have here a widening separation of subject matters and modes of thought in prose and poetry—rather than any formal separation based on criteria such as vocabulary, meter, rhyme, or even imagery. This is a comparatively new emphasis in poetics. Eliot sums up the change: "Anything that can be said as well in prose can be said better in prose. And a great deal, in the way of meaning, belongs to prose rather than to poetry."[5] Thus poetry, reft of "a great deal, in the way of meaning," has one less leg on which to stand, but must run a faster and higher race. In short, it becomes harder to write poetry. And the logical solution, as Eliot sees it, is to rise to the challenge by writing poetry that *must* be difficult, and harder to read. In this respect poetry turns its back on the primitive and on a nostalgic search for essentials and sincerity. Instead, as a solution to the same, persisting pressures first faced in the mid-eighteenth century, poetry now becomes avant-garde, looks ahead and creates as the heroic task not what is narrated—but the study of poetry, which the reader creates as a new narrative with each reading. The knowledge now most pervasively developed in poetry is the knowledge how to read. The reader becomes the hero of modern literature.[6]

The form and nature of poetry increasingly bore these various pressures in the later eighteenth century. Milton condemned rhyme as "being no necessary Adjunct or true Ornament of Poem or good Verse, in longer Works especially . . . the jingling sound of like endings, a fault avoided by the learned Ancients." Few contended that rhyme could be the distinguishing factor. (Surprisingly, Goldsmith at times holds fast to it.) In his pseudo-ballad stanza "I put my hat upon my head," Johnson mocked the preconceived, simplistic ballad form in rhyme, meter, or an even easier combination of the two. Wordsworth quotes this parody in his 1800 Preface without realizing, I think, that Johnson is not questioning the language of "life and nature" or "real life;" the very thing he praises in Shakespeare's dialogue is that it is "level with life." As Coleridge would point out, once again agreeing with Johnson's practice while castigating him elsewhere, "Thirty days hath September, April, June, and November" is technically verse but hardly poetry. Or, as Coleridge says in one of the Shakespeare lectures, bad poetry is not poetry—it is not poetic language. Furthermore, by having primarily one meter—iambic—or, as Robert Frost says, only two meters—strict and loose iambic—English draws no clear line between prose and verse if only because so much prose and speech fluctuates to a loose or regular iambic stress. Artificial meters not encountered in the flow of colloquial speech would help "define" and set off poetry, but the thrust of versification in the eighteenth century presses toward meter less "artificial" and strictly regulated, one relying on an emphasis and accent coincident with measured speech where there is often a "continual opposition of actual sense stress to theoretical or artificial stress."[7] This suggests a particularly fruitful way of regarding Blake's blank verse. We might also think of Coleridge's reference to Cowper's "divine Chit chat," or to his own "conversation poems." In this spirit he subtitled an early work as "A poem which affects not to be poetry."

The necessity of a more or less strict meter as a criterion—or the sole criterion—of poetry was severely questioned. Pope observes the practice of his day, that "most by Numbers judge a poet's song, / And smooth or rough, with them, is right or wrong." So Chaucer had been viewed dimly for supposed roughness. But the primacy of "numbers" is stronger for Pope's contemporaries than at any other time in English verse. A drive for metrical perfection and flexible correctness, its consummate artist Pope himself, leaves prosody little room for further refinement along those lines. Johnson warns it would be "dangerous" to try. Other directions would have to be explored. As Emerson Marks notes, "Whether meter is an essential of poetic discourse or only a pleasing but dispensable embellishment has been debated since the beginning of Western literary criticism." Marks points out that Hazlitt, acting like a bellweather, ends by treating the subject contradictorily. But his "inconsistencies are . . . symptoms not so much of this author's befuddlement as of complexities inherent in the problem."[8] Meter might seem to have become one denominator of poetry in modern European languages. But Lowth's *Lectures,* extolling the poetic quality of Hebrew scripture not composed in strict meter but in rhythmical patterns and parallels, was only one of many influential counterexamples. Coleridge quotes the Book of Job in the *Biographia* to illustrate this unmetered poetry (as had Jacobi, already familiar with Lowth, several decades earlier). He also views Jeremy Taylor as a poet, a verdict he perhaps first read in Francis Jeffrey's praise: "we will venture to assert, that there is in any of the prose folios of Jeremy Taylor more fine fancy and original imagery—more brilliant conceptions and glowing expressions—more new figures, and new applications of old figures—more, in short, of the body and soul of poetry, than in all the odes and epics that have since been produced in Europe."[9] Joining Sidney and others, Coleridge considers Plato a great poet whose "dismissal" of poets ran counter to his own practice. Hazlitt already speaks of prose poems, pointing to Burke and other orators whose prose soared "nearest to the verge of poetry."[10]

In the context and turmoil of redefinitions, a short time after Pope died the question arose whether he was a poet at all (tantamount to asking, in 1920, whether Dickens was a novelist—as many then denied). A set of assumptions about the nature, form, and purposes of poetry had altered markedly for the generation following Pope. Johnson felt compelled to address these changes in his *Life of Pope* and concluded, "If Pope be not a poet, where is poetry to be found? To circumscribe poetry by a definition will only show the narrowness of the definer." But for a critic often blithely labeled neoclassical, Johnson's criteria for poetry are not formal, but require acquaintance with many writers and their works, past and present. The fact that Johnson—supposedly an authority, and by that time in his life regarded as one—refuses to define poetry says a good deal about the metamorphoses in ideas of poetry at large. In addition, in his discussion of genius earlier in the *Life of Pope,* he prefigures Coleridge's question, What is a poet?

It was becoming more difficult to identify "the essential nature of poetry" on grounds of diction, meter, line, stanzaic shape, or any formal pattern. The development of free verse and the prose poem become the ultimate recognition of (and for some the solutions to) this changed state of affairs. Some attempts at definition associate poetry with metaphor, metonymy, synecdoche, or prosopopoeia, but for critics familiar with the body of classical rhetoric and earlier English prose, this proves uncomfortable and restricted. The doctrine of poetic diction with levels of vocabulary appropriate to certain subjects or genres continues slowly to evaporate. Wordsworth claims no "essential" difference exists. Genre distinctions grow less durable. Few linguistic features now seem solely or even predominantly appropriated by either poetry or prose. Yet poetry is potentially crowded into smaller literary space.

New scrutiny of poetry is thus producing a potentially jumbled set of theoretical positions. A substantial body of stanzaic forms, line lengths, and metrical experiments had been accumulating since the sixteenth century. Poetry relinquishes to prose fiction and essays a few more leaves on the palm of belles lettres. Thomson and Young, Cowper and Wordsworth, stretch blank verse until it becomes several distinct voices, not just an echo of Milton but a flexible stress pattern bearing the successive stamp of individual masters. The traditional ideal of poetic mimesis or imitation mutates—it does not change categorically—and still lives robustly in Hazlitt, Coleridge, and Wordsworth. But it is an altered view in which descriptive imitation of outward nature and action hold a diminished place, expressive emotion and the auxiliar light of the perceiving eye an elevated one. Deep erosion occurs in the primary didactic or ethical purpose of poetry, a potential fissure between art's moral function and the ideal of maximum pleasure in disinterested aesthetic contemplation. Yet, at the same time, poetry is taken as a "higher" function of language, a "purer" form of knowledge that poeticizes the world.

Defining poetry has become unsettling and paradoxical, full of difficult, novel combinations and contradictions. Many critics will eventually demand from poetry those very qualities. It might be said that the eighteenth century and the early nineteenth witnessed a de-definition of poetry on the formal, practical level (not to be interpreted as a loss in vitality), and a redefinition of poetry on theoretical levels of knowledge and special, figurative combinations of words as "*the* poetic function." This is the watershed for modern poetics and explains Barthes' use of "post-classical" to describe that poetics as a whole. "Post-romantic" further describes its loss of idealism and uneasiness with any mission of transcendence. When agreement on a subject wears thin, as it does on the nature of poetry beginning in the latter half of the eighteenth century, one symptom is a surge to reestablish and redefine, which assumes a theoretical cast: present theoretical debate about literature and literariness indicates general lack of agreement on those subjects. But that debate may also be considered a new watershed.

Changes in Theory

Coleridge asserts that if we ask what poetry is, we must ask related questions: what is a poem? a poet? We shift to philosophical and psychological grounds—the quality of an experiencing, sentient mind as it writes, observes, and expresses itself in a stylistic whole, connected with its particular vision and reconstruction of the world: what we mean when we identify something as "Yeatsian" or "Joycean." In some (older) cases the identification, out of convention, remains based on formal qualities, such as "Spenserian" stanza or "Miltonic" blank verse. But qualities now sought in a poet could be seen as having little or nothing to do with the act of written— or even verbal—composition. "A great poet," Coleridge insists, "must be, implicitè if not explicitè, a profound metaphysician."[11] Wordsworth calls his brother John a true poet, though John never wrote a poem. Carlyle takes the stance that a poet might write prose or verse—or nothing at all.[12] Mill ventures that poetry is "something which does not even require the instrument of words." Friedrich Schlegel and Novalis espouse poetry as a visionary process by which the world might be transformed. Yet this psychological, visionary premise of poetic spirit does not require actual composition or a specific vocabulary. It may be interpreted as empowering readers, who in their own way become poets by imaginatively completing texts given to them as suggestive fragments or hieroglyphics. Oscar Wilde would say as much in his aphorism prefacing *Dorian Gray:* "It is the spectator, and not life, that art really mirrors." Poetry, or the psyche producing it, transforms and catalyzes into activity the psyches of listeners and readers, who in turn become viceregents or final authors. In other words, one way to reground poetry is to rise through the mystery embodied in words to a region pointed to but not occupied by language, to appeal to something ineffable as the ultimate goal of poetry. Silence assumes a wholly new meaning in post-romantic criticism and philosophy.

Other attempts at definition try to contain the fluid and imprecise nature of poetry, to set it aright after it had seemed to grow too correct and enervated. One bit of advice, its success largely underestimated, was to regard Pope and didactic verse as abberant, to retreat from the "good sense" of Pope (and some French critics)— to fly back to Milton's sublime and Spenser's fairy imagination. To recapture "real" poetry becomes the theme of many poems. Public poetry, poetry enmeshed in civic, social or moral issues, becomes less poetic. If *volk* sources of poetry were actually drying up and the solitary reapers growing less numerous, there was a rush to find— or to fabricate—them, all culturally related to phenomena such as ornamental hermits and architectural "follies." Throughout, Joan Pittock notes, "Attention is increasingly focused on the essential nature of poetry and on the kind of genius shown by the poets of the past."[13] The eighteenth and nineteenth centures often conceive this recapturing as fundamentally backward-looking, connected with the cult of primitivism and original genius. But turning back to Spenser, Milton, or Fingal threatens the premium on originality and uncovers few new subjects. It has a half-life of two, at most three, generations. Tennyson takes the epic story Milton had put aside, but the *Idylls* signal an end to older poetic mythology in English in the traditional sense, and Yeats's plays are that end. In modern poetry we see, without hermits and Druid temples, an analogous attempt to recapture or reinamate some essential or original use of language, to reestablish the revelatory novelty, the incarnation, of world in word. This helps explains Pound's fascination with ideograms and Stein's efforts to reinvent English.

A related attempt, free from liabilities of trying to recapture an uncertain, idealized past or an equally uncertain future, identifies and valorizes "pure poetry." Such poetry can be regarded as a form both of refinement *and* primitivism, yet historically less rooted than the latter. It is a more purely theoretical concept. The term does not originate with Mallarmé, but finds its way through the later eighteenth century in Britain in Joseph Warton, Alexander Gerard, James Beattie, and Anna Laetitia Barbauld, then in the United States with William Cullen Bryant and Edgar Allan Poe—thence to France—forming a line of descent in which each critic alters the principle of "pure" to fit a present theoretical need or justification of practice. In the *Essay on Genius* (1774) Gerard, for instance, separates eloquence from poetry, a move soon commonly taken for granted with an ease that would have puzzled Ben Jonson. It culminates in Mill's statement that "eloquence is *heard*" and "poetry is *over*heard." For Gerard, eloquence moves the reader but "pure poetry" chiefly "pleases." It requires no public or social (and hence no historical) context. Beginning with A. C. Bradley's inaugural address as Professor of Poetry at Oxford in 1901, concepts of pure poetry have continued to punctuate twentieth-century critical discussion, influencing Yeats, Valéry, Ransom, R. P. Blackmur, Alfred Noyes, Ernest de Selincourt, and others, including Allen Tate. Louis Macneice even began his preface to *Modern Poetry* (1938) with a counterstatement: "This book is a plea for *impure* poetry, that is for poetry conditioned by the poet's life and the world around him."[14]

For literature and poetics the issue of defining poetry involves not only what, if anything, differentiates poetry from prose, but what is the most poetical or purest of poetry, what lays claim to its highest offices and ideal purposes, and in what language or imaginative cast is that quintessential poetry found? This question had once been roughly settled by ranking genres and modes—epic/tragedy, greater ode, elegy, lyric, pastoral, satire, and so forth. Now, with kinds of literature—"kinds" being the English term before "genre" was adopted—fluctuating in relative value and undergoing metamorphosis in practice, older generic guidelines soon begin to lack authority. They already mean little for Johnson, who is distinctly uncomfortable in relying on them. The push for an ideal of poetic discourse could not be addressed by a hierarchy of genre, which relied too heavily (though not exclusively) on subject matter, meter, and appropriate individual word choice. It becomes part of modern poetics actively to scrap such strictures.

In late-eighteenth-century and romantic criticism the question of the "highest" or most essential poetry often is answered "Shakespeare." The reply is valid for Hazlitt and Coleridge and tantalizes Keats. But the elevating of dramatic and fictive verse—and the weight of individual phrasing—begins to crowd out other uses of poetry, once legitimate and accepted. The didactic, scientific, or narrative historical poem—anything dealing with fact and experience rather than with imaginative conception or personal expression—now in more direct competition with intellectual and narrative prose, could seem less poetic, not *echt* poetry at all. The immense popularity followed by the precipitous falling off of Erasmus Darwin's poems is one example. The explanation for his popularity, while it lasted, was not so much scientific or intellectual interest—not the subject matter as such—but Darwin's gift of glittering phrase.

Another strategy for distilling the essence of poetry was to retrench and insist on meter, but with a new rationale. This line of argument feeds into a larger theoretical position that promotes "pleasure" rather than "truth" or instruction as the primary or even sole aim of poetry. Richard Hurd defines "universal poetry" on the grounds (similar to Gerard's) that if the function of poetry is to achieve maximum pleasure, meter supplies that pleasure more consistently than any other single formal element. He admits that one "may include, or not include, the idea of metre" in the "complex idea" of what is called a poem. But in the same breath he contends "that *metre,* as an instrument of *pleasing,* is essential to every work of poetic art."[15]

Curiously, the impetus for Schlegel's "universal transcendental poetry," or *Universalpoesie,* probably came from Hurd's attempt to define "universal poetry." German intellectual circles avidly read him in translation. But in Schlegel the emphasis, by way of proclaiming a poetic cum philosophic revolution, is on "progressive" and "transcendental" rather than on prosody or pure pleasure. A kiss, a sign, a glance, *are* poetry if acted in the context of poetic spirit infusing perception and feeling. This *Universalpoesie* is, Erich Heller states, "an extraordinary notion, never clearly expressed but often hinted at with intellectual passion and aphoristic force. If we piece together many fragments on the subject, what we arrive at is a scintillating manifesto of absolute poetic imperialism: poetry must conquer the world, the world must become poetry."[16]

New definitions of the function of poetry alternate, remarkably, from stressing maximum pleasure to that of transforming the world. With the latter we are back again at issues of wisdom and knowledge. Keats calls this "philosophy," the value of which he debates with himself, and in his poetry, to test whether it lives at the core of poetry or is entirely foreign to it. In this dialectic, pure or disinterested aesthetic judgment is held in solution, or entertained simultaneously with poetry as a radical reassessment of reality itself, something necessary to "complete" philosophy—an interested and ethically charged undertaking if there ever was one! In Schlegel's universal poetry the aesthetic experience not only differs from concepts of the understanding, it replaces or becomes understanding. No wonder Coleridge and Schelling said that the poet's imagination must reconcile opposites—as must the reader and critic in regarding the function and definitions of poetry.

What distinguishes poetry from other forms of writing—or the "poetic function" from poetry in general? These questions still preoccupy major critical movements of the twentieth century.[17] Russian Formalism, the Prague Circle, the New Criticism, linguistic analyses, deconstruction, literary theories in general—all approach the subject from linguistic features and formal properties of poetry or the poetic function, from figures and tropes examined through readings of texts. The inquiry into poetry and poetic language will continue as long as rigid authority in criticism is, thankfully, in abeyance. But the lively, frequent theoretical shifts and the scope of this inquiry are comparatively new phenomena. They commence with the eighteenth century, experience relative quiescence in the later nineteenth and earlier twentieth centuries, and then return strongly. Johnson's observation can be quarreled with but not overturned: before Dryden, English had "no poetical diction." Yet even in Johnson's lifetime that diction, other formal mechanisms, and then the philosophical expectations placed on poetry undergo increasing scrutiny. What Barthes calls "the unity of language" has been broken, and so, not coincidentally, has the unity of knowledge.

Although Jakobson is speaking about poetic function, which occurs in verse and prose, and Johnson about poetry distinguished from prose, they share a sense that "happy" *combinations,* that is, successful and new combinations, constitute what we call poetic—not lists of figures of speech as such, nor lists of individual words admitted or proscribed from certain types of poetry. In this sense of word combinations, the poetic function of language is less predictable than that of prose. As James Merrill puts it in his foreword to Richard Kenney's *Evolution of the Flightless Bird,* we look for "a hole in one at word golf." The poetic is fusive and inventive, exhibiting a degree of what might be called natural novelty, attractive yet unsettling. It plays on the expected and familiar in order to introduce new verbal arrangement. Increasingly, what has been sought since the time of Pope are individual words in unique, successful combinations never previously encountered in the language. But increasingly with this variation on Pope's definition of true wit: the new combinations of words do not seek to express what "oft was thought." Instead, they become more ends in themselves, and their agency creates the highest form of originality in writing.

A reconsideration of the nature of poetry can help to keep poetry vital, a different matter entirely than circumscribing it by definition. Even in one language or national tradition, poetry is not a static property of linguistic signs, nor a stable psychological profile of the poet, nor a set of aesthetic or ethical criteria imposed by society. Poetry is none of these exclusively, yet it partakes of each, shifting emphasis between them to meet varied demands: adverse reaction to—or admiration of—past poetry and tradition ("revisionism"), the advent of philosophical ideas or theories of psychology, a culture's dominant values, and poets who establish a new mode.

In all these theoretical reassessments of poetry two main sources of torque from 1660 to 1820 still exert great force. One, the belief that poetry creates greatest pleasure by imitating feeling or passion, I shall examine near the end of this chapter. The second concerns poetry as the most "efficient" use of language—not that it provides more information, but that poetry calls on more rseources of language simultaneously. Greatest linguistic economy and play, and, not inconsequentially, greatest psychological effectiveness result. The language is compact or compressed. (Earned silence, silence after speech, is a special case of this efficiency.) This reverses the classical notion, albeit simplified, of poetry as thought plus ornamentation and meter, which makes poetry more enjoyable but presumably less "efficient" because of its amplitude and dilation. For the poet, the reversal that occurs in the later eighteenth century means more formal license and freedom, but also more expectation, more weight on magic of phrasing, and a more symbolic, suggestive use of words. The symbol—or symbolism in general—may be viewed as a specially adapted technique to achieve efficiency in language, as well as one that splits what Barthes calls "the unity of language" wide apart. The more the unity of language is violated, potentially the greater is its efficiency, for the violation (in this case the symbol) becomes a code that not only expresses but reflects and recalls the common usage from which it has distinguished, but not divided, itself.

A "unity" of effect in poetry, the interpenetration of parts, is a favorite theme of Coleridge and helps explain his reliance on phrases such as "multeity in unity." It achieves its most rational, rather flat formulation in Hegel.[18] No single element in poetry is exclusively and at all times, as Wordsworth said of meter, merely a "superaddition" in the sense of being tacked on without acting upon—and reacting with—the whole. Everything stirs, at once catalytic and reactive. Hence any definition of poetry short enough to remember will inevitably prove inadequate. Its purpose will be polemical, or an attempt to correct some perceived defect in actual practice. Some poems are classics, but a classic definition of poetry cannot exist.

In accord with the stress on efficiency or unity, poetry as a speaking picture, *ut pictura poesis,* is replaced more by *ut musica poesis.* Music has temporal harmony and rhythm, which though not synonymous with rhyme and meter, nor with any specific features such as assonance, alliteration, vowel interplay, or caesuras, nevertheless form in musical composition an ensemble unique to each work and analogous to effects in poetry. (Art, harmony, and articulation share the same Indo-European root.) In addition, phrasing, theme, leitmotiv, beat, pitch, voice, quotation, tone, echo, mood—all come into play: even more than with literature or painting, critical vocabulary links music with poetry. Then, especially in the later eighteenth and early nineteenth century, the ideal nature of music, or of its ideal structural patterns, becomes related to the ideal nature of poetry. Beattie's *Essays on Poetry and Music as They Affect the Mind,* Daniel Webb's *Observations on the Correspondence between Poetry and Music,* Hurd's "Idea of Universal Poetry," Schelling's *Philosophie der Kunst,* Carlyle's paean to music, all descant on the subject. Webb makes a salient observtion about the effect of the musical analogy on the prizing of poetic form: "The constant and even tenor of the couplet secures it from falling into . . . relaxations; a security, however, in which the poet hath little reason to triumph, while the perpetual returns of similar impressions lie like weights upon our spirits, and oppress the imagination. Strong passions . . . were never destined to creep through monotonous parallels; they call for a more liberal rhythmus . . . measured by sentiment, and flowing in ever new yet musical proportions." As poetry focuses more on the individual voice and an inward emotional life, so music is similarly seen, in Schopenhauer's description, as the expression of individual will, "an objectification and copy of the will itself."[19]

Discrepancy in Practice

In definitions of poetry and in theoretical discussions of its aesthetic or stylistic values we always reckon with some discrepancy between criticism and contemporary practice. From 1660 to 1740 two central ideals in poetry—and, for many, the highest—were the heroic and the sublime. Criticism devotes comparatively less space to satire and virtually none to mock heroic. Yet poetry during that same period exhibits the greatest mock heroic and satire in the language.

In the Romantic period the plays of Shakespeare become the supreme English exposition of sympathetic, creative imagination. But romantic criticism—much of the best of it in Keats, Coleridge, De Quincey, and Hazlitt—centers on Shakespeare's characters and language, not his dramatic or structural gifts; no play in the Romantic period rekindles the form of Shakespearean theater. Better efforts strike us, in Byron's phrase, as "mental theater," usually where one individual character or the force of phrasing carry the production's weight. Hence romantic criticism sounds as if it is praising Shakespearean drama when it is really praising portrayal of psychology and those combinations of words that characterize poetry in general. The particular emphases of romantic Shakespearean criticism make it harder, not easier, to reproduce poetic drama for the living theater. Eliot recognized this; it explains why he called for a return to the "conventions" of the Elizabethan stage.

Though no strict rule applies, the larger picture is one where criticism is often out of phase. It does not always work synchronically with poetic production. Critics may valorize and analyze qualities that poets are not pursuing at the moment but have produced in the past or may be incited to produce in the future. Arnold saw a cycle of critical and creative ages. This is a partial truth, which should not be trivialized, but it oversimplifies matters. It would be better to say that the overall center of gravity shifts between creative and critical efforts. Sometimes one, sometimes the other heralds important change. Rarely do the two work in tandem. When they do, they signal a new and powerful sensibility. The inauguration of what, for better or worse, we call "periods" or "movements," points to that rare union, often in the figure of major poet-critics. The commencement and creation of literary movements may best be defined as the relative conjunction of new theory with new practice, one which is never perfect. Such conjunctions mark the inceptions of Romanticism and Modernism. Victorianism is a special case, for it is more a product of a cultural amalgam than a literary vanguard. Romantic practice changes, becomes acculturated, and then, during the aesthetic movement and its ensuing "decadence," rejects that acculturation. Arnold tries to steer that acculturation but simultaneously combats many of its aspects. Victorian literature constitutes a period but not a movement.

Interpretation, Ideality, and Poetry as a Double Sign

Newer definitions of poetry in the latter half of the eighteenth century create a potential impasse for interpretatiaon, one that has engaged criticism ever since and provided matter for an unending series of publications. With stress on immediate feeling and on the nature of words, especially figurative language, as not strictly logical and therefore not logical at all when pressed by readings only tepid for certainty, the poem becomes an utterance or composition that *must* escape pure ratiocination or understanding. It must escape any interpretation itself not expressed in figurative language. For example, in defining universal poetry Hurd says figurative expression "is universally pleasing"; therefore "truth of representation" is "of less account in this way of composition, than the livelines of it."[20] To escape, not only from "truth" but from "understanding," is part of its theoretical mission. As Hume pointed out in midcentury, although poetry is not totally unintelligible or perfectly irrational, it cannot justly be called rational either. And the more poetic composition is assumed to consist in impassioned figurative language, the more any paraphrase or interpretation based on analytic comparison and understanding alone will deny or run afoul of itself.

Schelling, the most idealistic of German aestheticians, insisted near
the end of *System of Transcendental Idealism* that the work of art,
especially the work of genius, presents a virtual infinity of perspectives, an irreducible number of interpretations (which is not to say,
however, that any and all interpretations are valid). In this manner,
we can see in poems the seeds of their own destruction or decomposition, their self-consuming and rebirth. That realization forms
the essential burden of much late-eighteenth-century and romantic
theory from the start: the irreducibility of imaginative language into
prose of the merely reflective faculty of Understanding. Furthermore, poetry itself—with its metaphors and feelings expressed in
figures and personifications—is often considered but a fading coal,
a shadow of the creating mind as it conceives of an ideal working
in and through the real. So any natural language of passion and its
leaps into imagery are not ways to recapture securely the soul's in-
spiration, but only to strive after the incommunicable, the ditties
of no tone. As Fichte said, when a painter puts brush to canvas, the
perfect form of vision is already vanishing. Poetry imitates, struggling through the sad incompetence of human speech to retrieve
something experienced which has not yet attained that happy combination of words suggesting its revelation and felt knowledge. Hegel, as he sums up this pressure toward the ideal, begins by asking,
"Is art to be poetry or prose?" His answer is that "the truly poetical
element in art is just what we have called the Ideal."[21] To find this
ideal, poetry becomes a naming and never-ending renaming.

When the New Criticism points out tension, paradox, and ambiguity in the interpretation of poetic language, or when deconstruction, its upside-down sibling, sees self-referential paradox and
rhetoric that takes its own figures as parallel mirrors of composition
and decomposition, both modes of interpretation rediscover what
romantic theory is professing from the start. A curious concept in
deconstruction is the suggestion that one might ever expect any
reader to entertain logic, cause and effect, or figuration as accessible
to a meaning or method constructed by the Understanding alone in
the first place. Such a critical method, especially when carried to
extremes, becomes positivistic or literal—"either/or"—for assuming

that anyone would even wish such an explication of poetry. As a strategy of interpretation it runs the risk of becoming superfluous, a feint that plays well in a society flooded with the critical prose of authority and understanding. The patron saint—in the sense of being much quoted and discussed—of deconstruction as practiced in America is not Fichte, Schelling, or perhaps most appropriately Oscar Wilde, but that idealistic archrationalist Hegel. "Reality is rational and rationality is real." True, he says poetry must avoid "the philosophical forms of judgment and syllogism," the realm of the Understanding. But ironically he lays down perfectly understandable rules and boundaries for poetry. Straining to be clear and concise, he places it in the scheme of things with rational judgment. Deconstruction, especially as practiced in the United States, may be seen in one light as an attempt to deny Hegel not on Nietzschean but on Hegelian grounds. Naturally it deconstructs itself and therefore cannot help but be endlessly successful.[22]

In justice to the New Critical emphasis on organic wholeness or "unity" of a poem, we should recall that such a tenet (if something so fluid and variously treated is a tenet) has nothing whatsoever to do with logical consequence or with unwrinkled meaning unfolding to the Understanding. Rather, that unity can imply a continually alternating, self-reflexive quality in all great poetry, the *Schweben,* or hovering and oscillating of imagination, described by Kant, Fichte, and Schelling. Although the sense of organic unity was pushed to extremes and became a kind of interpretive piety, such unity emphatically does not necessitate univocal, permanent interpretation. In such poetry the self-consciousness of its own creation is always part of, but not its exclusive subject.

Close interpretation, from whatever quarter, rarely supplements itself with one vital, elusive element of many poetic (especially romantic) texts. And that is the presence of ideals or, as Coleridge points out, the coexistence of ideals and ideas. Perhaps this is so because when we actually go through those interpretations we often find inadequate foundation in romantic or idealist philosophy, protests to the contrary. We find virtually no grounding in detailed, relevant critical theory of the later eighteenth-century, theory that fostered and fired, not angered, romantic poets. The relevant philosophical context is often as foreign to the interpreter as it is present to the poet. Tracing echoes and references to Proclus, Plotinus, Plato, Böhme, John Smith, Berkeley, Hartley, Campbell, Gerard, Schelling, and Fichte in Wordsworth, Blake, Shelley, Coleridge, Novalis, Friedrich Schlegel, and Schiller suggests that even as poetry is regarded in terms of its language, it is also defined as pointing not only to itself but also to something else. (Even Hegel agrees, though he believes that poetry is becoming obsolete as the World-Spirit completes its ultimate enlightenment and reveals the Absolute.) Poetry is a unique sign—signifier, signified, and sign all together. Like mythology, poetry tells about itself but also about nothing less than the burden of our mystery. Though not omnipotent, this intense drive toward the ideal stands behind romantic critical theory and poetry like a holy mountain looming behind the temples of several religions. Finally, this one feature most distinguishes it from modernist poetry and modern definitions of the function of poetry. At bottom it is a spiritual difference.

"Where I may find . . . human hearts"

The theory that poetry imitates and evokes primarily "the passions" gains force after 1750 and becomes omnipresent. It has many classical precedents, primarily Longinus, who connects strong feeling with the presence of meter. Dennis identifies passion as "the chief thing in poetry." And Pope claims its presence is Homer's great strength.[23] But passion increasingly becomes less weighed against an opposing balance pan of judgment. Shakespeare's plays draw scrutiny not so much for structure as for suggestive fidelity rather than dry description of passion. To say Shakespeare is the poet of nature means human nature. "Bardolatry" accompanies this shift in poetic theory. The transference of human feeling to natural or inanimate objects, the highest form of personification or prosopopeia (according to many rhetoricians in the latter part of the century)— what Coleridge calls Shakespeare's gift of "humanizing nature"—

this premise of feeling alters ideas about the essential and more profound mimetic function of poetry. In the pointed language of Joseph Warton, his comment prefiguring Hazlitt, "WIT and SATIRE are transitory and perishable, but NATURE and PASSION are eternal."[24]

Passion here should not be confused with "ruling passion," though some Shakespearean criticism does align major characters with single, overriding passions—for instance, Macbeth with ambition, Othello with jealousy. Coleridge calls poetry "the blending of passion with order." Hazlitt's famous term "gusto" entails "power or passion defining any object." Poetry aims immediately to arouse pleasure in the reader, imaginatively guided to recreate feelings within. "Passion" or "sentiment," what is "affecting," have changed connotations. We think of passion as strong or violent—a crime of passion—and connect it with heated, unreasonable desire, often sexual. But for the eighteenth and early nineteenth centuries, "passion" covers the gamut of feeling and emotion and includes all behaviors and motivations. Maurice Morgann makes this clear in his essay on Falstaff. And Joseph Warton even complains that French writers have ruined the idea of passion in dramatic representation by exerting too much ingenuity in love intrigue, one passion they let engross, and "impertinently introduced into, all subjects."[25] The passions extend instead to joy, hope, fear, laughter, anger, anxiety— and not only violent but also weaker or "finer" sensations. "Sentiment" is closer to the Latin root of feeling but, again, feeling in its widest sense, not just something opposed to reason. Burke's term "the affecting arts" implies whatever moves or arouses feeling; "affecting" could bring tears or soft meditation—or kindle anger or hate.

Increasingly throughout the century many theoretical reconsiderations revolve around Milton's definition of poetry, "simple, sensuous, and passionate." It finds scores of commonplace echoes. Hazlitt, even with his recast emphasis on imitation, places the stress on imitating passions. Dramatic tragedy thus reprsents the apex of poetry because there "nature" is most extensively imitated. Hume assumes that the imitation of passion precedes any ethical aim of literature. Earlier, in 1703, Locke wrote in "Reading and Study" that all who will carry responsibility in the world should read "books that of purpose treat of human nature, which help to give an insight into it. Such are those treating of the passions, and how they are moved, whereof Aristotle in his second book of *Rhetoric* hath admirably discoursed, and that in a little compass." It is not only possible but necessary to look at Johnson as a moral thinker, critic, and poet by first examining how he treats and analyzes human passion and feeling. Alan McKenzie has shown how rigorous and systemic this analysis is, and for W. J. Bate it undergrids all John son's intellectual premises and is what permits him to become a great moral wirter and critic.[26] The end—or at least a later way station— of this primacy of feeling is Wordsworth's definition: "the spontaneous overflow of powerful feelings . . . emotion recollected in tranquillity." For Wordsworth means strength of feeling, feeling and thought barely distinguishable, "the essential passions of the heart" that "speak a plainer and more emphatic language." Furthermore, in that Preface he specifically makes a final request "of my reader," that "in judging these Poems," that is, in critical as well as creative acts, the reader "decide by his own feelings genuinely, and not by reflection upon what will probably be the judgment of others."

How is emphasis on passion related to greater efficiency or compression in the combining, fusive nature of poetic language? Deep feeling stimulates the mind to use language in more compressed, elevated, and "emphatic" modes, to search out—through urgency or predominance of feeling—fresh combinations to galvanize attention and arrest the listener. Coleridge argues that meter channels power and, by casting a tinge of order over passion, adds to it, as a mill race channels and speeds water, making it do more work. He writes to William Sotheby in 1802: "*Metre itself* implies a *passion,* i.e., a state of excitement, both in the Poet's mind, & is expected in that of the Reader."[27] Coleridge's transatlantic student Emerson perceives a "fit" between meter and the passionate force of its argument. In feeling that musters itself to be regulated just enough to enhance its power, the cadence of its presentation is created: "not metres, but a metre-making argument" makes poetry.

In another perspective, feeling and passion ultimately tell stories about individuals, tales the reader "cannot choose but hear." They depict what Keats early called "a nobler life, / Where I may find the agonies, the strife / Of human hearts." The romantic poems that carry out this mission are many and varied: their subjects (and titles) are primarily individuals, usually caught up in actions and their aftermath. Most are narratives of some length. This indicates specific relations between poetic narrative, passion, individuals, and the lived experience of characters, or of the poet, in the world. These relations begin a long breakdown in the mid-nineteenth century.

Arnold believed imitation of passion—brought to life by creating specific characters—central to poetry. He had only to read in his father, Thomas Arnold, the then widely held premise: poetical feelings are the "highest and purest feelings of our nature."[28] Yet while upholding this principle, the young Arnold senses it as problematic and threatened—hence his conscious decision to suppress *Empedocles on Aetna* and to write, with mixed results, *Sohrab and Rustum*. The tendency toward portraying—in poetry—a more or less fully realized individual (other than the author), one whose life is either completely told or partially surmised, continues throughout the nineteenth century. We tend to forget this baldly obvious feature of premodernist poetry. From 1750 to 1900 the figure or feelings of the author often dominate poems; the verse frequently expresses the self writing. But from Thomas Blacklock's *The Graham* and John Langhorne's *The Country Justice* (both 1774), Hannah More's *Sir Eldred of the Bower* (1776), down well into romantic narratives and extending through Tennyson, Browning, and even the earlier Eliot (*Prufrock* and *Gerontion*), poetry creates individuals other than the author, individuals whose feelings and motivations are realized and complex. Such portraits, often full-length or at least three-quarters, as well as the meditative poems of personal expression in the voice of the author, invoke the principle enshrined by eighteenth-century criticism that poetry imitates many things but primarily the passions. It portrays and elicits sources of emotion experienced through memory and reflection, or through narrated encounters with others.

To use Wordsworth's distinction, poetry imitates emotion either meditatively or dramatically.

But with regard to characters and their passions, somewhere in the later nineteenth century romance—meaning a narrative of the passions of others—begins to disappear from poetry. Romance cannot exist without narration of events and depiction of characters' passions. Hence its absence, its conscious rejection, becomes one hallmark of modernist poetry. Perhaps this occurs because poetic techniques (with the exception of regular meter, eschewed in much modern verse) are being used with great success to portray human emotion and psychological motive by Flaubert, James, Proust, Lawrence, Joyce, and Woolf. This appropriation could be seen to limit the unique scope of verse (and once more the poetic function of language would have to take refuge in ever more original combinations of words per se, the extreme example of which in fact ends by occurring in the prose of *Finnegans Wake*). This development leads Edmund Wilson to ask, in his 1928 essay by that title, "Is Verse a Dying Technique?" In the modernist period, poetry becomes, on the whole, less dramatically "biographical" or personally narrative. It could be autobiographical or confessional, but by definition these modes center on the self. David Perkins notes this by collecting exceptions under the heading "The Narrative Protest," whre poets such as Kipling, Masefield, Chesterton, and Noyes "sought to be relevant to the actual experience of men and women in the modern world." Others, like A. E. Coppard, returned to ballads of rural characters such as "Betty Perrin."[29] We could think of Frost's *Death of the Hired Man* and perhaps Auden's elegy for Yeats, or Yeats's own Crazy Jane poems. Edward Arlington Robinson draws specific, living individuals. But these are exceptions, and many do not make the high modernist canon. The full and present living other, the dramatic individual, retreats as a vital subject of poetic narrative. Had "the passions"—to use the eighteenth-century term—or had "human interest," to use Johnson's phrase from the *Life of Milton,* reverted to the poet alone, or fragmented among nameless others—"I had not known death had undone so many"? The self, or a scattered world encountered by a not unsurprisingly fragmented self, supplants the presence of another self conceived in imaginative fullness—unless of course it is one's own "double."

In modernist poetry the lack of "human interest," as Johnson meant it, derives not from appeals to religious or anachronistic mythologies, but from a turning inward to myriad private mythologies, few of which seem cohesive enough to form the subject matter of a narrative poem. That function becomes, as it had been becoming ever since the seventeenth century, one of novels: *A la Recherche du temps perdu, Ulysses, Felix Krull, Mrs. Dalloway.* Could one claim Benet's *Western Star,* Robert Penn Warren's *Audubon,* or Berryman's *Dream Songs* as narratives of another person? Only with strong, almost insuperable qualifications. As Helen Vendler notes, in the *Dream Songs* "Henry is not Berryman, but neither is Henry not-Berryman."[30] Yet since modernist poetry often does reflect an inner life and spiritual condition, it remains in one sense mimetic to a high degree (and also in a very substantial way linked to romanticism and romantic theory). It represents states of consciousness, conditions of being and perceiving, but it no longer seeks to create a whole person as another. That is no longer the explicit or implicit essential of literary theory. There ceases to be anything "theoretical" about such a portrayal. In that special sense (not negative, but rather something poetry had to do to renew itself), modernist poetry and even poetic prose is "sterile," and sterility, dryness, and infertility form one of its great themes. *Buddenbrooks* is not the beginning of a career but a long farewell, at once loving and detached, to the end of an age Mann realized could not be successfully continued—a family without heirs. And who could be Hans Castorp's child? No one; he is the dying child himself. Finally, the boy in Grass's *Tin Drum* simply does not want to grow up.

What might be called "narrative or narrated passion" has assumed a comparative silence, passed over almost in embarrassment by the past generation or two of critics (especially academic scholars) in attempts to consider the nature of poetry. This is not wholly true of the poets themselves nor of reviewers writing for relatively wider audiences outside the academy. But the critic or scholar swept up by intellectual and textual analysis often appears aloof from the pulse of emotion. Going beyond ordered formalism has often seemed to mean forging ahead into the play of chaotic formalism. Perhaps by assuming so long in silence that poetry deals with passion, but rarely coming out with that statement and then being guided by it, or perhaps by letting linguistic and technical questions get the upper hand, the passionate and feeling side of poetry and poetic language has been squeezed out of most learned criticism. Combinations of words alone, Yeats's circus animals—and not those combinations in light of the feeling required to produce them and the feelings they imitate, the foul rag-and-bone shop of the heart—this has come to play the more important role in theory.

The critical trend away from discussing feeling is in part a question of subject matter, what is intended as the proper study of criticism. For critics often do want to talk primarily, and even exclusively, about language, tropes, encodings, decodings, or strategies. This discussion, after all, goes with the territory, part of the classifications and analysis that, as Aristotle knew, must characterize any systematic study.[31] Then too a breakdown of trust in mimetic power or referentiality, in the stability and "accuracy" of texts, and in the author's intention—all these issues, however genuine, help turn the focus away from communicable human experience and feeling; and constant mistrust of any mimetic or intentional nature of texts soon makes that very distrust, and all its byplays, a primary subject of criticism, saturating all acts of writing and reading with a light polarized through powerful lenses of ambiguity or professional virtuosity. Psychological approaches such as Freudianism prove limitless in utility and insight, but are rarely used with a capaciousness that would provide an examination of passion, motivation, and behavior as general and varied as that envisioned by earlier literary theory.

Works of criticism attracting widespread attention and picked up by readers beyond academic specialists tend to be biographies of writers—often critical biographies—editions of authors' letters, or essays that discuss writers as living minds and sensibilities or express a distinct critical personality and tone. If criticism loses human interest, it will lose itself in the process—human intrest as genuine *inter esse,* discussing or revealing the pressure of a particular mind, an individual sense of feeling and reacting that cannot be equated with (but need not oppose) method or theory.

How we define poetry—that is to say, how we talk about poetry in a theoretical fashion—reflects what we value and also what we sense is possible in poetic practice. Definitions offered by linguists and definitions hinted at or offered by poets rarely square. Theory changes as practices become exhausted and others are developed. These lasting questions and proposed answers heighten awareness of the possibilities and uses of poetry: the inexhaustible resources of word, music, rhythm, syntax, figure, and idea that are not always already there, but that the poet and critic search for and invent. In Keats's phrase, English must be kept up. Asking What is Poetry? What is Poetic Language? or What is a Poem or a Poet? never yields stable answers. Criticism is often seduced into concentrating on one or two answers as somehow more essential than others. Theories defining poetry display a tendency to become narrow and parochial if concentrated on from an exclusively linguistic perspective.

Before Dryden, no system of English poetic diction existed; the nature of poetry and the function of poetic language were generally agreed upon. As critics elaborate those issues throughout the eighteenth century, definitions become more interesting and varied not only in formal concerns: literary theory reflects debates about human nature, its proclivities, innate qualities (if any), passions, pleasure, and knowledge, how we control and express both feeling and knowing. To define poetry could now be seen as one way of implying general views of human nature, knowledge, destiny, and even of different cultures—definitions that go beyond Aristotle's observation in the *Poetics* that humans have two instincts, one for harmony and one for imitation. New urgency attends the question What Is Poetry?

Janus: Criticism and
the Contemporary

The book is not . . . a means for any end whatever; the end
to which it offers itself is the reader's freedom.
SARTRE, *WHAT IS LITERATURE?*

In reading as in experience, every registering on the pulse, and each
articulated interpretation, manifests a world of infinite receptions
and re-creations that evolve over a lifetime of reading and feeling.
With centuries of criticism at our disposal—and with texts potentially accessible to everyone—the individual reader nevertheless
forms a unique universe of reference and inner connection. Each act
of reading is an act of rethinking and refeeling, bringing to bear
not less than everything as we re-create it in and for our being. In
readings we cherish, a book or a text reshapes the whole of the
"read" universe we had constructed to that moment; it also mysteriously realigns the related universe we cohabit with fellow readers
and sufferers. The uses of literature become the uses of freedom.

No critic is completely objective or subjective, though if we admit no difference between the terms or else see them as mutually
exclusive antipodes, we stand on a slippery slope. (A good deal of
the subjective-objective debate in literary interpretation could be
scrapped if we studied those terms in several philosophical contexts
instead of relying on a crude sense of "objective" as true and unpre-
judiced and "subjective" as personal and opinionated.) The humanities are maddeningly irreducible, fraught with disagreement and

imprecision. They are often a celebration of ambiguity and dialogue; one rarely deals with accepted fact but rather with opinion,
to varying degrees informed or misinformed—with little in the way
of demonstrable proof. Each critic has—and perhaps that is what
we really value in critics we like—a specific Emersonian "angle of
vision." And we may like it the more because it compliments or
challenges our vision, not because it reaffirms it.

Two points can be underscored. Saying a critic has an ideology
or ideological point of view does not remove that critic from the
realm of moral choice or ethical value; rather it places the criticism
squarely within that framework. An ideology may be viewed as a
coherent set of values that inescapably involves moral and ethical
dimensions. Ideology entails values about society and human relations, about economies and power. Unless one wishes to speak about
a purely aesthetic ideology (if such extreme purity exists), or unless
one takes a reductive definition of moral value, ideology is another
way of talking about moral system with the advantage, for some,
of avoiding the word "moral."

Second, some critics bring their moral values or ideologies to bear
with full force in a programmatic or polemical way. We can sense
what template criticism is. That is, while every critic carries an
ideology or set of values that may or may not be more sensitive or
informed than another critic, not all critics bring those values to
bear with equal force. Many critics who rely heavily on a political
ideology, or on religious or cultural values, are more engaging than
critics who are not ideologues. But the point is, saying we all have
an "ideological" point of view becomes so loose and meaningless we
might as well say we all have tongues. In terms of application to
literary criticism, not all ideologies are equally coherent or well-
articulated. And what is relevant to one text might be inappropriate
for another. Although we cannot escape ideology or moral value,
their exercise does not flatten everyone's ideology to the same impact of intelligence, strength, or relevance. Some critics orient their
theories or interpretations around one coherent ideology. Others orient theirs around a less formulated set of values or, to use Henry

James's key word, around impressions. When we start throwing a term like "ideology" around, we need to examine carefully what it is we mean; otherwise it becomes a sack into which we can throw almost anything and sling it on our back.

In less than twenty years we have seen structuralism and post-structuralism come and go; structuralism hardly had time to blossom in the United States before its promise was cut short. And post-structuralism is often charaterized by deconstruction or "pragmatism," two modes of thought in which, carried to extremes, the text either means ultimately nothing except difference or anything including all differences. Perhaps the modes of criticism that will come out most clearly from the challenge to the older orthodoxies are neo-Marxism and feminism, not because they will gain the most adherents but because they deal with literature in real and demanding political, historical, and social contexts. They take up literature in relation to life and manners, or at least have the power to do so if they do not waste energy in internal conflict, often more bitter than disagreements with those outside the camp. The next major movement may be in the sociology of literature. This, however, demands more than theory, it requires historical knowledge, social research, and acquaintance with intellectual, religious, and political movements. As a sociology of literature is pursued, mimesis or "representation" will again occupy a key place in critical theory.

Terry Eagleton's provocative, brief survey *The Function of Criticism: From The Spectator to Post-Structuralism* (its main title derived from Arnold, through Eliot), contends that "Modern European criticism was born of a struggle against the absolutist state."[1] This is one of those fractional truths carrying enough worth to keep it alive and packaging enough authoritatively stated misinformation to guarantee novelty of approach. Eagleton's argument—that criticism in the eighteenth century became part of a more or less monolithic public discourse propelling a "bourgeois power bloc" into prominence—is suggestive in its reach, but it overreaches. The idea that a nonspecialist critical discourse on matters of general cultural and intellectual interest reared its head out of some vaguely defined yet apparently conscious political conspiracy, a plan to subvert absolute monarchy but also to silence or, better yet, to coopt the coarse malcontents of the proletariat, pulls up short on fact, glosses decades of highly complicated history with labels that are violent clichés, and basically fails to quote much criticism in context at all. "The *Tatler* and *Spectator* are projects of a bourgeois cultural politics, whose capacious, blandly homogenizing language is able to encompass art, ethics, religion, philosophy, and everyday life; there is here *no question*," Eagleton contends, "of a 'literary critical' response which is not *wholly determined* by an *entire* social and cultural ideology." Who can doubt it? One always feels more comfortable and courageous in intellectual riposte if it can be made to appear that everyone who seems to disagree with you is made to plot their disagreement together, and for the same reasons.[2] The argument moves beyond the traditional *post hoc ergo propter hoc* to a more inventive *post hoc ergo propter hac*.

Eagleton's skimming survey asserts that in the early nineteenth century a consensus of "general humanism" split on the rock of political disagreement and radicalization. Victorian sages could not put Humpty-Dumpty back together again. Soon "the market" determined everything. But Eagleton's comments on the directions of twentieth-century criticism, especially in the university, are shrewd and informed. Like others before him, he sees the split of popular and sophisticated tastes in the later nineteenth century as a fascinating and continuing cultural event. Amid his labels and loaded nouns (bourgeois, middle class, ruling bloc, and always "late" capitalism) strewn without specific explanation and buckling under the weight of facts and texts not provided, he does raise an urgent question and registers a crucial plea. Even if one disagrees with his interpretation of critical history and its motives, his fundamental contention deserves our closest scrutiny. The main point—and lament—is "that criticism today lacks all substantive social function." By securing a limited specialization within the academy, it has committed political and social suicide. (I take it he means criticism as an institution generally, for this could not be accurate as a blanket statement about all critics either in or out of the academy.) Especially for university criticism produced in the explosion of specialism since World War II, then, Eagleton's charge of a lack of substantive social function is a challenge worth soul searching. He ends by calling on the critic once again to shoulder a *"traditional"* role, and "not to invent some fashionable new function for it." This involves a scrutiny of language, discourse, and society, not just mastering "the conventionally valued writings of the past." The solution Eagleton offers to save criticism from having "no future at all," would for him enlist critics in a battle "against the bourgeois state."[3] Here the book ends.

Critics will engage themselves because they are intellectuals, because they read and think widely, are familiar with human character and history, and ponder ethical motives and social institutions. In order to be critics in the full-fledged sense of that word, those who read and write do these things. But if critics are merely masters of technical approaches to texts, none of this can be done. When Arnold called for criticism to be disinterested, he did not intend it to withdraw from the public sphere, but rather not to champion the cause of power or gain for personal or class reasons, least of all to stabilize the status quo. He intended for criticism not only to sympathize with new, even subversive ideas, but actually to champion them. (Curiously, Eagleton avoids discussing Arnold.) He spoofed the isolation of British letters and its limited canon by writing reviews of nonexistent French poets to see who would catch him at it. He saw the aristocracy as unidea'd "Barbarians," the middle class as "Philistines," and the only hope for social integration as a genuine liberation, not a coopting, of the Populace.

A Profile of Criticism

Literature is the only art in which the practice of the art, its criticism, scholarship, and analysis, are all performed in the same medium. If for this reason only, criticism can justly lay claim to the title of literature. The implications of this are many—we can assume a closer symbiosis between "literature" and "literary criticism," a blurring of borders between (not separating) them. But we also confront a lack of extrinsic signs, the absence of a different perspective intrinsic to another medium. In the arts as a whole, literary criticism thus presents a special situation. No critique or body of knowledge can be completely systematic or even offer a wholly new perspective on its subject if its measuring stick or instrument operates in the same medium as the subject it examines. There is no way to step completely outside the medium. This is one kind of prison or wilderness.

Yet the fact that literary criticism belongs in the wider sense to literature is supplemented by the recognition that it is a subset of criticism in general. Criticism of other arts is carried out in language too, and often we may think of that criticism as literature as well, especially if we believe that literature includes any form of writing when it attains a certain level of articulation and resourcefulness. (That level, itself a subject of literary theory, is hard to define accurately.)

More than two hundred years ago Johnson commented that in literature a very extraordinary book could no longer appear. Some are more remarkable than others, but Johnson meant no *extra*ordinary book, no book that would turn the whole subject inside out with lasting effect. Although there have been lasting movements and essential changes in literary form and cultural values, there have been few if any Copernican revolutions in literature or criticism. Any that have been achieved, such as Romanticism or the Modern movement, have encompassed a number of writers and views held in concert, often so loosely that genuine disagreement arises over specific characteristics of the movement and its proper definition. *Farenheit 451* shows that even measures that eradicate the past to establish a new order cannot erase human memory. Literature is too accumulative and assimilative, language too slow and communally possessed, to change completely in anything less than generations.

Structures of modern scholarship may actually make it harder for change to develop from internal pressure and theory, more likely to come from events and views in other fields, from political revolutions and social movements. At any rate, no literary construct comparable to the periodic table or to the theories of evolution or relativity will set radically new boundaries.

Who can say what the enduring criticism of today will be? It may turn out to be comprised of fugitive pieces, prefaces to short volumes of verse, personal journals come to light posthumously, collections of letters waiting to be published sometime in the next century; or diaries, or series of articles in small magazines written by young poets; or interviews, or lectures like Saussure's on linguistics, Adam Smith's on rhetoric, and Coleridge's on Shakespeare—in all cases saved primarily through attentive students and auditors who transcribed their contents, often unpublished for decades.

We tend to forget that in the ordinary way we now understand it Johnson never wrote a book of criticism. Neither did Dryden, Addison, Hazlitt, Keats, Shelley, or Wilde. Johnson's *Shakespeare* edition follows an enduring Preface and his *Lives* originally introduced fifty-two separate volumes in a bookseller's money-making series of English poets. Neither project, nor the periodical essays, was originally a book in the sense we think of it now. Coleridge's only criticism published as a book in his own lifetime, the *Biographia Literaria,* is notoriously uneven in its self-proclaimed "immethodical miscellany" of "sketches," including some parts of his own lectures, marginalia, earlier periodical efforts, reviews, travel letters, and numerous quotations, as well as some parts transcribed, with varying attribution, from German writers. And even that book was first conceived as a preface to the poems in *Sibylline Leaves,* in order to answer Wordsworth's 1815 Preface and the ghost of the one published in 1800.

Arnold wrote essays in criticism, as did Emerson, Poe, Hawthorne, and James. (Arnold's long books on religion and literature receive least attention of his work.) All of T. S. Eliot's books of criticism are essays. The one systematic book-length study he determined to write, on Elizabethan and Jacobean poets and playwrights, remains scattered in essays and shorter pieces. Naturally there are books of criticism—Aristotle's *Poetics,* combined with the apparently lost treatise on comedy, would make a short book. And in the period I have been concentrating on we have many: Rymer, Campbell, Blair, Gerard, Hurd, and more. Yet it remains to be seen whether criticism—as opposed to scholarly investigation of literary history and biography—has found its most accommodating length in the "book." It is sometimes ironic that modern universities usually demand—and the more self-consciously prestigious the university the greater the demand—at least "a book" (and better two, or one "big" book) before intellectual imprimatur is granted to the critic. The book of criticism or even of literary scholarship is a relatively recent genre, the creation of which is in part institutional and professional. Attaching reverence to it as the highest, most comprehensive critical genre entails assumptions worth questioning.

Attempts to orient criticism schematically have been presented by, among others, M. H. Abrams, Northrop Frye, Harry Levin, Claudio Guillén, René Wellek and Austin Warren. The orientation that follows is not meant to contradict or supersede them, but to supplement them and to stress that all orientations, like models of a national economy, inevitably select and simplify. My headings or schema suggest that before, during, and in the reflective afterwash of reading, both critic and reader come to texts with several foundations no less broad than experience itself—a mixture of assumptions and knowledge, fact and opinion, "ideology" and values—that actually orient critical theories in a way perhaps as important as placing stress on the specifically "literary" qualities evinced by reader, writer, or text. The massively complex series of perceptions we call, by innocent shorthand, "the act of reading" triggers unforeseeable reactions and further perceptions, though not of course from scratch. We come to texts, to read and to write them, not only encountering and creating what is new but as individuals already formed and informed, yet forming still. For such an orientation of broad critical response, we might select as headings the world, time, the human, and the medium (one facet of which is the "text"). Without introducing words as technical terms and without eliciting specific historical or philosophical significations, but simply in order to help remember these four schema, they could be called *cosmos, chronos, psyche,* and *logos.*

Cosmos, or the world • The nature of the world, the "universe," or cosmos can quickly get pretentious or silly, as implied by Emerson's unjustified put-down that he was glad Margaret Fuller had finally come to accept the universe. Or we might recall the volume dedicated by one of Johnson's school teachers "to the universe"; it was a spelling book. But the critic (reader and writer) does have values, tacitly if not explicitly—an "ideology" or Weltanschauung, a perspective or stance about the nature of reality or objective experience. So we say T. S. Eliot's view of this elusive reality or world picture was influenced by Bradley, or that Dante in some manner epitomizes or expresses a medieval worldview, or that Milton is a Christian humanist, Hume an atheist who blends skepticism with realism, Austen a moralist whose small world, as she described it, painted in miniature on a square of ivory, contains the deepest ethical insight. Eliot himself, who expresses a preference for poets with some philosophical approach or coherent worldview, uses that as a yardstick to measure Shakespeare. Derrida and Lukács exert strong force in literary circles because of their particular philosophical or political stances. There is always an appeal open from literary criticism to the critical intellect at large. The text allows—insists— that worldviews of author and reader interpenetrate to form a new or "third" view that could not have existed as an interpretation or mimesis for either one alone.

Chronos, or time • What we call history occurs in and by means of time, but history is not time's essence. Time always involves a sense of process; history is a more restricted process of our selection, expression, and interpretation, which though not identical to, is related to, chronology. In one sense history is what has happened to other people; we can ignore it until we realize that we are those other people. In another sense history is the hand we have drawn, the cards we have elected to pick up from the discard pile, itself placed there before us and therefore already limiting our choice. Without history we cannot be redeemed from time. C. V. Wedgwood in her biography of William the Silent says, "History is lived forwards but it is written in retrospect. We know the end before we consider the beginning and we can never wholly recapture what it was to know the beginning only."[4] The same thing can be said about individual lives—Wedgwood is paraphrasing Kierkegaard: life is lived forward but understood backward.

Time is the medium of change in literature and, what is not quite the same thing, the necessary condition of constructing all literary histories and all traditions, even different ones, drawn from the same body of material. Whatever we call that history, its traditions, processes, novelty, originality, chronology, or influences—all these occur in and through time but are not by their occurrence established *for us* by time: our active, informed, selective, and partial awareness of what happens in time must create those concepts and their applications to works, writers, movements, and styles. This awareness must be won, rescued. It might entail obvious problems. In "The Author's Advertisement" to the *Lives,* Johnson remarks that "in this minute kind of History the succession of facts is not easily discovered, and I am not without suspicion that some of Dryden's works are placed in wrong years. . . . and if I shall hereafter obtain a more correct chronology will publish it."[5] But even this does not mean, as Johnson knew, that literary history is a catalogue of fact. Time in criticism implies mental activity, a projecting and remembering—in short, an imagination able to grasp continuities and discontinuities, influences and originality, changes in language and usage—all of these, and more, as mutually acting upon each other. Our own understandings are historically conditioned too, and our awareness of literature in time is like the blinking of our eyes, sometimes automatic, sometimes willed, during which we cleanse and refresh our vision but through which we blind ourselves momentarily and return to a world not quite the same as our last glimpse of it. Ultimately, very few critical concepts are able to sever themselves from a sense of literature occurring in and over time.[6] Therefore, literary history can never be discarded as such; but in method, narrative, and values it is difficult to define and must be refashioned by every generation.

Time is in the works themselves, such as *Tom Jones,* Proust, or the great brooding on time that is *Burnt Norton;* time is with related concepts in narration, such as Bakhtin's chronotope, or Barthes's meditation on History, the novel, and the preterite tense in French narration (*Writing Degree Zero*), where he quotes the sentence Valéry considered to epitomize generic conventions of the novel: the marchioness went out at five o'clock. In *1984* the clock strikes thirteen, a special way to announce its new realism. More recently, historical and philosophical studies have made use of the term archaeology: Derrida and others employ this sense of unearthing and reconstructing the past from its minute particulars, missing shards, and confused strata. Such "archaeology," which is a special kind of history, rests on an acute sense of process.

Literary history does not so much describe events that happened as examine a series of texts created under different conditions by different individuals, who nevertheless often shared certain things because of their connection in time, culture, nationality, or in what they read. We receive a cultural inheritance, but through our historical sense, through partial and rarely impartial glimpses into the past, we have an opportunity to remold our culture and field of study. Literary history exists largely to serve social and cultural purposes. Even if this cultural inheritance seems to have been created predominantly by a ruling class or clique, even if it appears to enshrine a set of exclusive, unquestioned values, it is still essentially neutral in its value to the individual mind. Like imagination or originality, it can be used well or poorly. One can identify it as an edifice of oppression and dogmatism, or one can revere and cherish it—or a mixture of both. No matter which way we view it, it will not go away; it will continue to change not only because of events but through constant reinterpretation of them. It presents us with inescapable yet shifting conditions, not just for critics but for all readers, even those who do not reflect on it as such. Literary histories, which are highly complex and diverse projects, take on as many forms and methods as history at large. Thus to speak of "literary history" or the "historical approach" is a radically naive simplification.

Psyche, or the human • Human nature here implies a broad range of inquiry and different ways of knowing the human: psychology, anthropology, psychoanalysis, a view of what it means to be human in various social contexts, or what human nature is intrinsically (if, indeed, it has an intrinsic "nature"). This systematic study might include Aristotle, associationist psychology, Vico, Freud, Jung, Neumann, Lacan, and Bettleheim. And naturally it includes literature itself. If one does not believe there is anything intrinsic or essential to human nature except the ability to reproduce, that not even some passions and behaviors are inherent but that life is structured out of unique social and linguisitc circumstances, then the study of these human natures nevertheless survives as an inquiry into how and why human beings create or acquire such different characteristics and unique behaviors. Since language and literature represent better than any other single human expression, institution, or endeavor the multifaceted quality of experience and action, both literary creation and criticism draw upon and actually help to create theories and understandings of the human psyche and its social existence. Since Hobbes or even Vives, interest in systematic psychology has been not only one of the major tools of the critic, but an essential characteristic of the intellectual atmosphere in which all writers work.

Logos, or the medium • The medium is language itself, of all the schema perhaps most central, but nevertheless a medium which, regarded as an abstract system in and of itself, says no more about human life and the world than reading dictionary definitions, or inventing illustrations for a handbook of rhetorical terms. Yet we can go on to include all that has been primarily treated by rhetoric and poetics, by the study of metaphor, philology, grammar, linguistics, and the comparative study of languages and translation—and even by language-based theories of psychology and society. It is interesting, and not coincidental, that Johnson and Coleridge, two of the greatest critics in English, are most deeply interested in, and knowledgeable about, language and words. (It is often on the question of language that Coleridge chooses to debate with Johnson.) What makes their criticism especially rich in this regard are their respective abilities to combine insight into language and words with interest in other areas: history, biography, psychology, or philosophy. It is barely possible to see the "medium" or language as a separate category, since it is the one through which our understanding and views of the others are primarily expressed. This makes it central and helps explain why the study of language, taking "the linguistic turn"—or, more broadly, into semiotics—has for a half century stimulated intellectual achievement in many fields: philosophy, literary criticism, psychology, religion, anthropology, and sociology.

The idea of language as a medium also touches on what might generally be called literary form—questions of narrative, genre, mode, or style. Clearly these topics are combined with other areas—as narrative may be with history, style with psychoanalysis, genre with ideology.

Cosmos, chronos, psyche, logos: fundamental changes or ruptures not only in criticism but in cultures at large, such as the shift from classic to romantic, involve changes in the basic conceptions of all these elements and must be seen in and through them and their interrelated complexity. In such shifts—what we often call new "periods" or "ages" or new epistemic views or paradigms—human nature acquires a new definition, creating one for itself, whether by Rousseau and the French Revolution, Schiller's *Aesthetic Letters,* or the reforming hopes of Shelley. Cosmology is changed from that of

Pope and the mechanizers and the makers of grand theodicies to a more open-ended, organic, and vital plan—or even lack of plan; the Great Chain of Being becomes Jacob's Ladder and organic plenitude. The sense of time is changed as well. The French Revolution turns the clock back to zero—Wordsworth's spots of time echo what Johnson said—that time is particularly malleable to human consciousness. Bishop Ussher's clock of creation becomes challenged by tiny fossils embedded in limestone, in Tennyson's elegiac mood, "a maniac scattering dust." And the medium, logos, is given new weight in the power of language, the figure of personification, and the symbol, the "mystery" of words to incarnate a truth other than that of science.

Significant changes in criticism also occur when one of these elements is, in relative isolation, scrutinized and newly redefined: for example, human nature by psychoanalysis, language by modern linguistic theories instead of comparative historical philology, the cosmos by relativity theory, and chronos by new methods of historical investigation. Critical approaches emerge from specific emphases on one or more of these orientations. Instances are numerous. The influence of Darwin and various forms of social Darwinism affected literary form. Structuralism in literary criticism derived from an intellectual paradigm first used in the social sciences to investigate the nature of human behavior, intellect, and culture. It proved disturbing and fruitful (and incapable of pat definition) precisely because it could encompass and present changes in all the schema: new views of human nature, history, the medium, and even of reality. Reader-response theory grounds itself in both psychology and sociology, new literary history in changed attitudes toward our conception of what has happened to society and to our interpretation of events and "mentalities." Critical biography centers on the relation between the individual life and the process of writing. When successful, it brings to bear a whole range of critical attitudes articulated in an inventive narrative akin to the novel. The New Criticism focused most exclusively on the medium, on poetic language, pattern, and texture. Textualism (including deconstruction) in a way continues that same stress, though from a different perspective.

Deconstruction is thus the latest in a series of moves precipitated by a changed view of language and rhetoric, but now also associated, by some of its adherents, with a philosophical point of view about the nature of reality and, more specifically, about the history of metaphysics. Feminist and Marxist criticism (with varying degrees of systematic coherence) rest on views of the world originally social, political, and economic, views directly related to convictions about reality and history. Freudian or neo-Freudian readings derive from a particular study of the psyche. And so forth. Each critical approach is grounded in and emerges from areas other than "pure" criticism or "pure" literature. Since that grounding is various and complex, the four categories proposed—not separate but always interpenetrating—should not reduce each approach to a formula, but are intended to highlight origins and combinations of emphasis.

Each critical point of view, like any philosophical investigation, starts from one or more assumptions or convictions about cosmos, chronos, psyche, or logos. And though criticism may question its own assumptions, it never escapes them: if one is discarded another replaces it. In this sense criticism can never be completely scientific, for its hypotheses never undergo genuine verification, and the more they tend to exclude in order to be controlled and accurate, the more they tend to distort what is occurring in the production and experience of literature.

Any one approach taken exclusively becomes sterile. One kind of meal, served repeatedly, is malnourishing. We die in pure oxygen as well as in a vacuum. Asking criticism to go on all fours in complete and docile "objectivity" is like demanding a metaphor to do the same. Criticism, again like a metaphor, stands on more than just one leg. In metaphor Aristotle saw more than an ornamental figure of speech; for him it is the characteristic mark of genius. To create a metaphor is an act of mind or psyche, expressed in the medium of language, that apprehends the world in new relations of identity, space, and time. The act of metaphor—for it is a genuine act—shows that the categories of mind, nature, process, and medium are not fully separable but wonderfully related through the imaginative genius of thinking metaphorically. Metaphor is powerful precisely because it calls on all categories together. It is the most compact version of what we lamely call "interdisciplinary"; it bridges, connects, and interpenetrates the larger "separate" schema that classification and analysis offer. A metaphor acts on cosmos, chronos, psyche, and logos (nature, process, mind, and language) all at once and in transformation. In criticism this metaphorical revelation translates into a series of views wrought together, at least potentially.[7] As Harry Levin describes this critical act, it unravels and unfolds, it seeks the implication of explication: "To interpret a text with due justice should be to analyze it linguistically, structurally, historically, comparatively; to keep a synchronic eye out for esthetic angles which have hitherto gone unobserved; and to retain a diachronic cognizance of what it has meant in other contexts and in variorum rereadings. Nothing need be excluded from thoughtful examination under the most flexible and pluralistic criteria, but no emergent points would be worth pursuing unless they could withstand convincing tests of internal coherence and external relevance."[8]

In his wide-ranging book *The World, the Text, and the Critic,* Edward Said suggests that commentators could profitably examine Swift's work using methods and theories developed during the past decade or two. Done with balance and moderation, this is undoubtedly true, and Said expresses some puzzlement why it has not happened. He offers several reasons, but at bottom I believe it is because Swift has already been there, time and again, himself. His personae unmask the darker, ludicrous sides of such projects and their projectors. Many of his writings emerge as a parodic triumph of excess, pedantry, and waste in "critical" thinking, method, and apparatus. A long, humorless, and, to the general reader, arcane theoretical study of *A Tale of a Tub* quickly turns on itself. Swift remains impervious to web-spinners. Approaching him with high-tech critical tools possessed by a few initiates is like trying to bribe Robin Hood with counterfeit money. Swift is a rebuke to the icon of methodology set up as an inner sanctum.

To take up Swift in a forum where values, history, and personalities are not paramount would miss completely the point of his writing. Naturally what he says depends on his technique, is made genius through that technique, but what he says transcends technique and is the motivation for it in the first place (Emerson's "meter-making argument"). His technique is part of his genius, not the other way around. By talking exclusively about theory, narrative, tropes, figures, and the nature of language and literary form, we can avoid talking about a lot of other things. And Swift, for one, saw folly in that. The reason W. J. Bate and Harold Bloom have been important to criticism is not only because they talk about greatness, genius, figuration, and misreading in and of themselves, but because they talk about what it means to be a human being writing, with all the burden and psychological complexity that such a risk involves.

David Lodge cautions that in today's criticism specialists "at the coal-face are unintelligible to the general public," and those "who are intelligible often have nothing valuable to say." His indictment needs to be taken seriously because it identifies a deepening trend. Yet criticism retains the potential to be a set of inhering formal linguistic structures and textual strategies in active confluence *with* questions of human relevance in behavior, values, and action. Criticism can connect its own proper "essentially contested concepts" with essentially contested concepts in human value, moral and intellectual life, ethics, education, and government. Here the key word is not essential in the sense of settled or permanent, but what is essentially worth debate. By returning to the question of meaning—in texts themselves concerned with meaning and value in human experience—and by using knowledge and approaches available to us "we might," as Todorov states, "transcend the sterile dichotomy between specialist critics who know but do not think, and moralist critics who speak while not knowing much about the works of literature they speak about."[9] The condition of possessing refined critical means without ends becomes a frenzied chase leading nowhere, "trim and high-powered intellectual machines," as Graham Hough describes them, "with their wheels spinning vainly in the air."[10]

Where All the Ladders Start

A history or archaeology of humanism might begin by noting that
"humanism" has changed signification repeatedly over the five centuries of its existence by that name. Relatively distinct, different
manifestations of it can be charted: in the English tradition alone,
Elyot and Erasmus, Milton's Christian humanism, Augustan humanism, Arnold, the genteel tradition, neohumanism, academic
humanism, and all their variations. We might now call for a critical
or self-critical humanism. In commenting on Robert Scholes's book
Textual Power: Literary Theory and the Teaching of English, Todorov
surveys the critical scene in the United States. He finds himself in
essential agreement with Scholes's observations: post-structuralism
has divided itself into deconstructionists and pragmatists, neither
of which proves satisfactory. The alternative Todorov sees as having
gained the most leverage in relating literature to human interests
and concerns in direct, coherent fashion is Marxism (he might have
included feminism, too). But his final point is that we have lost
sight of the human referent. We have created a paper, not an ivory,
tower. And it grows flimsy, combustible. Scholes writes: "We will
have to restore the judgmental dimension to criticism, not in the
trivial sense of ranking literary texts but in the most serious sense
of questioning the values proferred by the texts we study." The
quest for relevance, feeling, and value seems perennial. Though
from another color of the political spectrum, this is also what Eagleton argues.

In the *Life of Pope,* where Johnson thought the remark most appropriate, he says friendship is a virtue that does not secure veracity.
Literary criticism is an intellectual activity that does not always
establish honesty. Some academic critics have in the last generation
cast doubt on the judgmental basis of criticism—not just on glib
or passing fashions, the "stock market" approach to authors' reputations—but on the deeper, acquired, highly complicated systems
of knowledge, fact, comparison, and acquaintance that form taste
and conviction in letters as well as in politics. It is not without
irony that some of these same critics may breezily rank their colleagues, their colleagues' books, and go on to do the same with

academic departments and universities, all the while resorting to the judgmental words (good, bad, weak, old-hat, exciting, lightweight, stuffy, traditional, risky) they would banish from "serious" professional work and criticism. If some of these views became critical law, an author's life would become suspect in thinking about that author's writing, yet a colleague has his or her personal history, education, and institutional alliance dissected in a search to explain or to expose critical preferences and points of view.

A humbling element accompanies any consideration of literature; so many have gone before. "Axioms in philosophy are not axioms until they are proved upon our pulses." How does Keats gloss his own? "We read fine things but never feel them to the full until we have gone the same steps as the author." In that spirit we might recognize reading and criticism as both a private and a communal enterprise. Yet academic criticism is a limited preserve. Only 30 percent of institutions that offer a BA or MA in literature even give courses in literary theory or criticism (and only half the Ph.D.-granting institutions).[11] The diet we as readers like is varied; so much is there. We respond to critics variously and personally, and there is no reason why critics who happen to be in the academy should think "academic criticism" synonymous with criticism at large. There is a real point to Johnson's assertion in *Rambler* 146 that of those "devoted to literature very few extend their views beyond some particular science, and the greater part seldom enquire, even in their own profession, for any authors but those whom the present mode of study happens to force upon their notice; they desire not to fill their minds with unfashionable knowledge, but contentedly resign to oblivion those books which they now find censured or neglected."

Our minds seem to have a proclivity to make an analogy between values and aesthetics, between concepts of worth and meaning and feelings of pleasure and displeasure. (Kant thought so, and this analogy works in either direction, whether life imitates art or art life.) We do not need to call this analogizing power—as Addison, Hume, Kant and many others did—taste. We could use another word. Greek philosophers and poets repeatedly asked themselves, What is Pleasure? The question implies a range of answers touching on moral life, the sensory world, the nature of human individuality and the worthiness—the value—of pursuing certain experiences or qualities we find in people; or pursuing erotically, in the more capacious sense of that word, the people who, as individuals, embody those valued qualities. Whatever kind of pleasure and worth we find in literary texts, critical questions soon stretch as broadly. By electing to banish values or ideology, history or psychology, linguistics or philology—or whatever might be relevant to the text, to its world, to its creator, and to its readers and the world they live in— we make the task of criticism easier and neater, but less authentic. And in the end I suspect we make it more boring.

By taking up criticism in exclusive ways it becomes possible to avoid talking about a great deal of what actually goes on as we read and write. One may construct systems and vocabularies that are self-sufficient and specialized, but the test then comes as one reintegrates them into other systems and finally into the larger system of art itself. Perhaps this larger integration could serve as a gloss to Arnold's cryptic remark about Sophocles: "To see life steadily and see it whole." That statement does not prize simplicity; it is not self-confident or optimistic or superior, but terrifying. We can see that command, like the voice of Apollo at the end of Heine's poem, drenched in an effort to confront complexity, doubt, and limitation. *Du musst dein Leben ändern.* Such a meaning moves behind Nietzsche's statement in *The Birth of Tragedy* that our systems of knowledge become limited even as we stand at the periphery of them and look out, that they come around to sting us like a scorpion's tail, to "deconstruct" us, their creators, as they must. And that, even as system within system is constructed for human knowledge, they all require, for full expression, the larger system of art— and the tragic, vital sense only art can bring. With such beauty and wonder that we do not feel rebuked but are changed and modified within, art serves as pastime, devotion, even addiction. Art reveals the limits of knowing, the joy and suffering of strange journeys. For criticism to participate in that revelation is difficult but possible.

NOTES • INDEX

_____

NOTES

Introduction: The Originating Force of
Eighteenth-Century Criticism

1. "Essentially Contested Concepts" is the title of an essay by W. B. Gallie in *Philosophy and the Historical Understanding* (London: Chatto & Windus, 1964), chap. 8. It is applied to literary studies by René Wellek and also by M. H. Abrams in "Rationality and Imagination in Cultural History: A Reply to Wayne Booth" in *Critical Inquiry* 2 (Spring 1976): 451. Abrams' reply is as much to J. Hillis Miller as to Booth; see also Wayne C. Booth, "'Preserving the Exemplar': or, How Not to Dig Our Own Graves," *Critical Inquiry* 3 (Spring 1977): 410–412.

2. For quotations and excellent discussion, see *Literary Criticism in England, 1660–1800,* ed. Gerald W. Chapman (New York: Alfred A. Knopf, 1966), pp. 3–10, esp. remarks on the critical "mind," p. 9.

3. J. H. Plumb, *Georgian Delights* (Boston: Little, Brown, 1980), pp. 8–48, 68–69, 76–77.

4. Campbell anticipates a modern debate; see Geoffrey Hartman "Crossing Over: Literary Commentary as Literature," in *Comparative Literature* 28 (1976): 265; also Murray Krieger, "Literary Criticism: A Primary or a Secondary Art?" chap. 2 of *Arts on the Level: The Fall of the Elite Object* (Knoxville: University of Tennessee Press, 1981), pp. 27–48 (originally The John C. Hodges Lectures, 1979).

5. Eric Rothstein, *Restoration and Eighteenth-century Poetry 1660–1780* (Boston and London: Routledge & Kegan Paul, 1981), p. 99; see also p. 165.

6. Hugh Blair, *Lectures on Rhetoric and Belles Lettres,* 3 vols. (London and Edinburgh: W. Strahan, 1783), I, 276.

7. James Boswell, *Life of Samuel Johnson,* ed. George Birkbeck Hill, rev. L. F. Powell, 6 vols. (Oxford: Clarendon Press, 1934–1950), IV, 381, n. 1.

8. *PMLA* 99 (October 1984): 991.

9. Tzvetan Todorov, *Introduction to Poetics,* trans. Richard Howard (Minneapolis: University of Minnesota Press, 1981), p. xxi.

1. Practical Theorist: Dryden's "Variety of Models"

1. George Watson, ed., Dryden's critical *Essays,* 2 vols. (London: J. M. Dent, 1962), I, ix: "Corneille's justifications are of the past, Dryden's of the future: the Englishman is the first European poet to make a habit of so preparing his critical ground in advance."

2. A similar dialectical, undogmatic quality works in Dryden's verse. For recent commentary see Ruth Salvaggio, *Dryden's Dualities* (Victoria, B.C.: ELS Monograph Series No. 29, 1983). Salvaggio sees Dryden's "otherness" in his dramatic structures, forms of debate in prose and verse, and fondness for intelligent paradox. "It is impossible," she says (p. 7), "to form a critical estimation of Dryden without taking into account the interplay involved in his dualistic vision," and she sees this vision stemming in part from a need both to satisfy and to anticipate and answer his audience, for example as a political writer in *Absalom and Achitophel* (p. 63).

3. Eric Rothstein, *Restoration and Eighteenth-century Poetry* (Boston and London: Routledge & Kegan Paul, 1981), p. 102; Edward Pechter, *Dryden's Classical Theory of Literature* (London and New York: Cambridge University Press, 1975), pp. 91–112; Robert D. Hume, *Dryden's Criticism* (Ithaca, N.Y., and London: Cornell University Press, 1970), p. 29: "In critical theory as in literary practice, Dryden is a syncretist, trying to reconcile and use what he finds best in the English, French, and Classical traditions."

4. "A conscious self-projection as a modernist occurs not just in the *Essay,* but, in one form or another, in practically every piece of criticism that he wrote" (Pechter, *Dryden's Classical Theory,* p. 113, with "conscious" the key adjective, as T. S. Eliot earlier noted).

5. For the concept of character and its connection with Johnson's criticism, see Jean Hagstrum, *Samuel Johnson's Literary Criticism* (Minneapolis: University of Minnesota Press, 1952), pp. 38–41.

6. Pechter, *Dryden's Classical Theory,* pp. 151–188, 197; John C. Scherwood, "Precept and Practice in Dryden's Criticism," *JEGP* 68 (1969): 432–440; and Hoyt C. Trowbridge, "The Place of Rules in Dryden's Criticism," (1946), rprt. in *Essential Articles for the Study of John Dryden,* ed. H. T. Swedenberg, Jr. (Hamden, Conn.: Archon Books, 1966). Eliot remarks on the solid and "sane" nature of Dryden's criticism. The commentary by George Saintsbury, Mark Van Doren (on poetry es-

pecially), and penetrating essays by Eliot himself remain fresh and balanced.

7. See Mark Van Doren, *The Poetry of John Dryden* (New York: Harcourt, Brace and Howe, 1920), pp. 119–120.

8. Louis I. Bredvold, *The Intellectual Milieu of John Dryden* (Ann Arbor: University of Michigan Press, 1934), pp. 67–72.

9. Bonamy Dobrée, "Dryden's Prose," in *Dryden's Mind and Art,* ed. Bruce King (Edinburgh: Oliver and Boyd, 1969), p. 181; see also Hume, *Dryden's Criticism,* pp. 43–44, and Pechter, *Dryden's Classical Theory,* pp. 29–35.

10. George Birkbeck Hill, ed., *Lives of the Poets,* 3 vols. (Oxford: Clarendon Press, 1905), I, 366. We might think of Johnson's many prefaces and dedications, often anonymous. For Dryden, Davenant's Preface to *Gondibert* would have provided one model.

11. See Don H. Bialostosky, "Dialogics as an Art of Discourse in Literary Criticism," *PMLA* 101 (October 1986): 788–797, esp. pp. 794–795; also Hume, *Dryden's Criticism,* pp. 13, 20.

12. "Of Dramatic Poesy," *Essays,* ed. Watson, I, 40.

13. "Defence of the Epilogue," *Essays,* I, 180.

14. "An Account of the Augustan Age of England" in *The Bee,* No. 8, *Collected Works of Oliver Goldsmith,* ed. Arthur Friedman, 5 vols. (Oxford: Clarendon Press, 1966), I, 500.

15. See Pechter, *Dryden's Classical Theory,* pp. 192–195, where he notes the "immediacy, the tone of direct address, the conversational tone" of these poems (p. 192); Van Doren provides an excellent summary in *The Poetry of John Dryden,* pp. 162–177.

16. *Essays,* ed. W. P. Ker, II, 43.

17. *Essays,* ed. Ker, II, 46–67, 97, esp. 46–47, 55–57, 61, 65, 67; Mikhail Bakhtin, "Epic and Novel: On a Methodology for the Study of the Novel" (1941) in *The Dialogic Imagination,* ed. Michael Holquist, trans. Carly Emerson and Michael Holquist (Austin: University of Texas Press, 1981), pp. 24–26. For Bakhtin and Pope, see Leo Damrosch, "Pope's Epics: What Happened to Narrative?" in *The Eighteenth Century* 29 (1988): 189–207.

18. Ludwig Feuerbach, *Grundsätze der Philosophie der Zukunft* (Frankfurt am Main: Klostermann, 1967), p. 69: "*Die wahre Dialektik ist kein Monolog des einsamen Denkers mit sich selbst, sie ist ein Dialog zwischen Ich und Du.*"

19. Katerina Clark and Michael Holquist, *Mikhail Bakhtin* (Cambridge, Mass.: Harvard University Press, 1984), p. 5, emphasis added.

20. See Douglas Lane Patey, *Probability and Literary Form: Philosophic*

Theory and Literary Practice in the Augustan Age (Cambridge: Cambridge University Press, 1984), pp. 314 n. 18, 141.

21. Van Doren, *Poetry of Dryden,* p. 206.

22. For the classical and Renaissance backgrounds of critical and philosophical dialogue in Dryden, see *The Works of John Dryden* (Berkeley: University of California Press, 1971), vol. XVII, *Prose 1668–1691,* ed. Samuel Holt Monk, A. E. Wallace Maurer, Vinton A. Dearing, pp. 348–359; on this topic the editors acknowledge the assistance of Philip Levine.

23. See Pechter, *Dryden's Classical Theory,* pp. 160–188; for analysis of theory and practice in *Mac Flecknoe,* esp. 187–188, 189, 196–197; also Van Doren, *Poetry of Dryden,* pp. 206, 276–277.

24. See Maximillian E. Novak, "Defoe's Theory of Fiction," *SP* 61 (1964): 668.

25. *Essays,* ed. Watson, I, 271–272.

26. Samuel Richardson, *Clarissa* (1747), I, A3^r.

27. "Of Heroic Plays," in *Essays,* I, 159.

28. Ibid., I, 219–220.

29. Ibid., I, 212–213, 216.

30. "Of Dramatic Poesy," ibid., I, 25, 41, 67, emphasis added.

31. Preface to *The Literary Criticism of John Dryden,* ed. Arthur C. Kirsch (Lincoln: University of Nebraska Press, Regents Series, 1966), pp. xiv-xv.

32. Robert Hume points out the shift in Dryden's criticism from the 1660s and 1670s to that of the last two decades, the 1680s and 1690s (pp. 15, 209, 216, 226–227); see also Pechter, *Dryden's Classical Theory,* pp. 151–160, esp. 157.

33. Roland Barthes, *The Pleasure of the Text,* trans. Richard Miller (New York: Hill and Wang, 1975), p. 3. *Le Plaisir du texte* (Paris: Editions du Seuil, 1973).

34. *Essays,* I, 58–59, and "A Defence of an Essay of Dramatic Poesy," I, 114.

35. Ibid., I, 82, 6, 84.

36. I am indebted to Stuart Cornfield for this observation.

37. Van Doren, *Poetry of Dryden,* p. 169.

38. See Kirsch's preface, pp. xii, xiv.

39. Barthes, *The Pleasure of the Text,* pp. 66, 67. Dryden's "sounding and significant" is related—with the terms reversed—to Barthes's "meaning, *insofar as it is sensually produced*" (p. 61).

40. Hume sees differences between the two, but Eliot is still "closest" to Dryden, closer than any other English critic (p. 20). Ronald Bush

observes, "Eliot opened and closed the decade of his poetic transformation with major essays on Dryden" in *T. S. Eliot: A Study in Character and Style* (New York: Oxford University Press, 1984), p. 114.

41. Francis Jeffrey, *Contributions to the Edinburgh Review* (1846), II, 144.

42. James Osborne, *John Dryden: Some Biographical Facts and Problems,* rev. ed. (Gainesville: University of Florida Press, 1965), p. 103; George Saintsbury, *Dryden* (New York: Harper Brothers, 1881), p. 127. For Dryden's relation to his predecessor, see Maximillian Novak, "Criticism, Adaptation, Politics, and the Shakespearean Model of Dryden's *All for Love,*" in *Studies in Eighteenth-Century Culture,* vol. VII, ed. Roseann Runte (Madison: University of Wisconsin Press, 1978), pp. 375–387.

43. "A Defence of An Essay of Dramatic Poesy," *Essays,* I, 120.

44. *Essays,* I, 44.

45. For the relation with Milton, see Anne Davidson Ferry, *Milton and the Miltonic Dryden* (Cambridge, Mass.: Harvard University Press, 1968).

2. The Paradox of Refinement: Progress and Decline in Literature

1. In this chapter I am indebted for observations and some quotations to Judith Abrams Plotz, "Ideas of the Decline of Poetry: A Study in English Criticism from 1700 to 1830," unpub. diss., Harvard University, 1965.

2. *Timber, or Discoveries,* in *Critical Essays of the Seventeenth Century,* ed. J. E. Spingarn, 3 vols. (Oxford: Clarendon Press, 1909), I, 27.

3. George Williamson, "Mutability, Decay and Jacobean Melancholy," *Seventeenth Century Contexts* (London: Faber, 1960), p. 24.

4. Dryden, *Of Dramatic Poesy and Other Critical Essays,* ed. George Watson, 2 vols. (London: J. M. Dent & Sons, Everyman's Library, 1962), I, 170, "Defence of the Epilogue to the Second Part of *Granada:* or an Essay on the Dramatic Poetry of the Last Age."

5. Dryden, *Essays* I, 178, 192, 181, passim; see W. J. Bate, *The Burden of the Past and the English Poet* (Cambridge, Mass.: Harvard University Press, 1970), pp. 26–27.

6. Dryden, *Essays* I, 180, "An Essay on the Dramatic Poetry of the Last Age"; "Preface to Fables Ancient and Modern," II, 246, emphasis added.

7. John Upton, *Critical Observations on Shakespeare* (London: Printed for G. Hawkins, in Fleet-street, 1746), p. 14.

8. See Maximillian E. Novak, "Shaping the Augustan Myth: John Dryden and the Politics of Restoration Augustanism" in *Greene Centennial Studies,* ed. Paul J. Korshin and Robert R. Allen (Charlottesville: University Press of Virginia, 1984), pp. 1–21, esp. pp. 10–16.

9. Quoted by Eliot in his Introduction to *Selected Poems* of Ezra Pound (London: Faber and Faber, 1928).

10. Sharon Turner, *History of England,* 2 vols. (London, 1814–1815), II, 555; Plotz, "Ideas of the Decline of Poetry," pp. 111–112, remarks that most literary histories of that time treat progress as a major theme.

11. Keats, *Letters,* ed. Hyder E. Rollins, 2 vols. (Cambridge, Mass.: Harvard University Press, 1958), I, 281–282.

12. *Edinburgh Review* (1802) in *Contributions to the Edinburgh Review by Francis Jeffrey* (London, 1846), I, 81, 160, 159.

13. *War and Peace,* trans. Rosemary Edmonds (Harmondsworth, Middlesex: Penguin Books, 1957, 1982 in one vol.), Epilogue, part 2, chaps. 2, 3, pp. 1406–1407, 1408, 1410.

14. For the best discussion on this aspect of the twin odes, see Howard Weinbrot, "Gray's 'Progress of Poesy' and 'The Bard': An Essay in Literary Transmission," in *Johnson and His Age,* ed. James Engell, Harvard English Studies 12 (Cambridge, Mass.: Harvard University Press, 1984), pp. 311–332.

15. *Preface to Shakespeare* in *Johnson on Shakespeare,* ed. Arthur C. Sherbo in *The Yale Edition of the Works of Samuel Johnson* (New Haven: Yale University Press, 1958-), VII, 81–82.

16. John Dennis, *The Advancement and Reformation of Modern Poetry* (London: Printed for Rich. Parker, 1701), chap. IV, pp. 20–21.

17. Letter VI, "Heroic and Gothic Manners" in *Hurd's Letters on Chivalry and Romance,* ed. Edith J. Morley (London: Henry Frowde, 1911), p. 114.

18. *Critical Essays,* ed. Spingarn, I, 27.

19. *Complete Poetical Works of James Thomson,* ed. J. Logie Robertson (London, 1908), p. 240.

20. Letter XL, *Letters from a Citizen of the World to his Friends in the East* in *Collected Works of Oliver Goldsmith,* ed. Arthur Friedman, 5 vols. (Oxford: Clarendon Press, 1966), II, 170; *Enquiry,* I, 257.

21. April 14, 1775 in *Boswell's Life of Johnson,* ed. George Birkbeck Hill, rev. and enlrg. L. F. Powell, 6 vols. (Oxford: Clarendon Press, 1934–1950), II, 358 and n.

22. "The Arts and the Idea of Progress," in *Progress and Its Discontents,* ed. Gabriel A. Almond, Marvin Chodorow, and Roy Harvey Pearce

(Berkeley: University of California Press, 1982), p. 450; Krieger's article, pp. 449–469, is one of a few recent critical essays to focus on progress and the arts. He anchors his wide-ranging and excellent discussion in the eighteenth century. The best recent book-length treatment of the concept of refinement, decline, and art in modern western Europe is Patrick Brantlinger's *Bread & Circuses: Theories of Mass Culture as Social Decay* (Ithaca, N.Y.: Cornell University Press, 1983).

23. Robert Nisbet, *History of the Idea of Progress* (New York: Basic Books, 1980), pp. 151–156.

24. I am indebted to Max Byrd for the observation; see his "Sterne and Swift: Augustan Continuities," in *Johnson and His Age,* ed. James Engell, pp. 509–530, p. 521.

25. See Krieger, "The Arts and . . . Progress," pp. 454–455.

26. *Memoirs of the Literary and Philosophical Society of Manchester,* I, 65–66.

27. "Preface to Fables Ancient and Modern" in *Essays,* ed. Watson, II, 277.

28. "Of Simplicity and Refinement in Writing," in *Essays Moral, Political, and Literary,* collected in *The Philosophical Works,* ed. T. H. Green and T. H. Grose, 4 vols. (London: 1882; rpt. Aalen: Scientia Verlag, 1964), III, 243, emphasis added.

29. Robert Alves, *Sketches of a History of Literature* (Edinburgh: Alex. Chapman, 1794), pp. 151, 194.

30. Leslie Stephen, *English Thought in the Eighteenth Century,* 3rd ed., 2 vols., (London: John Murray, 1902), II, 446–447.

31. See Howard D. Weinbrot, "'An Ambition to Excell': The Aesthetics of Emulation in the Seventeenth and Eighteenth Centuries," *Huntington Library Quarterly* 48 (1985): 121–139, esp. 125–134, 139 n. 35.

32. John Newbery, *The Art of Poetry on a New Plan* (1762), "Of the Epic or Heroic Poem," p. 382.

33. See Robert Folkenflik, "Macpherson, Chatterton, Blake and the Great Age of Literary Forgery," *The Centennial Review* 18 (Fall 1976): 378–391.

34. *Spectator* 279, in *The Spectator,* ed. Donald F. Bond, 5 vols. (Oxford: Clarendon Press, 1965), II, 588; emphasis added.

35. Gilchrist, *Beauties of English Poetry* (London, 1786), p. 238.

36. Joseph Warton, *An Essay on the Genius and Writings of Pope,* 2 vols. (London, 1806), I, 198.

37. *Life,* III, 169, Sept. 19, 1777; IV, 338, June 30, 1784.

38. See Bate, *Burden,* pp. 80–84; Krieger, "The Arts and . . . Progress," p. 461.

39. Quoted by Bate, *Burden,* p. 84.

40. Pierre Bourdieu, *Distinction: A Social Critique of the Judgement of Taste,* trans. Richard Nice (Cambridge, Mass.: Harvard University Press, 1984), p. 33; originally *La Distinction: Critique sociale du jugement* (Paris: Editions de Minuit, 1979).

41. Thomas Blackwell, *Enquiry into the Life and Writings of Homer* (1735), p. 28.

42. *Edinburgh Review* (1810) in *Contributions to the Edinburgh Review* (1846), II, 244.

43. Thomas Warton, *The History of English Poetry,* 4 vols. (London, 1774–1790), II, 462.

44. *The Poetry and Prose of William Blake,* ed. David V. Erdman, commentary by Harold Bloom (Garden City, N.Y.: Doubleday, 1965, 1970). p. 396.

45. See W. J. Bate, "The English Poet and the Burden of the Past, 1660–1820," in *Aspects of the Eighteenth Century,* ed. Earl Wasserman (Baltimore: Johns Hopkins University Press, 1965), pp. 245–264.

46. Richard Hurd, *A Discourse on Poetical Imitation* in *The Works of Richard Hurd, D.D.,* 8 vols. (London: T. Cadell & W. Davies, 1811), II, 235.

47. Letter to Thomas Curnik, April 9, 1814 in *Collected Letters of Samuel Taylor Coleridge,* ed. Earl Leslie Griggs (Oxford: Clarendon Press, 1959), I, 469–470.

48. *Critical Essays of the Seventeenth Century,* ed. Spingarn, II, 263, 264.

49. *The Works, in Verse and Prose, of Leonard Welsted, Esq.,* ed. John Nichols (London: printed by and for the editor, 1787), pp. 123–124, 122.

50. *Contributions to the Edinburgh Review* (1846), II, 38–39; "An Account of the Augustan Age in England," *The Bee,* No. 8, *Works,* ed. Friedman, I, 498.

51. *Life,* IV, 217.

52. *The Pamphleteer,* XI, 507–535, pp. 514–515.

53. Joseph Warton, *Essay on the Genius and Writings of Pope* (1782), II, 211.

54. Goldsmith, *Works,* ed. Friedman, I, 268.

55. *Tour,* Aug. 31., in Boswell's *Life,* V, 138 n.

3. "So Far Retir'd from Happy Pieties": The Rise of Modern Myth

1. Samuel Johnson, *Lives of the English Poets,* ed. George Birkbeck Hill, 3 vols. (Oxford: Clarendon Press, 1905), II, 294.

2. The best anthology, with detailed introductory essays to individual authors and a superb bibliography, is *The Rise of Modern Mythology 1680–1860,* ed. Burton Feldman and Robert D. Richardson (Bloomington: Indiana University Press, 1972); see pp. 1–295 for the eighteenth century.

3. Although it discusses primarily poetry and not prose criticism or commentary, still indispensable is Douglas Bush, *Mythology and the Romantic Tradition in English Poetry* (Cambridge, Mass.: Harvard University Press, 1937; rpt. New York: Pageant, 1957). The neoclassic age, says Bush, witnesses "almost fruitless generations" in its attempts at mythological poems and "is almost completely barren, at least of good ones" (pp. xi, 5).

4. Frank Manuel, *The Eighteenth Century Confronts the Gods* (Cambridge, Mass.: Harvard University Press, 1959), contains a fine treatment of the cultural and religious character of mythology in the eighteenth century. Manuel also examines crosscurrents of mythography between France and England. See also Stefano Cochetti, *Mythos und "Dialektik der Aufklärung"* (Königstein: Anton Hain, 1985, Monographien zur philosophischen Forschung, Band 229). Cochetti supplements Horkheimer and Adorno's analysis of the Enlightenment with a plea to appreciate the importance of old mythology, not modern "myths." While granting that such appreciation is deserved, we can argue for a more overarching perspective and establish the tendency and emphases of English thinkers on the subject.

5. This question, expanded to the range of English poetry and literature in the eighteenth and early nineteenth centuries, forms the subject of W. J. Bate's *The Burden of the Past and the English Poet* (Cambridge, Mass.: Harvard University Press, 1970). Bate discusses "the neoclassic dilemma" of admiration without the hope of original imitation in chap. 2, pp. 29–57, esp. 34–36.

6. Thomas Blackwell, *Letters Concerning Mythology* (London, 1748), p. 5.

7. Thomas Blackwell, *Proofs of An Enquiry into the Life and Writings of Homer* (1748), pp. 36–38; Blackwell, *An Enquiry into the Life and Writings of Homer* (1735), p. 148.

8. "Art and Politics," *Harvard International Review,* November 1983, p. 7.

9. Charles Cowden Clarke, in his *Recollections* (London: Silow, Marston, Searle, & Rivington, 1878) of John Keats (pp. 123–124), says Keats knew basic handbooks: Andrew Tooke's *The Pantheon* (1698), John Lemprière's *Bibliotheca classica; or, a Classical Dictionary* (1788), and Joseph Spence's *Polymetis* (1747): "This was the store whence he acquired his in-

timacy with the Greek mythology." To which could be added incidental and secondary sources, such as Burton's *Anatomy of Melancholy,* which Keats uses for *Lamia.*

10. Johnson, *Lives,* I, 295, see Addison's *Spectator* 523; *Lives* I, 213; II, 17.

11. Johnson, *Lives,* III, 436; II, 204.

12. Samuel Taylor Coleridge, *Biographia Literaria,* ed. James Engell and W. J. Bate, 2 vols. (Princeton and London: Princeton University Press and Routledge & Kegan Paul, 1983), II, 75. (Vol. 7 of *The Collected Works of Samuel Taylor Coleridge,* ed. Kathleen Coburn and Bart Winer.)

13. Johnson, *Lives,* II, 311.

14. Coleridge, *Biographia,* I, 10.

15. James Beattie, *Essays on Poetry and Music, as They Affect the Mind,* 2nd. ed. (Edinburgh, 1778), p. 259. Beattie apparently learned from the failure of his lifeless poem *Judgment of Paris* thirteen years earlier in 1765. See Emerson Marks, "In Search of the Godly Language," *Philological Quarterly,* 54 (Winter 1975): 289–309.

16. Johnson, *Lives,* II, 68, 283; I, 291; see *Rambler* 37: "Mythological allusions," especially in pastorals, are an "absurdity."

17. Johnson, *Lives,* III, 233.

18. Johnson, *Rambler* 37.

19. René Wellek, *The Rise of English Literary History* (Chapel Hill: University of North Carolina Press, 1941), p. 70.

20. A modern companion comes from William Alfred's poem "In Memory of My Friend Robert Lowell." Alfred speaks first, then Lowell: "Where you are Christ only knows. I'm in Harvard Square. / 'We found it brick; we're leaving it prefab.'"

21. For instance, Blackwell, *Life and Writings of Homer,* pp. 60–61, discusses Fénelon's work.

22. Bush, *Mythology and the Romantic Tradition,* p. 40n.

23. "The Passions: An Ode for Music," l. 188.

24. Wellek, *Rise of English Literary History,* p. 77; see Howard D. Weinbrot, *Augustus Caesar in "Augustan" England* (Princeton: Princeton University Press, 1978), p. 127.

25. Blackwell, *Life and Writings of Homer,* p. 32.

26. Ibid., p. 86; see also pp. 136–137.

27. Blackwell, *Letters Concerning Mythology,* p. 372.

28. Ibid., pp. 405–411, 372; Andrew Ramsay's *Discourse upon the Theology and Mythology of the Pagans* (1730), pp. 79–88. The *Discourse* is appended to *Travels of Cyrus* (1728).

29. Ramsay, *Discourse,* p. 88.

30. *Critical Opinions of Samuel Johnson,* ed. J. E. Brown (Princeton: Princeton University Press, 1926), pp. 159–160.

31. Blackwell, *Letters Concerning Mythology,* pp. 12, 406.

32. *Faust,* I, 392–397.

33. William Hazlitt, *Complete Works,* ed. P. P. Howe, 21 vols. (Toronto and New York: J. M. Dent & Sons, 1930–34), XX, 296, 61; IV, 18–19, 34; see James Engell, *The Creative Imagination: Enlightenment to Romanticism* (Cambridge, Mass.: Harvard University Press, 1981), pp. 211–212.

34. See Coleridge, *Wallenstein,* part 2 (*The Piccolomini*), II, iv, 123–131; Bush, *Mythology and the Romantic Tradition,* pp. 58–59. Bush connects Wordsworth's sonnet to Thomas Taylor's translation of Proclus in Taylor's *Plato*; compare *The Excursion,* IV, passages beginning at lines 717 and 847.

35. Wellek, *Rise of English Literary History,* p. 123.

36. Ibid., pp. 35–44, 70–71.

37. Blackwell, *Life and Writings of Homer,* pp. 148, 28–32; see also pp. 167–168, 213.

38. See Wellek, *Rise of English Literary History,* pp. 74–81; Bate, *Burden of the Past,* pp. 55–58; Blackwell, *Life and Writings of Homer,* p. 99.

39. William Duff, *An Essay on Original Genius in Philosophy and the Fine Arts, Particularly in Poetry* (1767), pp. 124, 192–193n, 181, 186–187.

40. Blackwell, *Life and Writings of Homer,* p. 78; see Bate, *Burden of the Past,* pp. 82–84; Wellek, *Rise of English Literary History,* pp. 72–73, 39.

41. See Harry Levin, "Some Meanings of Myth," *Daedalus* 88 (Spring 1950): 223–231, rpt. in *Myth and Mythmaking,* ed. H. A. Murray (New York, 1960). For *myth* and *mythology,* see Robert D. Richardson, "The Enlightenment View of Myth and Joel Barlow's *Vision of Columbus,*" *Early American Literature* 13 (1978); also Ben Halpern, "'Myth' and 'Ideology' in Modern Usage," *History and Theory* 1 (1961): 129–149.

42. *MND* V, i, 23–27. Perhaps for this reason Douglas Bush says that as far as English literature is concerned, everyone interested in mythology sooner or later collapses in the bosom of Shakespeare or, it might be added, in the bosom of Arthur, which Falstaff did—and Milton nearly followed.

43. Claude Lévi-Strauss, *Structural Anthropology,* trans. Claire Jacob-

son and Brooke Grundfest Schoepf (Penguin, 1972 [*Anthropologie Structurale,* Paris: Plon, 1958]), p. 210; Northrop Frye, *The Secular Scripture: A Study of the Structure of Romance* (Cambridge, Mass.: Harvard University Press, 1976), p. 9.

44. *Confessions,* Bk. 7 (1747–1749). Booksellers had conceived translating Chambers. Of course, Diderot greatly expanded that plan.

45. William Warburton, *The Divine Legation of Moses Demonstrated,* 2 vols. (1737–1742), II, bk. 4, sec. 4.

46. Roland Barthes, *Mythologies,* trans. Annette Lavers (New York: Hill and Wang, 1975 [Paris: Editions du Seuil, 1957]), p. 114.

47. Claude Lévi-Strauss, *The Savage Mind* (London: Weidenfeld and Nicolson, 1966 [Paris: Plon, 1962]), p. 263.

48. Ramsay's *Discours sur la poésie épique* (1797 ed.), p. 11 (prefixed to Fénelon's *Avantures*). On "secret symbols" and on allegory versus parable see Blackwell, *Life and Writings of Homer,* pp. 84–86, and *Letters Concerning Mythology,* pp. 56–57, 76.

49. Robert Lowth, *Lectures on the Sacred Poetry of the Hebrews,* trans. G. Gregory, ed. Calvin E. Stowe (Andover, Mass.: Crocker & Brewster), 1829, pp. 88–90 (Lecture XI, "Of the Mystical Allegory"). The *Lectures* first appeared in Latin as *De Sacra Poesi Hebraeorum Praelectiones Academicae* (1753) when Lowth was Professor of Poetry at Oxford. Coleridge, *Statesman's Manual* in *Lay Sermons,* ed. R. J. White, in *The Collected Coleridge,* ed. Kathleen Coburn and Bart Winer, 16 vol. (Princeton and London: Princeton University Press and Routledge & Kegan Paul, 1969-), VI, 29, 30, 30n. Paul de Man, "The Rhetoric of Temporality" in *Blindness and Insight* (Minneapolis: University of Minnesota, 1983). The 1971 Oxford Press edition does not include this essay.

50. Coleridge, *Statesman's Manual,* pp. 29–30 and n., 73, 79. See also Coleridge's *Miscellaneous Criticism,* ed. T. M. Raysor (Cambridge: Harvard University Press, 1936), pp. 28–29; and his *Notebooks,* ed. Kathleen Coburn, 4 vols. (New York, Princeton, and London: Princeton University Press, 1957-), III, 3325, 4183, 4498 and nn.

51. F. W. J. Schelling, *Sammtliche Werke,* ed. K. F. A. Schelling, 14 vols. (Stuttgart and Augsburg: Beck, 1856–1861), V, 399–423; I, 406.

52. See Blackwell, *Letters Concerning Mythology,* p. 395.

53. Wellek, *Rise of English Literary History,* p. 187.

54. Blackwell, *Letters Concerning Mythology,* p. 301.

55. See Engell, *The Creative Imagination,* chaps. 2, 3, 6–12, 16, 19.

56. Blackwell, *Letters Concerning Mythology,* pp. 231–233, 283.

57. Blackwell, *Ibid.,* pp. 155, 349–350, 23–24, 119, 283; see also pp. 130–131.

58. Ibid., pp. 387–388, 408.

59. For extended discussion, see Robert Folkenflik, "The Artist as Hero in the Eighteenth Century," *The Yearbook of English Studies* 12 (1982): 91–108; and Haskell M. Block, "The Myth of the Artist" in *Literary Criticism and Myth,* ed. Joseph P. Strelka (University Park: Pennsylvania University Press, 1980), pp. 3–24. In the phenomenon of artist or poet as hero, Folkenflik sees "the English . . . for a change in the avant-garde" (p. 92) in an evolution moving from Dryden through Coleridge. Block, who concentrates on the nineteenth and twentieth centuries, notes: "we may see that the scholars of the enlightenment who explored primitive society and religion, in their quest for the origins of modern culture, pointed the way to a recognition of the special place of myth as the groundwork of literature" (p. 3).

60. Walter Jaeschke, "Early German Idealist Reinterpretation of the Quarrel of the Ancients and Moderns," *Clio* 12 (Summer 1983): 313–331, p. 321.

61. For one view of modern political implications of myth, see Barthes, *Mythologies,* pp. 156–158. Paul Cantor's *Creature and Creator: Myth-making and English Romanticism* (Cambridge: Cambridge University Press, 1984) provides general discussion of this and other basic concerns.

62. Blackwell, *Life and Writings of Homer,* p. 154.

4. *Non Disputandum:* Hume's Critique of Criticism

1. Johnson, *Lives of the English Poets,* ed. George Birkbeck Hill, 3 vols. (Oxford: Clarendon Press, 1905), III, 441.

2. Preface to *All for Love,* the only play Dryden claimed he wrote to please himself and not his audience.

3. René Wellek, *History of Modern Criticism,* 5 vols. to date (New Haven: Yale University Press, 1955-), I, 109; cf. Ernst Cassirer, *The Philosophy of the Enlightenment,* trans. F. C. A. Koelln and J. P. Pettegrove (Princeton: Princeton University Press, 1951), pp. 275–278.

4. Coleridge, *Biographia Literaria,* ed. John Shawcross, 2 vols. (Oxford: Oxford University Press, 1907), II, 247.

5. Johnson, *Lives,* I, 410, 412.

6. Samuel Butler, *Satires and Miscellaneous Poetry and Prose,* ed. René Lamar (Cambridge: Cambridge University Press, 1928), "Upon Critics Who Judge of Modern Plays Precisely by the Rules of the Antients," pp. 60–62; and in Butler's *Characters,* ed. A. R. Waller (Cambridge: Cambridge University Press, 1908), "A Modern Critic," p. 32; emphasis added.

7. Johnson, *Lives,* II, 145.

8. W. Jackson Bate, *From Classic to Romantic: Premises of Taste in Eighteenth-Century England* (Cambridge, Mass.: Harvard University Press, 1946), pp. 113–114.

9. Edmund Burke, *Enquiry,* ed. J. T. Boulton (New York: Columbia University Press, 1958), p. 13.

10. Oliver Goldsmith, *Works,* ed. Peter Cunningham, 4 vols. (London: John Murray, 1854), IV, 203. The sentence occurs in a contribution to *The Critical Review* attributed, but not with certainty, to Goldsmith. *The Collected Works,* ed. Arthur Friedman, 5 vols. (Oxford: Clarendon Press, 1966), omits this review of Ralph Church's edition of *The Faerie Queene.*

11. Cassirer, *Philosophy of the Enlightenment,* p. 305; see also pp. 311–312.

12. Coleridge, *Biographia Literaria,* ed. James Engell and W. Jackson Bate, 2 vols. (Princeton: Princeton University Press, 1983), II, 84; I, 264.

13. Ibid., II, 9–11, 119.

14. David Hume, "Concerning Moral Sentiments" in *Essays Moral, Political, and Literary,* ed. T. H. Green and T. H. Grose, 2 vols. (London, 1882; Aalen: Scientia Verlag, 1964), II, 265, 268 (vol. IV of *The Philosophical Works*). Pierre Bourdieu, *Distinction: A Social Critique of the Judgement of Taste,* trans. Richard Nice (Cambridge, Mass.: Harvard University Press, 1984), p. 11.

15. The potential split between genius cultivated with a reflexive, self-conscious understanding and that of a more spontaneous, "natural" gift runs throughout eighteenth-century criticism—e.g., Addison's *Spectator* 160, Alexander Gerard's *Essay on Genius,* and Schiller's *Naive and Sentimental Poetry.*

16. For discussion in light of recent critical theory, see Frank Lentricchia, *After the New Criticism* (Chicago: University of Chicago Press, 1980), chap. 2, "Versions of Existentialism," esp. pp. 35–60. This potential psychic split is discussed by Paul de Man with regard to Yeats in *Blindness and Insight* (New York: Oxford University Press, 1971), pp. 170–172, and by Jean Hagstrum with reference to "wit" in "Johnson and the Concordia Discors," in *The Unknown Samuel Johnson,* ed. John J. Burke, Jr. and Donald Kay (Madison: University of Wisconsin Press, 1983), pp. 39–53, esp. 51–52.

17. For Hume's persisting relevance, see Murray Cohen, "Eighteenth-Century English Literature and Modern Critical Methodologies," *The Eighteenth Century: Theory and Interpretation* 20 (1979): 5–23, esp. 11–

15; and Mary Carman Rose, "The Importance of Hume in Western Aesthetics," *The British Journal of Aesthetics* 16 (1976): 218–229. Rose contends that Hume made vital "contributions to modern aesthetics" (p. 220) and that "the aesthetic inquiry of twentieth-century American and British language philosophers has explicitly been an appropriation but also a development of Hume's empirical approach to aesthetics" (p. 224).

18. "Of the Standard of Taste," in *Essays Moral, Political, and Literary,* I, 266, 267, 266. Hereafter cited as "Standard."

19. T. S. Eliot, *The Use of Poetry and the Use of Criticism* (London: Faber and Faber, 1933), pp. 141–142.

20. "Standard," p. 271; emphasis added.

21. Ibid., p. 272.

22. Hugh Blair, *Lectures on Rhetoric and Belles Lettres,* 2 vols. (London: W. Strahan, 1783), I, 32n.

23. For interplay of sense and sentiment, reason and feeling, see Ralph Cohen, "The Rationale of Hume's Literary Inquiries," in *David Hume: Many-sided Genius,* ed. Kenneth R. Merril and Robert W. Shahan (Norman: University of Oklahoma Press, 1976), pp. 99, 105; Teddy Brunius, *David Hume on Criticism* (Stockholm: Almquist & Wiksell, 1952), pp. 37, 39, 53; and Nicholas Capaldi, "Hume's Theory of the Passions," in *Hume, A Re-evaluation,* ed. Donald W. Livingston and James T. King (New York: Fordham University Press, 1976), pp. 172–190, esp. 175–176.

24. "Standard," pp. 277–278.

25. Capaldi notes that for Hume, "the test of all philosophical speculation is its relevance to our common experience. Common sense is not something to be explained away but something which calls for explanation" ("Hume's Theory," p. 176). Kant's *Critique of Judgment* notices the easily misunderstood signification of common sense and the abuse of it that Hume is fighting: "Common human understanding . . . has the doubtful honour of having the name of common sense . . . bestowed upon it; and bestowed, too, in an acceptation of the word *common* (not merely in our language, where it actually has a double meaning, but also in many others) which makes it amount to what is *vulgar (das Vulgare)*—which is everywhere to be met with—a quality which by no means confers credit or distinction upon its possessor." Kant's "das Vulgare" means vulgar in the sense of found in many instances or many places, not necessarily low or inferior.

26. "Standard," p. 269, emphasis added.

27. Adam Smith, *Lectures,* ed. John M. Lothian (London: Thomas

Nelson and Sons, 1963), p. 51; see also pp. xiii-xvi, and Cassirer, *Philosophy of the Enlightenment,* p. 308.

28. *Lives,* III, 441, emphasis added. For philosophically oriented discussion, see Chester Chapin, "Samuel Johnson and the Scottish Common Sense School," *The Eighteenth Century: Theory and Interpretation* 20 (1979): 50–64.

29. "Standard," p. 270.

30. Ibid., pp. 274, 275. Ralph Cohen, "David Hume's Experimental Method and the Theory of Taste," *ELH* 25 (1958): 270–289, remarks: "The most significant element of Hume's essay on taste is its insistence on method, of the introduction of fact and experience into the problem of taste" (p. 270). The method, however, is not demonstrable and scientific.

31. "Standard," p. 273.

32. Ibid., p. 279. See Brunius, *Hume on Criticism,* where Brunius sees Hume "creating a dialog about the great questions to which there are no definite answers" (p. 15).

33. On Hume's relativism limited by his insistence on a broadly catholic standard, see Cohen, "Hume's Experimental Method," p. 278, and "The Rationale," p. 114; also Brunius, pp. 75, 85.

34. Ernest Campbell Mossner, "Hume's 'Of Criticism,'" in *Studies in Criticism & Aesthetics: Essays in Honor of Samuel Holt Monk,* ed. Howard Anderson and John S. Shea (Minneapolis: University of Minnesota Press, 1967), pp. 232–248, puts the case bluntly: "In the realm of matter of fact, demonstration cannot be reached" (pp. 234–235).

35. "Standard," p. 279. Cohen, "Hume's Experimental Method," states: "It has cometimes been overlooked that Hume's explicit purpose . . . was to prove that some tastes are better than others and to provide a basis for this distinction" (p. 272).

36. "Standard," pp. 276, 280.

37. Cohen, "The Rationale," thus speaks of the critic undergoing a "*de*-conversion" (pp. 109–110).

38. Jacques Derrida, "Structure, Sign, and Play in the Discourse of the Human Sciences," in *The Structuralist Controversy: The Languages of Criticism and the Sciences of Man,* ed. Richard Macksey and Eugenio Donato (Baltimore: Johns Hopkins University Press, 1972), p. 264.

39. See "Christie's Chairman Quits in False Sale Case," *The New York Times,* July 20, 1985, pp. 1, 9.

40. Gerald Chapman, ed., *Literary Criticism in England: 1660–1800* (New York: Alfred Knopf, 1966), p. 273 (from "The Anglo-Scots Inquiry," pp. 265–276). On Hume's breaking the neoclassical mold, see also

Cohen, "Hume's Experimental Method," p. 280, and Mossner, "Hume's 'Of Criticism,'" pp. 237, 239. No recent commentator identifies Hume with neoclassical criticism.

41. For the combination of skepticism and realism in Hume, see John P. Wright, *The Sceptical Realism of David Hume* (Minneapolis: University of Minnesota Press, 1983).

42. No other single issue has led to more disagreement than Hume's views relating aesthetics to morality. William H. Halberstadt, "A Problem in Hume's Aesthetics," *The Journal of Aesthetics and Art Criticism* 30 (1971): 209–214, remarks, "There are good grounds for maintaining . . . that Hume treated aesthetics and ethics similarly" (p. 213)—though independently(?). Rose, in "The Importance of Hume," contends: "Hume interprets both the development and the functioning of the individual's moral stature as independent of the development and the functioning of his aesthetic sense" (p. 223). Mossner states ("Hume's 'Of Criticism,'") that "Morality, for Hume, may legitimately enter into the critical judgment of art" (p. 238). Cohen, in "Hume's Experimental Method," says Hume's procedure "helped separate art from morals," but it also implied that "no critic should give up his ideas of morality and decency in order to relish the work of art" (pp. 276, 277).

Compare Philip Flynn, "Scottish Aesthetics and the Search for a Standard of Taste," *Dalhousie Review* 60 (1980): 5–19, esp. p. 9: "Hume, Kames, Blair, Gerard, and Beattie noted that a just taste in the fine arts and a keen sense of virtue are not *always* joined in the same person. But most of the Scottish aestheticians agreed that art is an important force for moral instruction, operating more often through our sympathetic emotions than through our reason's grasp of moral principles." See also A. M. Kinghorn, "Literary Aesthetics and the Sympathetic Emotions—A Main Trend in Eighteenth-Century Scottish Criticism," *Studies in Scottish Literature* 1 (1963): 35–47.

43. "Standard," pp. 273–274. See Flynn, "Scottish Aesthetics," pp. 7, 11; Cohen, "The Rationale," p. 114; and Peter Jones, "Strains in Hume and Wittgenstein," in *Hume, A Re-evaluation*, pp. 191–209, and in the same volume his "Cause, Reason, and Objectivity in Hume's Aesthetics," pp. 323–342. Jones discusses a social and communal foundation of Hume's "general inalterable standard, by which we may approve or disapprove of characters and manners" (p. 330).

44. Jones, "Cause, Reason, and Objectivity," p. 331: "Hume also claims that certain fundamental 'rules of art are founded on the qualities of human nature.'" Cohen wrestles with the issue in "The Rationale":

"Perhaps one way to approach these inquiries is to ask why Hume does not undertake to define art . . . to him, art is important only in the sense that it engages human beings" (p. 101). But "Art was . . . for Hume . . . an enhancement of man's values" (p. 107) and "It was the value of art that in the end constituted the rationale of Hume's literary inquiries" (p. 115).

45. Quoted by Chapman, *Literary Criticism in England,* p. 273.

46. Goldsmith, *Works,* ed. Friedman, I, 294 and n., which connects Goldsmith's remark with Hume's essay "The Sceptic."

47. M. H. Abrams, "Art-As-Such: The Sociology of Modern Aesthetics," *Bulletin of The American Academy of Arts and Sciences* 38 (March 1985): 8–33, p. 26. Abrams procedes to "avert to social conditions in order to explain a drastic change in the general *theory* of art" (p. 14).

48. *The New Yorker,* July 15, 1985, p. 19.

49. Wordsworth, *Prose Works,* ed. W. J. B. Owen and J. Worthington Smyser, 3 vols. (Oxford: Clarendon Press), III, 84.

50. Francis Jeffrey, *Contributions to the Edinburgh Review* (1844 ed.), discussing Scott's *Lady of the Lake,* II, 483–519, p. 484.

51. Bourdieu, *Distinction,* p. 499.

52. Abrams, "Art-As-Such," p. 22.

53. Bourdieu, *Distinction,* pp. 499–500.

5. Estrangement: The Problem of Ethics and Aesthetics

1. Raymond Williams, *Marxism and Literature* (Oxford: Oxford University Press, 1977), pp. 45–54.

2. See *Critical Essays of the Seventeenth Century,* ed. J. E. Spingarn, 3 vols. (Oxford: Clarendon Press, 1908–1909; Bloomington: Indiana University Press, 1957), I, 221; for tension between delight and pleasure, see I, lxxiv-lxxv.

3. Blackmore, Preface to *Prince Arthur, An Heroick Poem* (London: Printed for A Wrisham and John Churchil at the black Swan in Paternoster-row, 1695, in *Critical Essays of the Seventeenth Century,* III, 229.

4. *The Yale Edition of the Works of Samuel Johnson* (New Haven: Yale University Press, 1958-), VII, 71 (from the *Preface to Shakespeare*).

5. *Critical Essays of the Seventeenth Century,* I, lxxxiv-lxxxv.

6. Reynolds, "Mythomystes," in ibid., I, 162–178.

7. Johnson, *Lives of the Poets,* ed. George Birkbeck Hill, 3 vols. (Oxford: Clarendon Press, 1905), III, 437; emphasis added.

8. *The Works, in Verse and Prose, of Leonard Welsted, Esq.* ed. John Nichols, (London: printed by and for the editor, in Red-Lion-passage, Fleet-street: 1787), p. 145; emphasis added.

9. "On the Idea of Universal Poetry," in *The Works of Richard Hurd, D.D.*, 8 vols. (London: Printed for T. Cadell and W. Davies, 1811), II, 16.

10. William Webbe, "Of English Poetry," in *Elizabethan Critical Essays*, ed. G. Gregory Smith, 2 vols. (Oxford and London: Oxford University Press and Humphrey Milford, 1904), I, 232; emphasis added.

11. M. H. Abrams, "Art-as-Such: The Sociology of Modern Aesthetics," *Bulletin of The American Academy of Arts and Sciences* 38 (March 1985): 8.

12. Kant, *Critique of Judgment,* trans. J. H. Bernard (New York: Macmillan, 1951), II, ii, §59, p. 200. For Kant's sense of analogy see also chap. 90; II, ii, §52, p. 170.

13. Kant, *Critique of Judgment,* II, ii, chap. 59, "Beauty as the symbol of morality"; emphasis added.

14. *The Spectator* (Friday, May 11, 1711), ed. Donald F. Bond, 5 vols. (Oxford: Clarendon Press, 1966), I, 268.

15. William Melmoth, *The Letters of Sir Thomas Fitzosborne with a Dialogue on Oratory,* 6th ed. (London: 1763), pp. 317–318.

16. *The Works of the Right Honourable Edmund Burke,* 12 vols. (Boston: Little Brown, 1865–1867), III, 379.

17. Ralph Cohen, "On the Interrelations of Eighteenth-Century Literary Forms" in *New Approaches to Eighteenth-Century Literature,* ed. Phillip Harth (New York: Columbia University Press, 1974), p. 75.

18. Alastair Fowler, *Kinds of Literature: An Introduction to the Theory of Genres and Modes* (Cambridge, Mass.: Harvard University Press, 1982), p. 224.

19. Jonathan Swift, *Irish Tracts 1720–1723 and Sermons,* ed. Louis Landa (Oxford: Basil Blackwell, 1948), pp. 329–330, 328–329. I have modernized the text and added emphasis. Cf. pp. xxiv–xxv.

20. Goldsmith is writing in *The Monthly Review,* in *Collected Works,* ed. Arthur Friedman, 5 vols. (Oxford: Clarendon Press, 1966), I, 11.

21. *The Life and Works of Charles Lamb,* ed. Alfred Ainger (London: Macmillan, 1899) IV, 50–51. For a recent study of this question from a flexible psychoanalytic approach, see Robert N. Watson, *Shakespeare and the Hazards of Ambition* (Cambridge, Mass.: Harvard University Press, 1984). Dostoevsky remarks in *The Brothers Karamazov* that characters become attractive because of their energy, not their moral qualities.

22. Oscar Wilde, "The Critic as Artist" in *The Artist as Critic: Critical Writings of Oscar Wilde,* ed. Richard Ellmann (New York: Random House, 1969; University of Chicago Press, 1982), p. 406.

23. Wilde, Preface to *The Picture of Dorian Gray,* in *Critical Writings,* ed. Ellmann, pp. 235–236.

24. Rymer, *Tragedies of the Last Age* in *The Critical Works of Thomas Rymer,* ed. Curt A. Zimansky (New Haven: Yale University Press, 1956), p. 75; emphasis added.

25. John Newbery, *Art of Poetry on a New Plan* (London: printed for J. Newbery, 1762), I, 41; II, 160, 181.

26. Johnson concluded, "that more influence has been ascribed to 'The Beggar's Opera,' than it in reality ever had; for I do not believe that any man was ever made a rogue by being present at its representation. At the same time I do not deny that it may have some influence, by making the character of a rogue familiar, and in some degree pleasing" (*Boswell's Life of Johnson,* ed. George Birkbeck Hill, rev. L. F. Powell, 6 vols. [Oxford: Clarendon Press, 1934–1950], II, 367); see Brian Corman in discussing "Johnson and Profane Authors: The *Lives* of Otway and Congreve" in *Johnson After Two Hundred Years,* ed. Paul J. Korshin (Philadelphia: University of Pennsylvania Press, 1986), pp. 225–244; on *The Beggar's Opera,* esp. p. 240 and n. Corman notes that others, including Sir John Hawkins, held the play's influence to be pernicious. In Johnson's qualification, "At the same time," is a response typical of the contraries of his criticism, discussed in Chapter 7.

27. In *The Bard,* Johnson finds little of use: "we are affected only as we believe; we are improved only as we find something to be imitated or declined. I do not see that *The Bard* promotes any truth, moral or political."

28. Rymer, *Tragedies of the Last Age* in *Critical Works,* ed. Zimansky, p. 75.

29. For one of the few recent extended examinations of the role of literature in depicting fundamental motives that give human life shape and pressure, and a study that itself turns to specific works, see Warner Berthoff, *Literature and the Continuances of Virtue* (Princeton: Princeton University Press, 1986).

6. Kinds, Canons, and Readers

1. For the chocolate connection, see *National Geographic,* 166 (November, 1984): 664–686, esp. p. 676.

2. Modern critical theory discriminates variously between *kind* and historical genre, type, mode, subgenre, and so forth. These distinctions, often elaborate, are necessary. But here I use *kind* and *genre* interchangably,

for the focus is on historical genre and its treatment in literary theory. Furthermore, *kind* is the single term most familiar to eighteenth-century English critics (they do not use *genre*); it has enjoyed a sophisticated revival.

3. For the concept of antigenre, see Alastair Fowler, *Kinds of Literature: An Introduction to the Theory of Genres and Modes* (Cambridge, Mass.: Harvard University Press, 1982), pp. 174–178, 216. Significantly, Fowler's examples from English begin mostly in the mid seventeenth century, and it is with Gay's *Shepherd's Week* that "antigenre in some ways more radical began" (p. 176).

4. Ralph Cohen, "On the Interrelations of Eighteenth-Century Literary Forms," in *New Approaches to Eighteenth-Century Literature,* ed. Phillip Harth (New York: Columbia University Press, 1974), p. 47. Margaret Doody, *The Daring Muse: Augustan Poetry Reconsidered* (Cambridge: Cambridge University Press, 1985), speaks of a new "generic self-consciousness" and states the new Augustan poet "had to face the job of creating each poem as its own genre" (p. 67). She calls this "the poem *sui generis*" (p. 77).

5. Doody, *The Daring Muse,* speaks of the novel not as a genre but as "a large loose idea, capable of apparently almost perpetual variation and innumerable idiosyncracies" (p. 200).

6. Richard Hurd, "On the Idea of Universal Poetry" in *The Works of Richard Hurd, D.D.,* 8 vols. (London: Printed for T. Cadell and W. Davies, 1811), II, 19–21.

7. Jean Hagstrum, *Samuel Johnson's Literary Criticism* (Minneapolis: University of Minnesota Press, 1952), p. 33, states that concerning attempts at generic criticism, "Johnson's heart was not in them." See also Leopold Damrosch, Jr., *The Uses of Johnson's Criticism* (Charlottesville: University Press of Virginia, 1976), p. 78: Johnson's "reaction to existing theories of genre, and a submerged theoretical argument underlies some of his best-known critical discussions"; cf. also p. 94.

8. For instance, David Lodge expressed a tepid but necessary rationale in his Inaugural Address on taking the Chair of Modern Criticism at the University of Birmingham. For a more spirited *apologia,* "The Relevance of Genre," in Fowler, *Kinds of Literature,* pp. 24–26, is succinct and eloquent.

9. See Fowler, *Kinds of Literature,* pp. 159 and esp. 23: "Every literary work changes the genres it relates to. This is true not only of radical innovations and productions of genius. The most imitative work, even as

it kowtows slavishly to generic conventions, nevertheless affects them, if only minutely or indirectly." He notes how Jurij Tynjanov's impressive system eventually becomes "too Darwinian" (p. 251).

10. For a well-argued view of understanding originality in the context of genre, see Ralph Cohen and Murray Krieger, "Innovation and Variation: Literary Change and Georgic Poetry" in *Literature and History* papers at the Clark Library Seminar, UCLA, 1973 (Los Angeles, 1974.)

11. Fowler, *Kinds of Literature,* pp. 26–27. On p. 37 he states that Blair and Kames had come to see this flexibility in genre, and while many thus started to regard genre as useless, its importance began to shift from taxonomy to interpretation and reception.

12. John Newbery, *Art of Poetry* (London, 1762), I, 54.

13. Fowler, *Kinds of Literature,* p. 27. See also p. 182: "In the subsequent period [seventeenth and early eighteenth centuries], there was some recoil from the idea of generic mixture to the ideal of pure genre." He cites Rapin. On pp. 218–219 Fowler replies to Cohen.

14. Fredric Jameson, *The Political Unconscious* (Ithaca, N.Y.: Cornell University Press, 1981), p. 105, cited by Ralph Cohen in "History and Genre" in *New Literary History* 17 (Winter 1986): 203. Cohen's essay, pp. 203–218, and the commentary by Dominick LaCapra, pp. 219–221, discuss genre in sociological and economic contexts relevant to topics later in this chapter. In short, I believe with Jameson that genre is a contract between readers and writers, but I also agree with Cohen that it is a contract with some preconditions; and that genre theory is at present an empirical tool and not a prescriptive or repressive voice of authority.

15. See Cohen, "On the Interrelations," pp. 33–39.

16. One fine example is John Feather, *The Provincial Book Trade in Eighteenth-Century England* (Cambridge: Cambridge University Press, 1985). This eminently readable study provides statistical evidence to support general conclusions. About the new national book and periodical markets established particularly by London publishers and book sellers, Feather notes: "The social, political, and cultural influence of this achievement was out of all proportion to its economic scale. Although regional cultures survived, a uniform national culture was superimposed upon them through the uniformity of the printed word" (p. 123). See also Feather's "The Commerce of Letters: The Study of the Eighteenth-Century Book Trade," *Eighteenth-Century Studies* 17 (Summer 1984): 405–424. For general readership in the eighteenth century, see R. D. Altick, *The English Common Reader* (Chicago: University of Chicago Press, 1957), and Laurence

Stone, "Literacy and Education in England 1640–1900," *Past and Present* 62 (1969): 69–139.

17. See Pat Rogers, "Classics and Chapbooks," chap. 7 in his *Literature and Popular Culture in Eighteenth-Century England* (Sussex and New Jersey: Harvester and Barnes & Noble, 1985), pp. 162–182.

18. Many studies explore this aspect of eighteenth-century literature, particularly verse, among them Reuben Brower, *Alexander Pope: The Poetry of Allusion* (Oxford: Clarendon Press, 1959); Earl R. Wasserman, "The Limits of Allusion in *The Rape of the Lock*" in *Journal of English and Germanic Philology* 65 (1966): 425–444; more recently Bruce Redford, "The Allusiveness of Thomas Gray," chap. 3 in his *The Converse of the Pen: Acts of Intimacy in the Eighteenth-Century Familiar Letter* (Chicago: University of Chicago Press, 1986), pp. 95–132, which focuses on Gray's letters. Redford cites earlier essays by Roger Lonsdale and Christopher Ricks.

19. See Howard Weinbrot, "Johnson and the Arts of Narration: *The Life of Savage, The Vanity of Human Wishes* and *Rasselas*" in *Samuel Johnson: Commemorative Lectures* (Beirut: Librarie du Liban, Egyptian International Publishing, Longman, 1986), pp. 13–38, esp. 13–16, 19–22, 33–34.

20. Fowler, *Kinds of Literature,* pp. 230–231, appears, uncharacteristically, to commit the common mistake of assuming Johnson chose the poets for the *Lives.* For background see W. Jackson Bate, *Samuel Johnson* (New York: Harcourt Brace Jovanovich, 1977), pp. 525–526. Bate makes the point (p. 531) that already some of the poets were being forgotten.

21. Fowler, *Kinds of Literature,* p. 167. For discussion of canon in the context of genre, see pp. 214–234, esp. 214–216, 230–234.

22. J. Paul Hunter has demonstrated this by an exhaustive survey.

23. John Engell, "Walt and Sir Walter, or the Bard and the Bart.: Balladeers," *Walt Whitman Quarterly* 5 (Spring 1988): 1–15.

24. For provincial reading habits and discussion of newspapers, see Roy McKeen Wiles, "The Relish for Reading in Provincial England Two Centuries Ago," in *The Widening Circle,* ed. Paul J. Korshin (Philadelphia: University of Pennsylvania Press, 1976), pp. 85–115.

25. Francis Jeffrey, *Contributions to the Edinburgh Review,* August 1817 (1844 ed.), II, 315.

7. Johnson and The Contraries of Criticism

1. *Boswell's Life of Johnson,* ed. George Birkbeck Hill, rev. L. F. Powell, 6 vols. (Oxford: Clarendon Press, 1934–1950), App. A, IV, 431.

2. "The Character and Opinions of Dr. Johnson" (London: printed

for Thomas J. Wise by Eyre and Spottiswoode, 1918 [1858]), p. 8; rpt. by William B. Todd for The Johnsonians, 1985.

3. *Life,* IV, 338; III, 169.

4. Johnson, *Lives of the Poets,* ed. George Birkbeck Hill, 3 vols. (Oxford: Clarendon Press, 1905), I, 404.

5. *Life,* III, 191.

6. Ibid., IV, 216.

7. For discussion, see James Gray, *"Auctor et Auctoritas:* Dr. Johnson's Views on the Authority of Authorship," *English Studies in Canada* 12 (September 1986): 269–284. Gray notes, "No one in the history of literature can lay greater claim to being an authority than Samuel Johnson. Yet his own self-estimate was such that he would have spurned and perhaps even derided such an ascription" (p. 269).

8. *The Yale Edition of the Works of Samuel Johnson* (New Haven: Yale University Press, 1958-   ), vol. 7, *Johnson on Shakespeare,* ed. Arthur Sherbo, pp. 80–81.

9. John Newbery, *The Art of Poetry* (London, 1762), "Of Dramatic Poetry," II, 156.

10. *Contributions to the Edinburgh Review* (1846), II, 99; James Beattie, *Dissertations Moral and Critical* (Dublin: Exshaw, Walker, Beatty, White, Byrne, Cash, & M'Kenzie, 1783), pp. 186–188.

11. W. Jackson Bate, *Samuel Johnson* (New York: Harcourt Brace Jovanovich, 1977), p. 158; see also R. D. Stock, *Samuel Johnson and Neoclassical Dramatic Theory* (Lincoln: University of Nebraska Press, 1973); and Calhoun Winton, "The Tragic Muse in Enlightened England," in *Greene Centennial Studies,* ed. Paul J. Korshin and Robert R. Allen (Charlottesville: University Press of Virginia, 1984), pp. 125–142, p. 126.

12. See W. Jackson Bate, *The Achievement of Samuel Johnson* (New York: Oxford University Press, 1955), pp. 182–183.

13. *The Letters of Samuel Johnson,* ed. R. W. Chapman, 3 vols. (Oxford: Clarendon Press, 1952), I, 35–36; see also letter 49.

14. *The French Journals of Mrs. Thrale and Dr. Johnson,* ed. M. Tyson and H. Guppy (Manchester: Manchester University Press, 1932), pp. 85–86 and n.

15. *Life,* I, 200.

16. *The Percy Letters* II, *The Correspondence of Thomas Percy & Richard Farmer,* ed. Cleanth Brooks (Baton Rouge: Louisiana State University Press, 1946), pp. 84–85.

17. For a close study, see James Boyd White, *When Words Lose Their Meaning: Constitutions and Reconstitutions of Language, Character, and Com-*

munity (Chicago: University of Chicago Press, 1984), chap. 6, "Teaching a Language of Morality: Johnson's *Rambler* Essays," pp. 138–162. In examining *Rambler* 2, White observes, "The mind that follows each statement with a countering statement has gone as far as it can; it has arrived at a silence not unlike that of a participant in a Socratic dialogue. One kind of thinking has come to an end. What can Johnson do now? His turn out of this position is characteristically upon himself and his present circumstances" (p. 147). White sees Johnson writing by "opposition and complication" and thinking "by recognizing and including contraries" (p. 152).

For Johnson and bipolar oppositions, see Earl Wasserman, "Johnson's *Rasselas:* Implicit Contexts," *Journal of English and Germanic Philology* 74 (1975): 1–25; valuable for the issue of contradiction in Johnson's criticism is also Leopold Damrosch, Jr., *The Uses of Johnson's Criticism* (Charlottesville: University Press of Virginia, 1976), pp. 3, 21–22.

18. Hazlitt, "On the Periodical Essayists" in *Works,* ed. P. P. Howe, 20 vols. (Toronto and New York: J. M. Dent, 1934), VI, 102.

19. See, for example, Emerson R. Marks, "The Antinomy of Style in Augustan Poetics," in *Johnson and His Age,* ed. James Engell (Cambridge, Mass.: Harvard University Press, 1984), pp. 215–232, esp. pp. 224–227.

20. *Miscellaneous Works of John Dryden, Esq.,* ed. Samuel Derrick with "The Life of John Dryden, Esq."; 4 vols. (London: J. and R. Tonson, 1760), I, xiii–xxxiv; p. xxiv.

21. Thomas Tyers, "A Biographical Sketch of Dr. Samuel Johnson" (1785) in *The Early Biographies of Samuel Johnson,,* ed. O. M. Brack and Robert E. Kelley (Iowa City: University of Iowa Press, 1974), p. 67.

22. For a lucid defense of the need to search for "the personal elements that significantly condition . . . what the critic chooses to criticize and how he does so," see Murray Krieger, *Theory of Criticism: A Tradition and Its System* (Baltimore: Johns Hopkins University Press, 1976), chap. 3, "The Critic as Person and Persona," pp. 38–64, esp. 51, 64, 45 (quoted).

23. W. H. Auden, *The Dyer's Hand* (London: Faber and Faber, 1953), p. xii.

24. *Tour* in *Life,* V, 378; see also 378 n.

25. Niels Bohr, "Discussions with Einstein on Epistemological Problems in Atomic Physics," *Atomic Physics and Human Knowledge* (New York: Wiley, 1958), p. 66.

26. For discussion of this in Nietzsche see Erich Heller, "Nietzsche's

Terror," *Salmagundi* (Fall–Winter 1985–86): 89–90; for contradiction as a modern philosophical concept, see Willi Hayum Goetschel, "Zur Geschichte des Widerspruchs in der Neuzeit," in *Wege des Widerspruchs,* ed. Willi Goetschel, John G. Cartwright, Maja Wicki (Bern and Stuttgart: Paul Haupt, 1984), pp. 9–40.

27. *Johnsonian Miscellanies,* ed. George Birkbeck Hill, 2 vols. (Oxford: Clarendon Press, 1897), II, 92.

8. The New Rhetoricians: Semiotics, Theory, and Psychology

1. Longinus, *On the Sublime,* trans. W. Rhys Roberts (Cambridge, Mass.: Cambridge University Press, 1899), p. 81.

2. For general studies, see Wilbur Samuel Howell, *Eighteenth-Century British Logic and Rhetoric* (Princeton: Princeton University Press, 1971), pp. 441–691, esp. 536–691; George A. Kennedy, *Classical Rhetoric and Its Christian Secular Tradition from Ancient to Modern Times* (Chapel Hill: University of North Carolina Press, 1980), pp. 220–241, esp. 227–241.

3. For "theory," see, for example, George Campbell, *The Philosophy of Rhetoric,* 2 vols. (London: W. Strahan, 1776), I, 25–83. Campbell refers to "the theory now laid down and explained" (p. 83). Howell (pp. 616–633) treats Lawson "as much . . . for the new rhetoric as for the old" (p. 630). For Ward and Lawson, see Kennedy, *Classical Rhetoric,* pp. 228–229. Vincent M. Bevilacqua and Richard Murphy, editing Joseph Priestley, *A Course of Lectures on Oratory and Criticism* (Carbondale: Southern Illinois University Press, 1965 [rpt. 1777 ed.]), refer to Ward and Lawson as "the culmination of classical rhetoric in the eighteenth century" (p. xxii).

For background, see Victor Anthony Rudowski, "The Theory of Signs in the Eighteenth Century," *Journal of the History of Ideas* 35 (1974): 683–690. Studies of eighteenth-century semiotics and rhetoric have tended to cluster around Germany and France: e.g., David E. Welberry, *Lessing's Laocoon: Semiotics and Aesthetics in the Age of Reason* (London: Cambridge University Press, 1984); Tzvetan Todorov, "Esthétique et sémiotique au XVIIIe siècle," *Critique* 29 (1973): 29–39; and Wolfgang Bender, "Rhetorische Tradition und Ästhetik im 18. Jahrhundert," *Zeitschrift für deutsche Philologie* 99 (1980): 481–506.

4. Adam Smith, *Lectures on Rhetoric and Belles Lettres . . . Reported by a Student in 1762–63,* ed. John M. Lothian (London: Thomas Nelson and Sons, 1963), p. 23. The manuscript is not in Smith's hand; some lectures may have been recorded partly from memory. On the persistent view of

rhetoric as mere terminology, see Wayne C. Booth, "The Scope of Rhetoric Today: A Polemical Excursion," in *The Prospect of Rhetoric,* ed. Lloyd F. Bitzer and Edwin Black (Englewood Cliffs, N.J.: Prentice-Hall, 1971), p. 94. Jonathan Culler, *Structuralist Poetics: Structuralism, Linguistics, and the Study of Literature* (Ithaca, N.Y.: Cornell University Press, 1975), p. 179.

5. Campbell, *Philosophy of Rhetoric,* I, 95.

6. Hugh Blair, *Lectures on Rhetoric and Belles-Lettres,* 3 vols. (London and Edinburgh: W. Strahan, 1783), I, 8–9.

7. George Saintsbury, *A History of Criticism and Literary Taste in Europe,* 3 vols. (New York: Dodd, Mead, 1900–1904), I, 4, 72.

8. Ibid., II, 463, 470–471.

9. Karl Richards Wallace, *Francis Bacon on Communication & Rhetoric* (Chapel Hill: University of North Carolina Press, 1943), pp. 32–33, 217–218, 222–223.

10. Quintilian, *Institutio Oratoria,* trans. H. E. Butler (Cambridge, Mass.: Harvard University Press, Loeb Classical Library, 1958), I, bk. I, pref. 18 (p. 15; see also pp. 9–14).

11. See J. Hillis Miller, "The Function of Rhetorical Study at the Present Time," *The State of the Discipline 1970s–1980s, ADE Bulletin* 62 (Sept.-Nov. 1979): 10–18, esp. 12–13.

12. Saintsbury, *History,* I, 36–37, 4.

13. Blair, *Lectures,* I, 276.

14. Johnson defines *critick* as "A man skilled in the art of judging literature," but the second definition under *critick* (critique) is "Science of criticism." See also Harry Levin, "Why Literary Criticism is Not an Exact Science," *Grounds for Comparison* (Cambridge, Mass.: Harvard University Press, 1972), pp. 40–56.

15. Aristotle, *The "Art" of Rhetoric,* trans. John Henry Freese (Cambridge, Mass.: Harvard University Press, Loeb Classical Library, 1975), bk. I, i, 1 (p. 3).

16. See, e.g., Campbell, *Philosophy of Rhetoric,* I, vii–x, 155–159, 367–370. Quintilian, I, bk. II, xiv, 1–38 (pp. 299–319) provides a classical answer to "what is rhetoric?" For the leeway of interpretation, see Paul B. Armstrong, "The Conflict of Interpretations and the Limits of Pluralism," *PMLA* 98 (1983): 341–352.

17. Campbell, *Philosophy of Rhetoric,* I, 96.

18. O. Hobart Mowrer, "The Psychologist Looks at Language," *The American Psychologist* 9 (November 1954): 660, as quoted by Marie Hochmuth Nichols, *Rhetoric and Criticism* (Baton Rouge: Louisiana State Uni-

versity Press, 1963), p. 28. Nichols' first chapter, "Rhetoric and Public Address as Humane Study," pp. 3–18, is illuminating.

19. Quintilian, II, bk. VI, ii, 8–9 (pp. 421–423).

20. Priestley, *Oratory and Criticism,* ed. Bevilacqua and Murphy, pp. 3–4.

21. Campbell, *Philosophy of Rhetoric,* I, vii, 12. See also Campbell's *Philosophy,* ed. Lloyd F. Bitzer (Carbondale: Southern Illinois University Press, 1963), which reprints the 1850 London ed. By 1912 *The Philosophy* had entered eleven editions. In New York it was reprinted nineteen times between 1845 and 1887 (see Bitzer, pp. xxx-xxxi). The first edition (1776) is quoted here.

22. Samuel Taylor Coleridge, *Biographia Literaria,* ed. James Engell and W. Jackson Bate, 2 vols. (Princeton: Princeton University Press, 1983), II, 84.

23. Campbell, *Philosophy of Rhetoric,* I, 16; see Karl R. Wallace, "The Fundamentals of Rhetoric," in Bitzer and Black, *The Prospect of Rhetoric,* p. 11.

24. Hans Aarsleff, *The Study of Language in England 1780–1860* (Princeton: Princeton University Press, 1967), p. 23, cf. 20–25. Aarsleff states (p. 53) that Horne Tooke conceived of language *as* thought, not merely as that which makes thought possible. For general background, see also Murray Cohen, *Sensible Words: Linguistic Practice in England, 1670–1785* (Baltimore: Johns Hopkins University Press, 1977).

25. John Hoskins, *Directions for Speech and Style,* ed. Hoyt H. Hudson (Princeton: Princeton University Press, 1935), p. 8.

26. Thomas Gibbons, *Rhetoric* (London: J. and W. Oliver, 1767), p. 448.

27. Campbell, *Philosophy of Rhetoric,* I, 200. This seems to concern what Susan Sontag calls an erotics of art.

28. Blair, *Lectures,* II, 6.

29. Campbell, *Philosophy of Rhetoric,* I, 187.

30. Blair, *Lectures,* I, 296, 275.

31. Thomas Sheridan, *A Course of Lectures on Elocution* (London: J. Dodsley, 1787 [1st ed. 1762]), p. xii.

32. Ibid., p. xii, emphasis added. Recall T. S. Eliot's remark that communication alone does not explain poetry; or Coleridge's, that poetry is most enjoyed when *im*perfectly understood.

33. E.g., see Blair, *Lectures,* I, 94–95, on the difference between describing and actually imitating nature; also Johnson in *Rambler* 36, where he says the effects of nature on the ear and eye are "incapable of much variety of description."

34. For another view, see M. H. Abrams, *The Mirror and the Lamp: Romantic Theory and the Critical Tradition* (New York: Norton, 1958 [rpt. 1953 Oxford University Press ed.]), pp. 53–54.

35. See Gibbons, *Rhetoric,* p. 392; Campbell, *Philosophy of Rhetoric,* I, 242–248. James Beattie, *Essays on Poetry and Music as They Affect the Mind* (Edinburgh: William Creech, 1778), p. 194; see also Beattie, *Dissertations Moral and Critical* (London: W. Strahan, 1783), pp. 166–190.

36. Blair, *Lectures,* I, 327, 330, 332–334, 335.

37. Gibbons, *Rhetoric,* p. 394. See Morton W. Bloomfield, "Personification-Metaphors," *The Chaucer Review* 14 (1980): 287–297; and Earl R. Wasserman, "The Inherent Values of Eighteenth-Century Personification," *PMLA* 65 (1950): 435–463.

38. Gibbons, *Rhetoric,* pp. 95–96; Campbell, *Philosophy of Rhetoric,* I, 306–309, 314–338; Kames, Henry Home, Lord, *Elements of Criticism,* 3 vols. (Edinburgh: A. Millar, 1762), I, 104–127; see also Abrams, *Mirror and Lamp,* pp. 270–271, 324–325. Erasmus Darwin emphasized this power of pleasing illusion and ideal presence in poetry and his view may have influenced Coleridge in the 1790s. See also Wallace Jackson, *Immediacy: The Development of a Critical Concept from Addison to Coleridge* (Amsterdam: Rodopi, 1973), chap. 3.

39. Blair, *Lectures,* I, 81, 75; Campbell, *Philosophy of Rhetoric* (I, 207), offers an interesting defense and definition of the "rather modern" term, "the *sentimental.*"

40. Leopold Damrosch, "The Significance of Addison's Criticism," *SEL* 19 (1979): 430. See also "William Warburton as 'New Critic'" in *Studies in Criticism & Aesthetics: Essays in Honor of Samuel Holt Monk,* ed. Howard Anderson and John S. Shea (Minneapolis: University of Minnesota Press, 1967), pp. 249–265.

41. Blair, *Lectures,* I, 410.

42. *Wordsworth's Poetical Works,* ed. E. de Selincourt and Helen Darbishire, 5 vols. (Oxford: Clarendon Press, 1940–49), II, 513; Coleridge, *Biographia,* ed. Engell and Bate, II, 57; Gibbons, *Rhetoric,* pp. 207–208, 210. Bishop Lowth also discussed the Song of Deborah in his *Lectures on the Sacred Poetry of the Hebrews.*

43. Beattie, *Essays,* p. 263.

44. Ibid., pp. 285, 285–286, 287. For another view of the stress on natural language, see Abrams, *Mirror and Lamp,* pp. 16, 288.

45. Smith, *Lectures,* ed. Lothian, p. 51.

46. Ibid., pp. 22–23; emphasis in original.

47. Jacques Derrida, "The Linguistic Circle of Geneva," trans. Alan Bass, *Critical Inquiry* 8 (1982): 675.

48. Derrida, *Of Grammatology,* trans. Gayatri Chakravorty Spivak (Baltimore: Johns Hopkins University Press, 1977), p. 75.

49. Jonathan Culler, *Ferdinand de Saussure* (New York: Penguin, 1976), p. 57.

50. Aarsleff, *Study of Language,* p. 127.

51. Culler, *Saussure,* p. 58.

52. Kennedy, *Classical Rhetoric* (p. 233), assesses Campbell as "innovative and challenging" and sees him departing "radically" from traditional terms and presentations.

53. Blair, *Lectures,* I, 138.

54. Campbell, *Philosophy of Rhetoric,* II, 125–129, 127–129n.

55. Hans Aarsleff, *From Locke to Saussure: Essays on the Study of Language and Intellectual History* (Minneapolis: University of Minnesota Press, 1982), p. 24; see also pp. 42–83, and 120–145 on Locke's reputation in the nineteenth century. An acute view of the philosophical context is provided by James G. Buickerood, "The Natural History of the Understanding: Locke and the Rise of Facultative Logic in the Eighteenth Century," *History and Philosophy of Logic* 6 (1985): 157–190, esp. 170–178, which traces the evolution of semiotics and logic as related concepts in Locke's thinking during the 1670s and 1680s. For additional background on the relation of rhetoric to knowledge, see Nancy S. Struever, "The Conversable World: Eighteenth-Century Transformations of the Relation of Rhetoric and Truth," William Andrews Clark Memorial Library Seminar Papers no. 65.

For words, ideas, and things, see, e.g., Thomas Gunter Browne, *Hermes Unmasked; or, The Art of Speech Founded on the Association of Words and Ideas* (London: T. Payne, 1795); and the earlier, anonymous *The Way to Things by Words, and to Words by Things* (London: Davies and Reymers, 1766).

56. Campbell, *Philosophy of Rhetoric,* I, 340; see also II, 112; I, 342; Blair, *Lectures,* I, 105; Culler, *Saussure,* pp. 10–15.

57. Campbell, *Philosophy of Rhetoric,* I, 38–39. Wordsworth's phrase appears not only in *The Prelude,* but in his 1815 Preface to *Lyrical Ballads* as well.

58. Quoted by Gibbons, *Rhetoric,* p. 69, from John Ward, *A System of Oratory* (London: printed for John Ward, 1759), II, 25–26. Harold Bloom makes metaleptic imagination a central act in his own new rhetoric of the psychology of poetic imagination.

59. Campbell, *Philosophy of Rhetoric,* I, 192; cf. Aarsleff, *Study of Language,* pp. 53, 20–25.

60. Campbell, *Philosophy of Rhetoric,* II, 112–113. For Addison's treatment of nature (things), description (signs), and the activity of mind involved with them, see *Spectator* 416.

61. *Rambler* 202 uses "vehicle" similarly, as does Blair, *Lectures,* I, 98, 289. In Johnson's *Dictionary* the second definition of "tenour" is "sense contained; general course or drift," and the illustration is from Locke: "Reading it must be repeated again and again with a close attention to the *tenor* of the discourse, and a perfect neglect of the divisions into chapters and verses." Under the third definition of "vehicle," Johnson quotes L'Estrange: "The gaiety of a diverting word, serves as a *vehicle* to convey the force and meaning of a thing."

The Collected Works of Ralph Waldo Emerson, vol. III. *Essays: Second Series,* ed. Joseph Slater et al. (Cambridge, Mass.: Harvard University Press, 1983), p. 20.

62. Priestley, *Lectures,* p. 47; cf. Campbell, *Philosophy of Rhetoric,* I, 39.

63. Priestley, *A Course of Lectures on the Theory of Language, and Universal Grammar* (Warrington: W. Eyres, 1762), pp. 163, 164.

64. Culler, *Structuralist Poetics,* p. 135.

65. Campbell, *Philosophy of Rhetoric,* II, 93. The chapter is vol. II, bk. II, ch. VII (II, 92–129).

66. Ibid., II, 96–97.

67. Ibid., II, 101, 102.

68. Blair, *Lectures,* II, 6. Edward P. J. Corbett, "John Locke's Contributions to Rhetoric," in *The Rhetorical Tradition and Modern Writing,* ed. James J. Murphy (New York: MLA, 1982), pp. 73–84, remarks: "The expansion of the province of rhetoric in the schools [in the 18th and 19th centuries] is probably due mainly to the influence of George Campbell, who proposed that the purposes of discourse were 'to enlighten the understanding, to please the imagination, to move the passions, or to influence the will,' or to the influence of Alexander Bain, who propagated the notion of the four modes of discourse—narration, description, exposition, and argumentation. It is clear, however, that the impetus for that expansion comes from Locke's *Essay*" (p. 75). Bain stressed the psychological basis of such figures as metonymy and synecdoche, not so much from the point of view of the writer, but of the reader.

See also in *The Rhetorical Tradition,* "Rhetoric in the Liberal Arts: Nineteenth-Century Scottish Universities," by Winifred Bryan Horner, pp. 85–94; "Nineteenth-Century Psychology and the Shaping of Alexander Bain's *English Composition and Rhetoric,*" by Gerald P. Mulderig, pp.

95–104; and "Three Nineteenth-Century Rhetoricians: The Humanist Alternative to Rhetoric as Skills Management," by Nan Johnson, pp. 105–117.

69. For theoretical discussion, see Campbell, *Philosophy of Rhetoric,* "Of the different sources of Evidence, and the different subjects to which they are respectively adapted" (I, 103–163).

70. Howell, *Logic and Rhetoric,* (p. 547) says Smith "made rhetoric the general theory of all branches of literature—the historical, the poetical, the didactic or scientific, and oratorical."

71. For discussion of Johnson's rhetoric, see Hoyt Trowbridge, "The Language of Reasoned Rhetoric in *The Rambler,*" in *Greene Centennial Essays,* ed. Paul J. Korshin and Robert K. Allen (Charlottesville: University Press of Virginia, 1984), pp. 200–216. Trowbridge ably discusses the use and limits of logic in Johnson's rhetoric.

72. Wallace, "The Fundamentals of Rhetoric," in Bitzer and Black, *The Prospect of Rhetoric,* p. 19, n. 7, cites Everett Hunt in *The Rhetorical Idiom,* ed. Donald Bryant (Ithaca, N.Y.: Cornell University Press, 1958), p. 4: "If we can keep as basic our conception that the humanities embrace whatever contributes to the making of free and enlightened choices, whether it be knowledge scientific, sociological, or poetic, and that in addition to adequate knowledge of all the alternatives there must be imagination to envision all the possibilities and sympathy to make some of the options appeal to the emotions and powers of the will, we can see that rhetoric is an essential instrument for the enterprises of the human spirit."

9. What Is Poetry?

1. Roland Barthes, *Writing Degree Zero,* trans. Annette Lavers and Colin Smith (New York: Hill and Wang, 1968 [1953]), p. 41.

2. Roman Jakobson, "Closing Statement: Linguistics and Poetics," in *Style in Language,* ed. Thomas A. Sebeok (Cambridge: M.I.T. Press, 1960), pp. 358, 370. Jakobson, like J. S. Mill and Lamb before him, was prompted to use the question What Is Poetry? as the title of an essay "Qu'est que c'est la Poésie?"

3. Terrence Hawkes, *Structuralism and Semiotics* (Berkeley: University of California Press, 1977), p. 79.

4. See Thomas McFarland on the soul in *Originality and Imagination* (Baltimore: Johns Hopkins University Press, 1985), pp. ix–xii, 88–89, 174.

5. T. S. Eliot, *The Use of Poetry and the Use of Criticism* (London: Faber and Faber, 1933), p. 152.

6. See Northrop Frye, *The Secular Scripture: A Study of the Structure of Romance* (Cambridge, Mass.: Harvard University Press, 1976), pp. 185–186.

7. See Paul Fussell, Jr., *Theory of Prosody in Eighteenth-Century England* (Connecticut College Monograph No. 5, 1954), pp. 113 and esp. 127–163. The New Rhetoricians, like the "liberals" in prosody, call for a "natural" or "actual" language of poetry (see Chapter 8).

8. Emerson Marks, "Meter in English Romantic Poetics," *Literary Theory and Criticism: Festschrift for René Wellek*, ed. Joseph P. Strelka (Peter Lang, 1984), pp. 975, 976.

9. Jeffrey, *Contributions to the Edinburgh Review* (1844 ed.), II, 287.

10. Hazlitt, "On the Prose Style of Poets" from *The Plain Speaker* in *Works*, ed. P. P. Howe (London and Toronto: J. M. Dent & Sons, 1930–1934), XII, 5.

11. Coleridge, *Collected Letters*, ed. E. L. Griggs, 6 vols. (Oxford and New York: Oxford University Press, 1956–1971), II, 810.

12. Thomas Carlyle, *Heroes, Hero-Worship and the Heroic in Poetry*, ed. P. C. Parr (Oxford: Clarendon Press, 1910), p. 96.

13. Joan Pittock, *The Ascendancy of Taste* (London: Routledge & Kegan Paul, 1973), p. 92.

14. See John Sitter, *Literary Loneliness in Mid-Eighteenth-Century England* (Ithaca, N.Y.: Cornell University Press, 1982), pp. 9, 13; also Clarice de Sainte Marie Dion, *The Idea of 'Pure Poetry' in English Criticism, 1900–1945* (Washington, D.C.: Catholic University Press of America, 1948).

15. Richard Hurd, "On the idea of Universal Poetry" in *Works*, 8 vols. (London: T. Cadell & W. Davies, 1811), II, 17; see also p. 11.

16. Erich Heller, "The Realistic Fallacy" in *The Artist's Journey into the Interior And Other Essays* (New York and London: Harcourt Brace Jovanovich, 1976), p. 92. Heller suggests that Hegel's all-consuming rational World-spirit is a mirrored reflection of the imaginative spirit of universal poetry, a reflection that appears as rational consciousness, and from this rational consciousness and its original image of universal poetry arise two realisms of post-romantic literature. One is the rational description of the novel as represented by Balzac, Tolstoy, and Flaubert. The other is an imaginative grasp of inner reality found in Baudelaire, *Ulysses*, or *The Death of Virgil*.

17. Greater emphasis now often falls on the difference between speech and writing. See, e.g., J. Douglas Kneale, "Wordsworth's Images of Language: Voice and Letter in *The Prelude*," *PMLA* 101 (May 1986):

351–362. Although such a difference is important, it does not fully re-place or deny perceived differences between poetry and prose, especially since those terms were themselves employed and, however problematic, remain vital.

18. G. W. F. Hegel, *Aesthetics: Lectures on Fine Art,* trans. T. M. Knox, 2 vols. (Oxford: Clarendon Press, 1975), II, 982–983.

19. Daniel Webb, *Observations on the Correspondence between Poetry and Music* (London, 1769), p. 113; Schopenhauer, *World as Will and Idea,* I, iii, 52.

20. Hurd, *Works,* II, 6.

21. Hegel, *Aesthetics,* trans. Knox, chap. III, "The Beauty of Art or the Ideal."

22. Heller, *The Artist's Journey,* p. 93: "It is a piece of profound Romantic irony that Hegel should have summed up and superseded all Romantic philosophizing with this excess of rationality, casting the sus-picion of poetic and intellectual irresponsibility . . . on the imperialists of poetry." We get instead the imperialists of criticism.

23. John Dennis, "Advancement and Reformation of Poetry," in *The Critical Works,* ed. Edward Niles Hooker, 2 vols. (Baltimore: Johns Hop-kins University Press, 1939–1943), I, 215. See Pope's Preface to Homer and, for extended discussion, Steven Shankman, *Pope's "Iliad": Homer in the Age of Passion* (Princeton: Princeton University Press, 1983).

24. Joseph Warton, *An Essay on the Genius and Writings of Pope,* 2 vols. (London: W. J. and J. Richardson, 1806), I, 330. For the premise of feeling as a major force behind taste and poetics in the second half of the eighteenth century, see W. J. Bate, *From Classic to Romantic* (Cam-bridge, Mass.: Harvard University Press, 1946), esp. chap. 5, "The Growth of Individualism: The Premise of Feeling," pp. 129–159. See also Douglas Lane Patey, *Probability and Literary Form* (Cambridge and New York: Cambridge University Press, 1984), p. 144: "By mid-century, 'na-ture' had in critical discourse come almost wholly to mean human nature, and especially passionate nature; at the same time, passion came more than ever to be considered the source and concern of all true poetry." For ex-tended study, see P. W. K. Stone, *The Art of Poetry 1750–1820: Theories of poetic compostion and style in the late Neo-Classic and early Romantic periods* (New York: Barnes and Noble, 1967).

25. Warton, *Essay on Pope,* I, 258.

26. Alan McKenzie, "The Systematic Scrutiny of Passion in John-son's *Rambler,*" *Eighteenth-Century Studies* 20 (Winter 1986–87): 129–152; W. J. Bate, *Samuel Johnson* (New York: Harcourt Brace Jovanovich, 1977), esp. pp. 296–317.

27. Coleridge, *Collected Letters,* II, 812. Coleridge says Wordsworth has not "done justice" to this argument, "nor has he in my opinion sufficiently answered it" in the Preface to *Lyrical Ballads.*

28. Thomas Arnold, *Miscellaneous Works* (London: B. Fellows, 1845), preface to "Poetry of Common Life," p. 252.

29. David Perkins, *A History of Modern Poetry,* 2 vols. (Cambridge, Mass.: Harvard University Press, 1976–1987), I, 60–83.

30. Helen Vendler, *Part of Nature, Part of Us: Modern American Poets* (Cambridge, Mass.: Harvard University Press, 1980), p. 120.

31. See David Lodge, *Modernism, Antimodernism, and Postmodernism,* inaugural address on assuming the Chair of Modern Criticism at Birmingham (Birmingham: University of Birmingham Press, 1977), p. 1.

Janus: Criticism and the Contemporary

1. Terry Eagleton, *The Function of Criticism: From the Spectator to Post-Structuralism* (London: Verso, 1984), p. 9. Frank Lentricchia's *Criticism and Social Change* (Chicago: University of Chicago Press, 1983), relying on the thought of Kenneth Burke, gives perhaps a more cogent and closely argued vision of the critic's involvement in ethical and politic considerations, but is in no way a survey of English criticism. Lentricchia's position is fundamentally NeoMarxist and he tilts at deconstruction, Paul de Man in particular, as being ingeniously "traditional" in avoiding social and political issues.

2. Eagleton, *Function of Criticism,* p. 18, emphasis mine. He says (p. 12) there was no "universal agreement," but he does posit an "increasingly self-confident ruling bloc in English society."

3. Ibid., pp. 7, 123, 124. Note how "traditional" here has the exact opposite connotation of Lentricchia's assessment of de Man, showing how one can invoke "tradition" for or against anything.

4. C. V. Wedgwood, *William the Silent, William of Nassau, Prince of Orange, 1533–1584* (New Haven: Yale University Press, 1944; rpt. 1948). *Lives of the Poets,* ed. George Birkbeck Hill, 3 vols. (Oxford: Clarendon Press, 1905), I, xxvi.

6. For instance, in eighteenth-century studies, see Phyllis Gaba, "'A Succession of Amusements': The Moralization in *Rasselas* of Locke's Account of Time," *Eighteenth-Century Studies* 10 (1977): 451–463; also Paul K. Alkon, "Johnson and Chronology" in *Greene Centennial Studies,* ed. Paul J. Korshin and Robert R. Allen (Charlottesville: University Press of Virginia, 1984), pp. 143–171, which focuses on the importance of chronology and time for Johnson as a thinker in general.

7. The importance of metaphor for critical theory is present, natu-

rally, from Aristotle. One good discussion in the context of critical theories and history is Willam K. Wimsatt, Jr., and Cleanth Brooks, *Literary Criticism: A Short History* (New York: Alfred A. Knopf, 1957), pp. 752–755.

8. Harry Levin, "The Implication of Explication" in *Poetics Today* 5 (1984): 109.

9. *TLS* October 4, 1985, p. 1094, "All Against Humanity," a review of Robert Scholes's *Textual Power;* Scholes's book and Todorov's review offer challenging analyses.

10. Graham Hough, *London Review,* October 17, 1985, in a review of *Criticism in the University,* ed. Gerald Graff and Reginald Gibbons.

11. *MLA Newsletter* (Summer 1986), p. 18.

INDEX

Aarsleff, Hans, 5, 202, 209, 210,
  300n24, 302nn55,59
Abrams, M. H., 5, 121, 123, 133,
  258, 273n1, 290nn47,52, 291n11,
  301nn34,38,44
Addison, Joseph, 6, 22, 47, 53, 56,
  60, 62, 64, 67, 84, 105, 106, 123,
  132, 136, 151, 163, 165, 167, 168,
  170, 181, 183, 185, 207, 259, 269,
  286n15, 303n60; *Spectator,* 60, 67,
  123, 136, 254; *Tatler,* 207, 254
Aeneas, 83
Aeneid, 27, 78
Aeschylus, 84
Aesthetics, 1, 127–149; values, 206
Agrippa, 82
Akenside, Mark, 79, 80, 84, 88, 188;
  Hymn to the Naiads, 80, 84, 88
Alexander, Keith, x
Alfred, William, 282n20
Alison, Archibald, 63, 64, 106
Alkon, Paul K., 307n6
Allegory, 91, 94, 95; mystical, 95
Allusion, 80, 81, 162
Altick, R. D., 294n16
Alves, Robert, *Sketches of a History of
  Literature,* 59
Analogy, between ethics and aesthetics,
  133–135
Ancients, 18, 30, 72
Anne (Queen), 69

Antigenres, 152
Apuleius, *Golden Ass,* 24, 78
Aristotle, 17, 34, 118, 128, 156, 197,
  217, 244, 248, 249, 258, 262, 265,
  308n7
Armstrong, Paul B., 299n16
Arnold, Matthew, ix, 8, 21, 30, 32,
  49, 65, 110, 115, 127, 148, 149,
  170, 217, 224, 225, 238, 239, 245,
  253, 255, 257, 268, 270; *Preface to
  Poems,* 21
Arnold, Thomas, 245
Association of Ideas, 159
Associationists, 201
Auden, W. H., 18, 38, 190, 246; *The
  Dyer's Hand,* 190
Auerbach, Erich, 17
Augustus (Caesar), 83
Austen, Jane, 28, 64, 139, 142, 153,
  259; *Northanger Abbey,* 28
Authority, 116, 147, 161, 180

Bacon, Francis, 4, 45, 53, 54, 78, 97,
  122, 154, 162, 198
Bain, Alexander, 303n68
Bakhtin, Mikhail, 15, 23, 24, 25, 26,
  27, 261, 275n17; *The Dialogic
  Imagination,* 24; *Epic and Novel,* 25
Balzac, Honoré, 305n16
Banier, Antoine, 86, 94
Barbauld, Anna Laetitia, 232